Contributions to International Relations

This book series offers an outlet for cutting-edge research on all areas of international relations. Contributions to International Relations (CIR) welcomes theoretically sound and empirically robust monographs, edited volumes and handbooks from various disciplines and approaches on topics such as IR-theory, international security studies, foreign policy, peace and conflict studies, international organization, global governance, international political economy, the history of international relations and related fields.

All titles in this series are peer-reviewed.

Daniel Beck · Julia Renner-Mugono
Editors

Radicalization and Variations of Violence

New Theoretical Approaches and Original Case Studies

Editors
Daniel Beck
Institute for Social Sciences
Otto-von-Guericke University Magdeburg
Magdeburg, Sachsen-Anhalt
Germany

Julia Renner-Mugono
Environmental and Social Expert
at an International Development
Organisation and Associate Fellow
Friedensakademie Rheinland-Pfalz
Landau, Germany

ISSN 2731-5061 ISSN 2731-507X (electronic)
Contributions to International Relations
ISBN 978-3-031-27010-9 ISBN 978-3-031-27011-6 (eBook)
https://doi.org/10.1007/978-3-031-27011-6

© The Editor(s) (if applicable) and The Author(s), under exclusive license to Springer Nature Switzerland AG 2023

This work is subject to copyright. All rights are solely and exclusively licensed by the Publisher, whether the whole or part of the material is concerned, specifically the rights of translation, reprinting, reuse of illustrations, recitation, broadcasting, reproduction on microfilms or in any other physical way, and transmission or information storage and retrieval, electronic adaptation, computer software, or by similar or dissimilar methodology now known or hereafter developed.

The use of general descriptive names, registered names, trademarks, service marks, etc. in this publication does not imply, even in the absence of a specific statement, that such names are exempt from the relevant protective laws and regulations and therefore free for general use.

The publisher, the authors, and the editors are safe to assume that the advice and information in this book are believed to be true and accurate at the date of publication. Neither the publisher nor the authors or the editors give a warranty, expressed or implied, with respect to the material contained herein or for any errors or omissions that may have been made. The publisher remains neutral with regard to jurisdictional claims in published maps and institutional affiliations.

This Springer imprint is published by the registered company Springer Nature Switzerland AG
The registered company address is: Gewerbestrasse 11, 6330 Cham, Switzerland

Preface

We want to thank all our supporters and contributors who enabled the process of publishing this edited volume on radicalization and violence over the last years.

We are especially grateful to the German Foundation for Peace Research (DSF), the German Association for Peace and Conflict Studies (AFK) and their executive boards for their generous support for the conference and for the support of the publication of this Edited Volume. All of them contributed to an important project for peace and conflict researchers on all career levels. Furthermore, we want to thank Alexander Spencer for his initial ideas, advice and ongoing patience when new questions arose.

We also thank our research assistants and proof-readers from Magdeburg University for their work. This project would not have been possible without the immense effort of Gabriela Pancheva, Ethan Smith and Leon Senger.

Due to COVID-19, our AFK Conference on Radicalization and Collective Violence was one of the first scientific conferences in March 2020, which had to be cancelled and rescheduled for one year later as an online conference. The COVID situation demanded our utmost stamina first for the hosting of the conference and then again for the later release of this publication. The motivation for our initial conference in 2019 was to add something substantial to contemporary debates in research, which were limited and unsystematic, and this is still the case.

In 2019, when starting to organize a conference on violence and radicalization, it was already clear that the topic was of high relevance in both academia and in many societies around the globe. Recent years only added more complications to processes of violence and radicalization in societies, which further shows the topic's relevance to Peace and Conflict Studies and to society in general. As a consequence, our timely topic for the conference has become even more relevant and relatable to debates in peace and conflict research.

The aim of this publication is to contribute to a current research topic, to provide a sustainable record of results and to strengthen the network of the German peace and conflict community. Our book therefore contributes to debates about radicalization in several areas, especially regarding visuality, emotions and narratives. In its final part, the book also contributes to these debates through new case studies. Particularly through a focus on international societal radicalization and prevention processes, we address an important gap in the scientific debate and bring new cases into the spotlight.

Institute for Social Sciences Daniel Beck
Otto-von-Guericke University Magdeburg
Magdeburg, Sachsen-Anhalt, Germany

Contents

Introduction 1
Daniel Beck and Julia Renner-Mugono

Part I   Causes and the Constitution of Radicalization

Organising Political Violence: Radicalisation and Militancy as
Narrative Activity 15
Maéva Clément

Making Sense of Terrorism and Violence: A Case Study 33
Ramzi Merhej and Ziad Fahed

Correlates for Foreign Fighters in Tunisia 51
Julius Strunk

Part II   Approaches to Prognosis, De-radicalization and Prevention

Radicalization and Public Discourse 75
Mareike Tichatschke

The (Non-)escalation of Violence During the Third Act of the Yellow
Vests Protests 97
Oliver Unverdorben

Elicitive Peace Education in Polarizing Conflicts over Democracy 113
Annalena Groppe

Part III   Selected Case Studies of Radicalization

Representation of Kurdish Female Combatants in Western Cinema 135
Nilgün Yelpaze

Manifestations of Violence in the Causality of a Radicalization
Episode 155
María Fernanda Córdova Suxo

Radical Politics in Post-Conflict Settings 173
Stratis Andreas Efthymiou

**Uncovering the Complexities of Radicalization and Violence:
A Summary** 195
Daniel Beck

Editors and Contributors

About the Editors

Daniel Beck is a research fellow at the chair of International Relations as well as lecturer in the Peace and Conflict Master Programme at Otto-von-Guericke University Magdeburg, Germany. He holds a Master degree in Peace and Conflict Studies from Magdeburg University and a Bachelor in History and Political Science. His research focus is on political humour, post-structuralist approaches and visuality in international politics. He was spokesperson of Junge AFK, the German Association for Peace and Conflict Studies. He published in journals like the Cambridge Review of International Affairs, the Journal of Multicultural Discourses and the Journal of War & Culture Studies. His most recent publication, titled "'Our Sofa was the Front'- Ontological Insecurity and the German Government's Humourous Heroification of Couch Potatoes During COVID-19", was published in German Politics.

Julia Renner holds a PhD on the topic of water-related conflicts in Kenya and Uganda. Her key research areas are conflict analysis and resource conflicts with a focus on East Africa. In particular, she researched how water shortages lead to individual and intra-community violence and how water shortages might be pathways for inter- and intra-ethnic radicalization processes. Moreover, she was regional-coordinator for South and East Africa at the Bertelsmann Transformation Index. She was spokesperson of Junge AFK, the German Association for Peace and Conflict Studies.

Contributors

Maéva Clément Institute of Social Sciences, Osnabrück University, Osnabrück, Germany

Ramzi Merhej University of Marburg, Marburg, Germany

Ziad Fahed Notre Dame University Louaize, Louaize, Lebanon

Julius Strunk Goethe University Frankfurt, Frankfurt, Germany

Mareike Tichatschke Mainz, Rheinland-Pfalz, Deutschland

Oliver Unverdorben Sciences Po Paris, Paris, France

Annalena Groppe Rheinland-Pfälzische Technische Universität, Landau, Germany

Nilgün Yelpaze University of Marburg, Marburg, Germany

Maria Fernanda Cordova Suxo University of Kassel, Germany

Stratis Andreas Efthymiou London Policing College, London, England

Introduction

Daniel Beck and Julia Renner-Mugono

This book focuses on the interaction between different kinds and levels of violence and various processes of radicalization. Currently, a growing political polarization can be identified in civil society, on a political-institutional level, as well as on an international level, which poses urgent questions for peace and conflict research. In particular, the connection between radicalization and the use of violence and force is a major object of investigation for science and politics, but there are multiple pathways and consequences of radicalization.

While the radicalization of parts of society has been a topic in many publications during the last years (Daase et al., 2019; Bosi et al., 2016; Kruglanski et al., 2019), the interest of this project is different. Our title aims at a more international readership and looks more at the *interaction* of violence and radicalization. Furthermore, it adds different perspectives on radicalization, like the role of narratives, visuality, and emotions, as well as the prognosis and handling of radicalization. It also provides new and original case studies which have not been focused upon before.

This book, therefore, will focus on the connection between radicalization and variations of violence. On the one hand, we define the individual use of violence as an integrated aspect of social and collective radicalization processes. On the other hand, the book focuses on specific situations of violence as a consequence of radicalization (Nassauer, 2011) while not excluding radicalization without violence, which is often seen as an emancipatory practice.

D. Beck (✉)
Institute for Social Sciences, Otto-von-Guericke University Magdeburg, Magdeburg, Sachsen-Anhalt, Germany
e-mail: daniel.beck@ovgu.de

J. Renner-Mugono
Environmental and Social Expert at an International Development Organisation and Associate Fellow Friedensakademie Rheinland-Pfalz, Landau, Germany

This introductory chapter first illustrates the state of the art concerning processes of radicalization in Peace and Conflict Studies. Therefore, we provide an investigation into variations of violence and seek to address reasons for individual and collective radicalization. Later, deradicalization is introduced. After that, the rest of the book is divided into three parts: Causes and the Constitution of Radicalization, Approaches to De-radicalization and Prevention and, finally, Selected Case Studies of Radicalization.

While radicalization is established in research, it is of special interest for Peace and Conflict Studies to discuss ideas and concepts surrounding deradicalization, which is also significant for understanding radicalization more deeply (Della Porta & LaFree, 2012). Currently, the term 'radicalization' is used for various phenomena, such as Islamist fundamentalism and terrorism, left-wing militant movements, and right-wing extremism (Amadeu Antonio Foundation, 2016). The same is the case for deradicalization.

Based on current shortcomings and key debates in the main literature, we identify some guiding questions for the study of radicalization processes which are covered by the different sections of our volume:

Why and how does radicalization happen?
    What contexts shape violence and radicalization?
    What socio-economic consequences does radicalization have?
    What is the role of narratives and emotions in shaping violence and radicalization?
    What can be done to counteract radicalization and to react adequately to it?
    What lessons can be learned from post-conflict societies?

These questions enable the central contributions of this book, which include new theoretical perspectives from a micro- to a macro-level analysis of individual and more collective radicalization movements.

Part one of the book is about the constitution of violence and radicalization. It provides a solid theoretical basis and new theoretical insights into the recently popular phenomenon of radicalization. Furthermore, it examines the interaction between different kinds of violence and radicalization. Overall, it looks theoretically at meaning-making, narratives, and emotions.

Part two is about reactions and prognosis of violence, as well as deradicalization and prevention. It includes political relevance by dealing with prevention and deradicalization, including peace education. Moreover, it adds new ideas and concepts to the debate with a specific focus on pathways for deradicalization and avenues for peace scholarship and conflict transformation. It also deals with the question of adequate responses.

Part three is about new case studies around the globe. It sheds light on conflicts about land and radical actors in post-conflict societies. The arguments refer to original cases and investigate new cases in Bolivia, Cyprus, and Western cinema. It also deals with phenomena like representations of radicalization and radical actors in the media, and the authors highlight new empirical insights regarding radicalization and point to open issues and controversies in and among Peace and Conflict Studies.

Overall, we identify promising avenues of future research: the role of emotions and opportunity structures, the connection between (non)violence and emancipation, the influence of narratives and representations and, lastly, new approaches and perspectives on deradicalization.

1 Problem Description

The definition of terms is a key task, as research into violence, for example, presents itself with numerous but conflicting definitions of the term "violence." Despite their differences, the majority of approaches and definitions are aligned by four essential elements which define violence: behavior that is (a) intentional, (b) unwanted, (c) nonessential, and (d) harmful (Hamby, 2017). A majority of the definitions are closely linked to the violent escalation of conflicts (Enzmann, 2013).

Collective violence is one form that is often at the center of research.[1] However, we aim to discuss the concept of violence more broadly, ranging from violence as a physical act or punishment to epistemic violence (Brunner, 2016). Instead of looking only at the causes, the focus of our chapters will also be on the emergence, practice, and dynamics of violence, which has not received enough attention so far (Walther, 2016). Additionally, the chapters focus on how non-violent behavior in situations where violence commonly would be expected is possible.

The challenge which remains in research is to nuance an intellectual understanding of the phenomenon, to provide better information on radicalization and how to prevent terrorism and violent extremism, how to deal with this phenomenon, and how far it can be predicted in specific situations. This edited volume, therefore, will focus on the connection between radicalization and violence in various forms and on various levels.

2 Defining and Understanding Radicalization

This section will provide a basic understanding of radicalization, before turning toward deradicalization. In peace and conflict research, radicalization is often understood as a kind of transitional moment between non-violence and the use of violence which, nevertheless, acts as a hinge and catalyst and provides explanatory approaches for the violent escalation of conflicts (Enzmann, 2013). Thus, it is important to address two important counterpoints in order to be able to specify the dynamics of radicalization and violence to be described. Firstly, radicalization does not describe a single moment, but rather a process that should not be understood as a spiral of violence with a fixed beginning and end (Kemmesies & Weber, 2019). Secondly, not every radicalization process leads to the use of direct violence or is

---

[1] For a long time one distinguished four forms of collective violence: lynching, rioting, vigilantism, and terrorism. The four forms differ in terms of their degree of organization and individual or collective (de la Roche, 2001).

linked to the use of direct violence at all (Maurer, 2017). Furthermore, radicalization must be understood as a relational concept that is strongly context-dependent, especially on the political system in which radicalization and radical movements take place.

Research on radicalization in connection with the use of violence has, in recent years, increasingly focused on the phenomenon of individual radicalization (Logvinov, 2017).[2] The focus of this edited volume will be on the connection between radicalization and forms of violence. On the one hand, we see individual use of violence integrated into social and collective radicalization processes. On the other hand, the question arises as to which specific situations violence can be the consequence of radicalization (Nassauer, 2011).

While research on violence is one of the foundational pillars of Peace and Conflict Studies, research on radicalization came more recently into the focus. Current research on radicalization criticizes linear models of radicalization and assumes that individuals are involved in radical actions, even without extremist preferences. In recent years, the research on radicalization and the use of violence has increasingly been focused on this phenomenon of individual radicalization (Williams, 2019).

It is furthermore essential to highlight certain aspects of the relationship between radicalization and violence in order to specify the dynamics of radicalization on the one hand and violence on the other hand. Radicalization is often understood as a kind of transitional moment between non-violent behavior and the use of violence. However, it will also be demonstrated that radicalization even without prior violence is possible. Apart from that, deprivation, dissatisfaction, and unsatisfied needs can provide factual and objective criteria for analyzing a social situation that contains the potential for the emergence of conflict (Piazza, 2006, p. 162).

Models of radicalization processes and their relation to collective violence, as well as measures for their prevention, are largely related to the individual realm. Critics thus see an empirical deficit in addressing the causes of violence applications at both a micro (intrapersonal), meso (inter-personal), and macro (social and group) level (Ahmed, 2016). This individual-based focus as explanation is not suitable for the complexity, especially because the role of ideology is limited and because every individual is a part/member of groups (Borum, 2011, p. 2).

As a discipline, it is of special interest for Peace and Conflict Studies to study violence. This factor of violence also helps to specify our understanding of radicalization. Thinking of violence and radicalization together helps us to build analytical categories which will appear throughout the edited volume. Abay Gaspar et al. (2018) distinguish between three types of radicalization: (1) radicalization leading to violence, (2) radicalization through violence, and (3) radicalization without violence, which is helpful here since the edited volume will focus on all three mentioned types. Thus, we adopt a thematic tripartition of the term and intend to

---

[2] See single perpetrator debates and rampages, jihadist radicalization models, radicalization through individual experience of violence.

strengthen radicalization as an analytical tool within peace and conflict research and make its normative implications explicit.

This theoretical structure of how violence and radicalization are linked can be extended by three levels of analysis: radicalization of individuals, groups, and society, which are all part of this book (and the consequences regarding (non)violence).

It remains to be said that the term radicalization is as wide and normative as it is controversial within peace and conflict research. Ambiguities remain, especially in connection with collective violence and its (non-)application. Radicalization can describe the development process from extreme belief structures to ideologies. A further understanding of radicalization refers to the process of diminishing acceptance of an existing order, which might be associated with a corresponding willingness to act (Kruglanski et al., 2014).

9/11 and other terrorist attacks had a huge impact on debates and understandings of radicalization. Security officials, because of the consternation about the 9/11 attacks, had problems understanding the processes by which individuals and groups radicalized and finally moved to terrorism. The hope was to achieve the capability of predicting and even preventing planned attacks. Therefore, with 9/11, "radicalization came to be the word used to refer to the human developments that precede terrorist attacks" (McCauley & Moskalenko, 2017, p. 205). The term radicalization is more manifold, as the negative connotation nowadays suggests. Even if both terms are today still often seen as the same (Kruglanski et al., 2019), one definitely has to differentiate between radicalization and terrorism (Daase & Spencer, 2011, p. 29).

What is especially problematic is that violence and terrorism are often seen as a logical end-point of radicalization. However, not every radicalization process leads to the use of direct violence or is linked to the use of direct violence at all (Maurer, 2017). Borum (2011) and Dalgaard-Nielsen (2010) studied radicalization without violence, for example.

Scholars see a pluralism of the term radicalization (Daase et al., 2019, p. 8), and there are various attempts at defining radicalization and bringing a systematization into the concept. Della Porta (2018) and Doosje et al. (2016, p. 79) see radicalization as a process which leads to violence. Neumann links the term radicalism to extremism and sees radicalism as a step toward extremism (Neumann, 2013). Often, a focus on radicalization within violence is missing. Some understand, for example, a radical as someone who is not normal (Sedgwick, 2010, p. 491).

The understanding of radicalization has increased since 2001. In particular, "the psychological, emotional, and behavioural processes by which an individual adopts an ideology that promotes the use of violence for the attainment of political, economic, religious, or social goals" gained a lot of attention (Jensen et al., 2020, p. 1067). Apart from individual radicalization, scholars have, over the last two decades, "identified a diverse set of structural (Crenshaw, 2011; Piazza, 2006), group-based (Sageman, 2004; Alimi, 2011) and individual-level (Horgan, 2014; Kruglanski et al., 2014) mechanisms as potential drivers of political extremism" (Jensen et al., 2020, p. 1067). While it is undeniable that these mechanisms are crucial for understanding radicalization, they do not, by themselves, offer adequate causal justifications for the majority of cases of extremism. (Jensen et al., 2020). To this end, radicalization experts have proposed that the phenomena of extremism be viewed as a collection of intricate causal processes in which a number of different variables interact to end with extremist results (Horgan, 2014 in Jensen et al., 2020).

It is assumed that individual radicalization is taking the person through a number of phases from a "cognitive opening," the meeting with an extremist ideology and the internalization of extremist ideas until eventually they reach the end destination: the perpetration of a terrorist attack (Crone, 2016). However, deprivation, dissatisfaction, and unsatisfied needs can provide factual and objective criteria for analyzing a social situation that contains the potential for the emergence of conflict. This role of social cleavages is strengthened by recent research. It is assumed that individual radicalization takes the person through a number of phases, starting from a "cognitive opening," the meeting with an extremist ideology and the internalization of extremist ideas, until they eventually reach the end destination: the perpetration of a terrorist attack (Crone, 2016). However, deprivation, dissatisfaction, and unsatisfied needs can provide factual and objective criteria for analyzing a social situation that contains the potential for the emergence of conflict. This role of social cleavages is strengthened by recent research (Minkenberg, 2017).

Despite the problematic negative connotation, there are further critical tendencies: initial concepts of radicalization perceived the phenomenon as an individual process through which a single person was transformed from a normal citizen into a budding terrorist (Crone, 2016). However, current research criticizes linear models of radicalization and assumes that individuals are involved in radical actions, even without extremist preferences (Williams, 2019).

Radicalization does not describe a single moment, but, rather, a process that should not be understood as a spiral of violence with a fixed beginning and an end (Kemmesies & Weber, 2019). Overall, current research assumes that individuals are involved in radical actions even without extremist preferences (Williams, 2019).

We want to stress the ambiguity of radicalization between threat and emancipatory chance and highlight the mechanisms of individual and more collective forms of radicalization. Radicalization without violence can often be seen as emancipation, as radicalization was previously seen as progressive (Daase et al., 2019, p. 15). Not every radicalization process leads to the use of direct violence or is linked to the use of direct violence at all (Maurer, 2017). Looking at history and who was called radical by whom and when, the third category of radicalization without violence also includes emancipatory ideas, such as the civil rights movement in the USA and also movements in the German Democratic Republic (GDR) (Steinbach, 2013). Furthermore, radicalization must be understood as a relational concept that is strongly context-dependent, especially on the political system in which radicalization takes place.

As has been shown, understanding why individuals and groups of people engage in extremist behaviors is seen as a crucial part of successful prevention efforts regarding violence and terrorism (Jensen et al., 2020, p. 1067). Therefore, our edited volume aims to provide new theoretical insights regarding radicalization in the areas of emotions, narratives, and ideology, but also regarding aspects of deradicalization.

3 Deradicalization

Scholars criticize that the term "deradicalization is used for various phenomena such as Islamist fundamentalism and terrorism, left-wing militant movements and right-wing extremism" (Amadeu-Antonio Foundation, 2016: p. 1). Radicalization and Deradicalization belong together and need to be considered together. While radicalization is established in academic research, it is of special interest for our subject to discuss ideas and concepts around deradicalization and prevention, which are significant to understanding radicalization as well. While radicalization is established in research in general, Peace and Conflict Studies as a discipline is specifically interested in discussing ideas and concepts around deradicalization, which is also significant to understanding radicalization more deeply (Della Porta & LaFree, 2012).

Like in radicalization, there is dissent about the specific use of the term. Thus, a distinction is made between state and civil society understandings and practices, but the fluid transitions between prevention and deradicalization should also be pointed out (Berrissoun, 2014). Lastly, our edited volume aims to shed light not only on the aspect of radicalization, which is most often negatively connoted but also to discuss the positive aspects of radicalization in shaping inter-state political and societal processes. In this edited volume, the term deradicalization is therefore also approached from different perspectives and connected to different approaches.

Furthermore, we look at factors that explain violence and that could be used to manage, restrict and prevent violence and radicalization. One contribution deals with the absence of violence, and another one with responsible reactions after terrorist attacks.

4 Book Outline

We use a very broad understanding of radicalization and look at theoretical conceptions around deradicalization, reaction and prognosis to radicalization and radical acts/movements. We, additionally, provide insights into conflicts where societal radicalization is present, but has not received much attention so far.

To this end, we address in the first part the most pressing issue: the nexus of violence, conflict, and radicalization. In the second part, we discuss forms of deradicalization and radicalization and the prevention of violence. The third section moves on to various new case studies of radicalization and collective violence. The edited volume allows for a contribution of new insights through (theory-driven) case studies in all three parts.

In the following, we will outline the specific content of the volume and how the individual contributions address central questions.

Our first part deals with the Causes and the Constitution of Radicalization. Here, Maéva Clément theorizes the role of emotions and narratives in "Collective emotions and organised political violence: Pathways to radicalization?" She offers a theoretical exploration of the relationship between organized political violence and emotional narratives. She interrogates conventional approaches to radicalization and questions assumptions about emotional dynamics in, and narratives' relevance to, radicalization processes. Clément introduces the concept of narrative emotionalization to grasp the process by which a political narrative becomes strongly emotionalized, which, in turn, impacts the possibilities of interpretation by the audience and, ultimately, the range of desirable collective actions. Finally, Clément argues that organizations mobilizing for political violence draw extensively on narrative emotionalization, resulting in demands for a most conform performance of emotions from members, high commitment, and decisive action.

Ramzi Merhej and Ziad Fahed explore political violence, including violent extremism and terrorism in their contribution, which can, according to them, be viewed as the results of a radicalization process. Their contribution, "Does Terrorism make sense? Motives and driving factors of radicalization," studies deradicalization to advance knowledge on how to prevent and mitigate political violence. The authors conducted interviews and focus group discussions with individuals engaged in the Lebanon civil war (1975–1990). The data were collected and analyzed using the Interpretative Phenomenological Analysis (IPA) method.

Julius Strunk analyzes fighter mobilization in his chapter, "Correlates for Foreign Fighters: Marginalization and protest as pathways to violence and radical behaviour." His paper assesses foreign fighter mobilization on the delegation level in Tunisia, and it aims to assess the factors responsible for the mobilization of foreign fighters in Tunisia. The author set out to verify the results made by Sterman and Rosenblatt (2018), who conclude a positive correlation between protest and foreign fighter mobilization. The replicative approach shows that the number of foreign fighter mobilization is positively correlated to protest, regardless of its demands. The number of foreign fighters is positively correlated to Ansar al-Sharia's activities, while he also states that two hypotheses by Sterman and Rosenblatt are not replicable.

The second part of the edited volume forms a bridge from different approaches toward radical acts, and prognosis of them, to deradicalization and prevention.

Mareike Tichatschke examines narratives used by European governments (France, Germany, and the UK) in reaction to terrorist attacks in pursuit to analyze in what ways they might provide compatibility for such used by extremist organizations. The research of her chapter "Radicalization and Public Discourse—Government Narratives in Reaction to Terrorist Attacks and their Relevance in Addressing and Preventing Violent Extremism" is conducted following pragmatist theoretical assumptions. Her discussion section of the paper elaborates on three complexes of issues that can be analyzed with the three narratives presented regarding the implications they might hold for countering and preventing violent extremism. These issues are: (1) whether to validate or to disregard the self-concept and situational definition of terrorist perpetrators and organizations in the plot, (2) the construction of groups and identities, especially of the question which groups are associated with the heroes or the villains in the narrative and, as a last issue, (3) the objective navigates the balance between reacting too heavily, or not reacting resolutely enough, both of which might play into the hands of extremist organizations.

Oliver Unverdorben brings visual analysis into the debate about radicalization and the prognosis of violence. In his chapter, "The (non-)escalation of violence: A critique of micro-sociological theories of violence," Unverdorben analyzes video footage of violent confrontations between protestors and the police during the third Act of the Yellow Vest demonstrations in Paris in 2018. The author contributes to the existing literature on interactional theories of violence by providing the first analysis of "the situation of immediate social interaction" (Collins, 2011). Furthermore, it is the first study that examines collective violence during the Yellow Vest movement through the visual analysis of video recordings. The author argues that Collins' theory is mainly descriptive and lacks explanatory value.

Annalena Groppe, in her contribution, looks at the role of peace education. Her chapter, "Peace education as an opportunity to prevent violence and radicalization?" is a case study of the New Hambach Festival. She explores how peace education could complement the prevention of radicalization approaches. Groppe uses Paul Lederach's elicitive framework to answer to two questions: (1) How can we understand the dynamics of radicalization, manifesting in the New Hambach Festival, in order to avoid onto-epistemic violence? and (2) How does peace education approach those dynamics accordingly and thereby complement an approach of "prevention"? The author proposes the concept of "polarizing conflicts over democracy" to analyze underlying dynamics from a transformative and relational perspective. As a consequence, transformation can occur by unfolding competences on both cultural and (trans)personal conflict dimensions in order to address radicalization from a whole society perspective.

Our third part finally introduces selected case studies from an international level. Here, a further contribution on the role of narratives and visuality in radicalization can be found in Nilgün Yelpaze's chapter, "Romantic narratives of Radicalization: The construction of Female Fighters in the Cinema," which looks at recent documentaries. Yelpaze analyzes the movies *Girls of the Sun* (2018) and *Sisters in Arms* (2019), proving the argument that the frames used in depicting Kurdish female combatants in these two films are in line with the media frames like depoliticization, personal-emotional motives, exceptionalism, and sexualization. Yelpaze uses feminist film criticism as a methodological framework.

María Fernanda Córdova Suxo sheds light on a new case study in Bolivia, which which has yet to receive much attention. In her contribution, "Living in Conflict and Violence: Radicalization in the context of territorial limits in Bolivia," Córdova Suxo argues that important reasons for the episode of violence are to be found in its causality, rather than in the episode as such. She uses the metatheory of Critical Realism to apply a stratified perspective of reality and thus analyze the episode of radicalization by questioning its ontology. Córdova Suxo examines the case of Macrodistrict VI—Mallasa to illustrate her argument. She identifies elements that perpetuate and reproduce dynamics rooted in causality, rather than in the radicalization episode.

Stratis Andreas Efthymiou uses the case of Cyprus and the radical right political party ELAM to illustrate how radical right organizations in post-conflict settings emerge. In his text, "Radical Politics in Post-conflict Settings," Efthymiou draws on elite interviews he conducted with radical right politicians, as well as drawing on ELAM's party materials and newspaper coverage of ELAM in his analysis. He explores how radical far-right ideological agendas can emerge in contemporary post-conflict settings. The Understanding of Cyprus through ELAM sheds light on the emergence of radical right organizations in post-conflict settings in the scope of the recent emergence of far-right radicalism in Europe and beyond.

A short conclusion appears at the end of the book. The conclusion briefly summarizes the issues and provides an outlook for further developments and areas for research.

References

Ahmed, K. (2016). Radicalism leading to violent extremism in Canada: A multi-level analysis of Muslim community and university based student leaders' perceptions and experiences. *Journal for Deradicalization, 6*(1), 231–271.

Amadeu Antonio Foundation. (2016). *A critique of "deradicalization" the task force on gendered right-wing extremism prevention*. https://www.amadeu-antonio-stiftung.de/wp-content/uploads/2019/01/deradicalization.pdf

Alimi, E. Y. (2011). Relational dynamics in factional adoption of terrorist tactics: A comparative perspective. *Theory and Society, 40*(1), 95–118. https://doi.org/10.1007/s11186-010-9137-x

Berrissoun, M. (2014). Extremismusprävention im Frühstadium. Initiative 180 Grad Wende als innovativer Lösungsansatz und Modellprojekt. *Zeitschrift für Außen- und Sicherheitspolitik, 7*(3), 389–401. https://doi.org/10.1007/s12399-014-0415-y

Borum, R. (2011). Rethinking radicalization. *Journal of Strategic Security, 4*(4), 1–6. https://digitalcommons.usf.edu/jss/vol4/iss4/1

Brunner, C. (2016). Das Konzept epistemische Gewalt als Element einer transdisziplinären Friedens- und Konflikttheorie. In W. Wintersteiner & L. Wolf (Eds.), *Friedensfoschung in Österreich: Bilanz und Perspektiven* (pp. 38–53). Drava Verlag. https://doi.org/10.25595/146

Collins, R. (2011). Reply to Kalyvas, Wieviorka, and Magaudda. *Sociologica, 13*(2). https://doi.org/10.2383/35867

Crenshaw, M. (2011). *Explaining terrorism. Causes, processes and consequences*. Routledge.

Crone, M. (2016). Radicalization revisited: Violence, politics and the skills of the body. *International Affairs, 92*(3), 587–604. https://doi.org/10.1111/1468-2346.12604

Dalgaard-Nielsen, A. (2010). Violent radicalization in Europe: What we know and what we do not know. *Studies in Conflict & Terrorism, 33*(9), 797–814. https://doi.org/10.1080/1057610X.2010.501423

Daase, C., Deitelhoff, N., & Junk, J. (Hg.). (2019). *Gesellschaft Extrem. Was wir über Radikalisierung wissen*. Frankfurt, New York: Campus Verlag.

Daase, C., & Spencer, A. (2011). Stand und Perspektiven der politikwissenschaftlichen Terrorismusforschung. In A. Spencer, A. Kocks, & K. Harbrich (Hg.), *Terrorismusforschung in Deutschland*. VS Verlag für Sozialwissenschaften. https://doi.org/10.1007/978-3-531-93040-4_2

Della Porta, D. (2018). Radicalization: A relational perspective. *Annual Review of Political Science, 21*(1), 461–474. https://doi.org/10.1146/annurev-polisci-042716-102314

Della Porta, D., & LaFree, G. (2012). Guest editorial: Processes of radicalization and de-radicalization. *International Journal of Conflict and Violence, 6*, 4–10. https://www.start.umd.edu/sites/default/files/publications/local_attachments/LafreeEditorial.pdf

Bosi, L., Demetriou, C., & Malthaner, S. (Eds.). (2016). *Dynamics of political violence: A process-oriented perspective on radicalization and the escalation of political conflict*. Routledge.

Doosje, B., Moghaddam, F. M., Kruglanski, A. W., de Wolf, A., Mann, L., & Feddes, A. R. (2016). Terrorism, radicalization and de-radicalization. *Current Opinion in Psychology, 11*, 79–84. https://doi.org/10.1016/j.copsyc.2016.06.008

Enzmann, B. (2013). *Handbuch Politische Gewalt*. Springer Fachmedien Wiesbaden.

Gaspar, A. H., Daase, C., Deitelhoff, N., Junk, J., & Sold, M. (2018). *Was ist Radikalisierung? Präzisierungen eines umstrittenen Begriffs* (Report 5/2018). PRIF & HSFK. https://www.hsfk.de/fileadmin/HSFK/hsfk_publikationen/prif0518.pdf

Hamby, S. (2017). On defining violence, and why it matters [Editorial]. *Psychology of Violence, 7*(2), 167–180. https://psycnet.apa.org/doi/10.1037/vio0000117

Horgan, J. (2014). *The psychology of terrorism* (2nd ed.). Routledge Taylor & Francis Group. https://doi.org/10.4324/9781315882246

Jensen, M. A., Seate, A. A., & James, P. A. (2020). Radicalization to violence: A pathway approach to studying extremism. *Terrorism and Political Violence, 32*(5), 1067–1090. https://doi.org/10.1080/09546553.2018.1442330

Kemmesies, U. E., & Weber, K. (2019). Frieden und Deradikalisierung. In H. J. Gießmann & B. Rinke (Eds.), *Handbuch Frieden* (pp. 319–329). Springer Fachmedien Wiesbaden.

Kruglanski, A. W., Bélanger, J. J., & Gunaratna, R. (2019). *The three pillars of radicalization. Needs, narratives, and networks*. Oxford University Press. https://psycnet.apa.org/doi/10.1093/oso/9780190851125.001.0001

Kruglanski, A. W., Gelfand, M. J., Bélanger, J. J., Sheveland, A., Hetiarachchi, M., & Gunaratna, R. (2014). The psychology of radicalization and deradicalization: How significance quest impacts violent extremism. *Political Psychology, 35*(2), 69–93. https://doi.org/10.1111/pops.12163

Logvinov, M. (2017). *Salafismus, Radikalisierung und terroristische Gewalt*. Springer Fachmedien Wiesbaden.

McCauley, C., & Moskalenko, S. (2017). Understanding political radicalization: The two-pyramids model. *The American Psychologist, 72*(3), 205–216. https://psycnet.apa.org/doi/10.1037/amp0000062

Maurer, T. (2017). Die Pluralität der Radikalisierung – Eine systematische Analyse der Theorieansätze zur Radikalisierungsforschung. *Journal for Deradicalization, 13*(1), 49–100.

Minkenberg, M. (2017). *The radical right in Eastern Europe*. Palgrave Macmillan US.

Nassauer, A. (2011). From hate to collective violence: Research and practical implications. *Journal of Hate Studies, 9*(1), 198–220. https://doi.org/10.33972/jhs.84

Neumann, P. (2013). Radikalisierung, Deradikalisierung und Extremismus. *Aus Politik und Zeitgeschichte, 29*(31), 3–10. https://www.bpb.de/system/files/dokument_pdf/APuZ_2013-29-31_online.pdf

Piazza, J. A. (2006). Rooted in poverty? Terrorism, poor economic development, and social cleavages. *Terrorism and Political Violence, 18*(1), 159–177. https://doi.org/10.1080/095465590944578

Sageman, M. (2004). *Understanding terror networks*. University of Pennsylvania Press.

Sedgwick, M. (2010). The concept of radicalization as a source of confusion. *Terrorism and Political Violence, 22*(4), 479–494. https://doi.org/10.1080/09546553.2010.491009

de la Roche, R. S. (2001). Why is collective violence collective? *Sociological Theory, 19*(2), 126–144. https://doi.org/10.1111/0735-2751.00133

Steinbach, P. (2013). Widerstand und opposition in der DDR. In B. Enzmann (Ed.), *Handbuch politische Gewalt. Formen-Ursachen-Legitimation-Begrenzung* (pp. 117–142). Springer VS.

Sterman, D., & Rosenblatt, N. (2018). *All Jihad is Local Volume 2: ISIS in North Africa and the Arabian Peninsula*. New America, Washington, DC.

Walther, R. (2016, January 31). "Tanz in der Flamme" – Kollektive Gewalt, *Süddeutsche Zeitung*. https://www.sueddeutsche.de/politik/kollektive-gewalt-tanz-in-der-flamme-1.2842689

Williams, T. (2019). Ideological and behavioural radicalisation into terrorism – An alternative sequencing. *Journal for Deradicalization, 19*, 85–121. http://journals.sfu.ca/jd/index.php/jd/article/view/215

Part I

Causes and the Constitution of Radicalization

Organising Political Violence: Radicalisation and Militancy as Narrative Activity

Maéva Clément

1 Introduction

Affection and compassion for the believers must be in all matters, hm? When a Muslim makes a mistake, then other Muslims have to defend him (…) and that counts for the *mujahideen* too. […] How can a person speak against someone who defends my and your honor? It cannot be. Where is *al-wala wal-bara*? Where is loving and hating for Allah? […]

How could you visit someone, show him friendliness (…) when this person, this *kafir* [disbeliever], slaughters your Muslim brothers and sisters, oppresses your Muslim brothers and sisters, subdues your sisters, rapes your sisters, occupies your countries (sic), hm? And what do these occupiers want? To implement their democracy (…) Since we hate *kufr* [disbelief] and abhor them (…) we stand up and don't keep our mouths shut, as many do because they fear that something happens to them.

On this path, we must be ready to give our life. To give our life. Why? Because our life, our death, our sacrifices and prayers, this is all for Allah the Mighty and Sublime, all of it! Thus we must talk and thus we must live, because talking alone is not enough, brother. (…) If you truly hate *kufr*, then you must get to work and you must work hard on this path.[1]

(Video entitled "Love and hate for Allah", *Millatu Ibrahim*, October 2012)

This passage from a video by the organisation Millatu Ibrahim exemplifies mobilisation by militant Islamist actors in Germany in the late 2000s and early 2010s. This video was produced in the context of the Syrian civil war and addresses Muslim audiences in Germany. The categorisation in friend—brothers and sisters in Islam—and foe—disbelievers (here, non-Muslim Germans)—is supported by the reference

---

[1] Author's translation of the original in German.

M. Clément (✉)
Institute of Social Sciences, Osnabrück University, Osnabrück, Lower Saxony, Germany
e-mail: maeva.clement@uni-osnabrueck.de

© The Author(s), under exclusive license to Springer Nature Switzerland AG 2023
D. Beck, J. Renner-Mugono (eds.), *Radicalization and Variations of Violence*, Contributions to International Relations,
https://doi.org/10.1007/978-3-031-27011-6_2

to the ideological precept *al-wala wal-bara* which translates as "loyalty to the Muslims and disavowal and rejection of the disbelievers". But, there is more to it: the narrator delimits the borders of affection and dislike towards fellow Muslims on one side and enemies on the other and declares which feelings are "right" for fellow Muslims and which are not. Further, he spells out the consequences derived from feeling appropriately: standing up to the enemies of Muslims, supporting the Mujahidin unconditionally and, ultimately, being prepared to give one's life. What is at stake in this passage is the management of followers' and sympathisers' emotions to mobilise for, and to sustain, organised political violence. It is not merely a video either, but a narrative occurrence in a larger narrative, constructing relevant local and international events alike as a systematic war against Islam and Muslims.

This chapter offers a theoretical exploration of the relationship between organised political violence and emotional narratives.[2] I start by interrogating conventional approaches to radicalisation and point to several issues relating to a superficial understanding of emotions in intersubjective relations. I then question assumptions about emotional dynamics in and narratives' relevance to radicalisation processes and ultimately argue for taking the emotional resonance of (militant) narratives seriously. I then take a literary-critical approach to the narratives at play in organised political violence. Section 3 conceptualises what political narratives do, how emotions are mediated in and through such narratives, and which narrative genre militant organisations draw upon. Therein, I introduce the central concept of *narrative emotionalisation* to grasp the process by which a political narrative becomes strongly emotionalised and explain how this, in turn, impacts the possibilities of interpretation by the audience and, ultimately, collective action. The last section discusses the combined effects of *narrative emotionalisation* and contextual-organisational dynamics within radicalising and militant organisations.

2   Reading Research on Radicalisation to Retrieve Emotional Dynamics

2.1   Radicalisation and Militancy Root on Emotional Experiences

Conventional approaches to radicalisation have produced analyses centred on the individual that aim to explain what causes participation in political violence, find patterns and generalise pathways to political violence (Malthaner, 2017). In the context of increasing militant activity by actors on the Islamist spectrum in Western Europe in the 2000s, this scholarly focus has led to the production of hyper-subjective accounts of radicalisation. This is problematic for at least two reasons: first, it bears the risk of pathologising individuals who turn to violence, thereby

---

[2] Sections 2, 3, and 4 of this chapter draw on work originally published in Clément, M. (2023). *Collective emotions and political violence. Narratives of Islamist organisations in Western Europe*. Manchester University Press. Reproduced with permission of MUP.

disqualifying both their agency and the political dimension of their actions; second, it reproduces the idea that social institutions bear little responsibility in such phenomena, be it the state, the radical milieu, or radical networks and organisations.

The literature of the late 2000s on so-called "lone-wolves" is symptomatic of this recurrent focus (for a critique see Gable & Jackson, 2011; Berntzen & Sandberg, 2014). For instance, the notion that individuals may "self-radicalise", i.e. turn via online contents to an ideology promoting violence and act upon it, is misleading. It reflects a poor understanding of the intersubjective and affective character of language. Online communication is social interaction, riddled with collectively constructed aesthetic and affective meanings. Processes of radicalisation cannot be but intersubjective.

Moreover, the literature tends to largely over-emphasise the role played by cognitive-ideological factors. Approaches that aimed to model radicalisation processes in the 2000s illustrate this tendency well. Rational cognition is held as the standard, while individual and collective emotions are given at most an instrumental function. Reviewing five prominent theoretical models,[3] King and Taylor argue that all five present two major "psychological factors" impacting radicalisation: "relative deprivation and an identity crisis" (2011, p. 609). The first is described as the "affective reaction" formed towards other groups when considering the in-group's relative situation. The second would refer to "managing a dual identity", which would create tension and negative emotions within the Self (King & Taylor, 2011, p. 611). Emotions are hence reduced to either the perception of group-based grievances or to identity processes at the individual level. While attributing a minor role to emotions, the five models miss emotions' fundamentally intersubjective character, their sociality, in that most models participate in reproducing individualistic accounts of radicalisation, albeit with a mild emotional colour.

Some former proponents have critiqued theories that are overly cognitive-ideological and have come to view radicalisation processes as fundamentally shaped by social interactions at multiple levels (Horgan, 2008; Borum, 2011). Yet, large parts of the scholarship nonetheless still imagine the emergence of political violence in narrow cognitive-ideological terms. Put shortly, it reproduces the belief that individuals would engage in violence when they come to believe in a violent ideology (Schuurman & Taylor, 2018). Approaches engaging theoretically with emotional dynamics in the context of radicalisation and organised political violence have had a hard time breaking through. As such, it should not come as a surprise that some scholars have endeavoured to bring emotions into existing theories and models of radicalisation (McCauley & Moskalenko, 2008; Rice, 2009; Cottee & Hayward, 2011; van Stekelenburg, 2017). However, such conceptual efforts have tended to present emotions as a mere "resource" within a larger repertoire at the disposition of propagandists. Such a perspective falls short of bringing to the fore the depth and complexity of affective modes of sensation, perception, and knowledge. Other scholars, for instance in social movement studies, consider that

---

[3] Those are the models by Borum (2003), Wiktorowicz (2004), Moghaddam (2005, 2006), Silber and Bhatt (2007), and Sageman (2008, 2009).

intersubjective emotional dynamics should not be studied from the viewpoint of approaches resting on theories largely disqualifying emotions (Calhoun, 2001; Goodwin & Pfaff, 2001; Goodwin & Jasper, 2004). In such a perspective, conceptual and theoretical efforts would draw on and develop alternative approaches giving emotions and affect their adequate place.

Indeed, viewing affective modes of knowledge and experience as the motivational force behind collective action allows for an alternative engagement with radicalisation and the dynamics of organised political violence. It calls our attention to how individuals experience *collective emotions*, how they *feel* like other group members. It means researching milieus, radicalising organisations, and militant groups as specific communities of emotions and interrogating the extent to which political entrepreneurs and leaders may be able to impact the management of collective emotions therein. In this regard, analyses of individuals' self-accounts of expressed motives (Copeland, 2019; da Silva, 2018) and organisations' narrative performance of collective emotions (Clément, 2019) interrogate how individuals' motivations for participation fit in with the larger narrative(s) re-produced by militant organisations. In short, it calls for exploring the relationship between narrative activity and the organisation of political violence.

2.2 Taking the Emotional Resonance of Narratives Seriously

The texts and visuals produced by militant groups and networks have become increasingly salient research objects in the context of massive access to online materials. In this literature, some have focused on "terrorist messages" and the seductive "themes" they contain, drawing attention to the form in which basic ideological elements are passed on. Such "messages" would deserve our attention because of their instrumental function (Gupta, 2010; Holbrook et al., 2013; O'Halloran et al., 2016). Others argue that their attractiveness goes far beyond propaganda purposes; what makes them resonate among audiences is their narrative character, i.e. whether they are "good stories" (Glazzard, 2017). Still, narrative effects are too often taken for granted in the literature on radicalisation. Consider the following statement regarding the appeal of al Qaeda's narrative:

> [...] it is not difficult to see why bin Laden's emphatic challenge to the Ummah to recognise the assault upon their faith, lands, and people, and to retaliate in kind, might strike powerful emotional chords with Muslim audiences everywhere. (Awan et al., 2011, p. 23)

First, this assumption is misleading because Muslim audiences do react differently to extremist propaganda (Leuprecht et al., 2010, pp. 60–62). Similar shortcuts are found in the literature on right-wing extremism, where the use of Nazi/Fascist symbols would have automatic affective power over right-wing audiences. This begs the question: how can we account for varied reception? As Aly points out, much research is still needed on the "interactive and dynamic process between message producers, the message and the receivers of the message", the latter being active audiences "who exercise agency" and should not be seen as mere passive recipients

(2016, p. 120). Second, assuming emotional effects on audiences prevents from asking the difficult question: where does the power of narrative lie? Is it in the very stories they convey, the simplification of events they offer or the emotions they weave in and mediate?

More recently, some authors have suggested conceptual avenues for exploring militant narratives that attend to their emotional underpinning. Braddock suggests three ways in which narratives promote extremist beliefs: "the encouragement of identification with story characters, the arousal of emotional responses, and the definition of boundaries that distinguish in-groups and out-groups" (Braddock, 2012). Together with Horgan, he contends that the narratives of extremist groups might be conceptualised as "vehicle[s] through which an ideology can be communicated" (Braddock & Horgan, 2016, p. 383). Others argue that studying narratives as mere vehicles proves too narrow. For instance, Glazzard argues convincingly that terrorist groups do not merely persuade their followers, they inspire them—he deplores that most of the literature has missed "the affective and aesthetic dimensions of narrative that are fundamental to its appeal" (2017, p. 9). He argues in favour of studying narratives by militant groups as narratives in *the literary sense*. Drawing on bin Laden's "Message to the American People"[4], Glazzard underlines that "this is a story and not just a message: the moral of the statement may be reducible to a short statement, but it is formed affectively as well as rationally; it is designed to affect our emotions, even if that is not immediately apparent" (2017, p. 15). In short, narratives are not just about content and should not be reduced to exercises in rhetoric. Literary-critical approaches to militant narratives thus go beyond identifying far-right or Islamist "extremist contents" and they take narrative as a discursive form and sociopolitical practice seriously (Shoshan, 2016; Clément et al., 2017; Pfeifer & Spencer, 2019; Copeland, 2019).

3 Narrative, Emotions and Mobilisation

This section builds on a literary-critical approach to narratives re-produced by radicalising and militant organisations. It offers a conceptualisation of what political narratives do, explains how emotions are mediated in and through such narratives and introduces the concept of *narrative emotionalisation* to grasp the process by which a political narrative becomes strongly emotionalised and how it impacts mobilisation for collective (violent) action.

3.1 Political Narratives: Definition, Characteristics and Functions

Telling, interpreting and trading stories represents a fundamental human activity (Fisher, 1984; Rabatel, 2008; Andrews et al., 2000). And political discourse is no

---

[4] The message was released to *Al-Jazeera* on October 29th, 2004.

exception to the universal practice of narrative (Wibben, 2011; Hammack & Pilecki, 2012; Krebs, 2015; Clément et al., 2017). If narratives are so widespread in political discourse, it is because they fit in well "with the political logic of trying to shape the present in light of lessons learned from the past" (Shenhav, 2006, p. 246). This does not only hold true for formal political narratives produced by institutional actors, but also for stories produced by other organised actors and more diffuse social movements, which routinely co-produce, reproduce or contest political narratives. To explore the narrative activities at play in organised political violence, researchers can draw on the long tradition of narrative research in literary studies, philosophy, and more recent engagements in political science.

In this chapter, narrative is understood as a discursive form, rather than a methodology.[5] In literary studies, a minimal conceptualisation refers to narrative as the "representation of at least two real or fictive events or situations in time sequence" (Prince, 1982, p. 4). In political philosophy and theory, narrative tends to be defined in relation to discourse. Hinchman and Hinchman define narrative "provisionally as discourses with a clear sequential order that connect events in a meaningful way for a definite audience and thus offer insights about the world and/or people's experiences of it" (1997, xvi). Similarly, in a poststructuralist perspective, narratives are discourses, as they re-present a specific social positioning (Andrews et al., 2013, 2015). However, it would be reductive to equate narratives with "discourses *plus* temporal sequencing". Because they organise events in a way that each event can be understood through its relation to the whole story, narratives are both "sequence and consequence" (Riessman, 2008). Foucauldian approaches thus argue that "rather than being considered as representing reality/ies, narratives should be seen as productive: narratives do things, they *constitute* realities, shaping the social rather than being determined by it" (Andrews et al., 2013, p. 15). Simply put, a narrative consists of beliefs and perceptions, put in story form, about one's collective and the world, which become thereby ordered and legitimised (Hammack & Pilecki, 2012, p. 78). While a political narrative may refer to one or several discourse(s), it is not a mere vignette which would serve to illustrate said discourse(s). It actively *re*-presents and constitutes reality and shapes and orients action.

Particularly cohesive narratives possess further structural components, be them a story and a plot (Franzosi, 1998) or a setting, a plot and characters (Kruck & Spencer, 2014; Spencer, 2016). In the following, I outline the characteristics that (political) narratives present:

i. A narrative involves at least one disruptive event, a break from what is seen as normal and to be expected (Franzosi, 1998; Kruck & Spencer, 2014), or else there would be no need to recount events.
ii. A narrative always contains a series of events, organised through time and, often indirectly, space. The temporal sequencing may be arranged in chronological

---

[5] For an introduction to narrative as a research methodology in the social sciences and the humanities, see for instance (Elliott, 2005; Riessman, 2008; Andrews et al., 2013).

order, i.e. organised according to the historic order of events, but not necessarily (Clément et al., 2017), especially if events are fictive.
iii. A narrative lets causal connections appear between specific events, while hiding other events and their potential relationships. This is not to say that it has to be factually true or logical in a scientific sense.[6]
iv. A narrative displays a set of characters, i.e. human or "human-like" protagonists (Kruck & Spencer, 2014, p. 148), whose characteristics are in parts elaborated within the narrative and in parts by the audience which is called to complete the construction of their image.
v. A narrative weaves together symbols, past experiences, collective memories, cultural scripts, complementary narratives (Hammack & Pilecki, 2012; Sakwa, 2012), i.e. all socio-cultural resources which might fit in the story it tells.

Importantly, each narrative is interpreted within a specific spatial-temporal setting—its composition interacts with the context of its production, narration and reception (Llanque, 2014)—meaning that interpretations will vary with changes to this context. Overall, a narrative calls its audience to interpret what is at stake in the story and what ought to be thought and done. It does not necessarily recount accurately "what happened", but engages the audience in reconstructing the motivations for, and consequences of, (fictive or real) events (Pearson & de Villiers, 2005, p. 695). By constructing an intersubjective reality in which power relations are either (re)produced or contested, political narratives provide justifications and incentives for political action. Thus, in terms of function, there is an intimate link between interpreting a narrative and committing to action: narrative defines the possibilities of knowledge and, hence, action in a given society (Lyotard, 1984; Wittgenstein, 1958). As I discuss in the next sections, some narratives provide justifications and incentives for non-violent forms of political action, while others legitimise and prioritise violent forms of collective action.

3.2 The Representation of Collective Emotions in Narrative Form

If narratives are so ubiquitous in the social world, it is not only because of what they *do*, but *how* they do it. Before processing their thematic content, audiences receive narratives aesthetically and affectively. Seen as socio-cultural practices, they follow the audience's aesthetic preferences,[7] draw on culturally-specific images, metaphors and popular myths. Furthermore, narratives draw their motivational force from the

---

[6] A narrative does not need to be factually true; what makes it strong is being internally logical. Glazzard, drawing on Fisher (1987), contends that "by satisfying an internal logic while remaining apparently true to the real world [...] narratives can appear to be more profoundly true than other, more factual forms." (2017, 15)

[7] As such, they cannot be completely freely chosen by political actors engaging in narrative activity.

performance of emotion. This section thus explores the intersection of narrative and emotions further.

One way to grasp this relationship is to view narrative as the *representation* of emotions[8] in language in the broadest sense. The latter encompasses linguistic text, images[9] and other aesthetic products and practices (Bleiker & Hutchison, 2018; Hutchison & Bleiker, 2014). It is a central site of inquiry for emotions are mediated in and through language. Emotion researchers stress that the experience of emotions is expressed in relation to others, communicated or, better said, *re-presented* in a language that others can understand (Searle, 1992; Fattah & Fierke, 2009; Fierke, 2012). Representations are the first attempts by social actors to articulate what they feel 'inside' and to produce effects on their social reality. Or, formulated in a Wittgensteinian perspective:

"We do not know our own emotions and feelings in a natural way or by observation. We produce spontaneous linguistic articulations of our feelings and impressions of the world. We express descriptive states of our affects" (Belli & Harré, 2010, p. 252, drawing on Wittgenstein, 1958).

The representation in language and (simultaneous or subsequent) meaning-making of our emotions is a powerful social practice (Bially Mattern, 2011; Schlag, 2018). Communicated to others, emotional experience forms an intersubjective reality in which certain interpretations and practices prevail over others. By reconstructing social actors' representations of emotional experiences (here, in narrative form), researchers interrogate how collectives make sense of emotions put into language, in their specific socio-historical context.

However, the expression of emotions in language is not a mere description of what individuals or collectives feel. Perhaps more fundamentally, emotions are evoked *through* language. This is most apparent in the experience of aesthetic products (e.g. being moved by a painting), but also holds true for language in a narrow linguistic sense. Much like novelists aim to both "put emotions in words" and "construct emotions through the use of words", social actors use words and construct contexts to *recreate* the experience of emotion, thereby creating a "performance" (Belli & Harré, 2010, pp. 254–255, drawing on Butler, 1993; see also Austin, 1975). The words used and images created by social actors are designed to produce real emotions in intersubjective interactions. Emotions work powerfully in discursive performances "by slowly entrenching—or gradually challenging—how we feel, view, think of the socio-political world around us" (Bleiker & Hutchison, 2018, p. 333). The interplay between emotions and discourse is fundamental in reproducing or contesting dominant interpretations of the socio-political world, especially

---

[8] Part of the scholarship on emotions and affect argues that some emotional phenomena escape representation in language or practices. Especially affect is viewed as beyond representation. For a critical discussion of the issues at stake in this debate, see Clément (2021, pp. 7–8).

[9] Language, strictly speaking, and images do not mediate emotions in the same way. Schlag points out that "language does not mirror reality", whereas "images—in particular, photographs—attempt to have a natural and mimetic relation to the depicted reality" (2018, p. 213). Although images are representations of reality as much as language is, because of their immediacy, images appear truer to reality.

those concerned with security (Wolf, 2012; Koschut, 2015; Van Rythoven, 2015; Clément & Sangar, 2018).

As a specific discursive form, narrative provides the performance of emotions *par excellence* (Clément, 2019, 2023). The characterisation of and interaction between the story's protagonists plays a central role therein. For instance, culturally specific scapegoat and enemy images participate in the differentiated characterisation of the story's protagonists, which allows the audience to reject specific characters and identify with others. By revealing part of the alleged motives and behaviour of its characters, a narrative gives the illusion of disclosing hidden truths about social actors and events. In short, it normalises what the characters feel, think and do, how events are linked to each other, what they mean and what consequences they have. For the audience, what happens in the story in general becomes less important than what happens to the protagonists with which it identifies. It is the fate of these characters, their struggles, successes and losses that *moves* an audience. Thus, by staging different social identities and their interactions, narratives affect audiences emotionally. Emotional experience, in turn, provides motivational force. Depending on the intensity and direction of the experience and the strength of their group identification, audiences are thus called to (re)act. This, in turn, bears upon the possibilities of organised political action.

3.3 Some Narratives Perform Emotions More Intensely Than Others

While narrative as a discursive form appears to offer the performance of emotions *par excellence*, not all narratives perform emotions in the same way, nor to the same intensity.[10] Indeed, some narratives rely more strongly on emotional experiences and meanings than others. This is partly due to the specific narrative *genre* on which a given narrative draws, i.e. tragedy, comedy, satire or romance. Compared with the other genres, romance is a particularly emotion-intensive narrative genre (Ringmar, 2006; Spencer, 2016). Ringmar characterises *romance* as the preferred mode of idealists who strive (often by fighting) to change the world; *tragedy* as the mode of pessimists who hold that there is no escape from the laws of nature and insecurity; *comedy* as the mode of liberal "institution-builders" who engage in conversations to win others to their views; and, finally, *satire* as the mode of distanced anti-war critics (2006, pp. 404–407). In short, the interpretation of political problems and diagnosis the four genres arrive at are radically different.

Romance is the genre that a wide range of state and non-state actors calling for profound political transformation and/or radical action draw upon. Romantic narrators call to embark on a quest and prepare to fight for their conception of a "better place" (Ringmar, 2006, p. 405). Audiences confronted with a romantic narrative

---

[10] This point goes beyond the issue of narrative cohesion or whether a given narrative rose to prominence over time (i.e. dominant vs. minority narratives). For an in-depth discussion of what it means for a narrative to become (temporarily) successful, see Krebs (2015).

cannot ignore the suffering of identifiable victims and the responsibilities attributed to identifiable perpetrators (Boltanski, 1999; Clément et al., 2017). Romance thus affects audiences identifying particularly strongly with victims and motivates them to take decisive action. Indeed, it is the genre that "takes itself most seriously" and that casts violence in a positive light (Ringmar, 2006, p. 406), both the violent action itself and its outcome in the form of a better future (Clément et al., 2017).

Yet, even within the narrative genre of romance, large differences can be observed. Clément (2023) shows, for instance, that the romantic narrative purported by Islamist organisations is not as intensely emotional in phases of radicalisation as in phases of violent extremism. How can we differentiate between lowly and highly emotionalised narrative? In the following, I draw on the concept of *narrative emotionalisation* to account for narratives in which emotions are particularly intensely performed and what it means for the possibilities of interpretation of such narratives.

The concept of *narrative emotionalisation* grasps the process by which a political narrative becomes increasingly emotionalised, i.e. to account for narrative change (Clément, 2023). I have defined narrative emotionalisation in the context of romance as

> the gradual process by which the texts and visuals pertaining to a narrative increasingly perform strong, non-conflicting, collective emotions towards distinct narrative objects and events, according to strict emotion rules (Clément, 2023, p. 100).

The overall process of narrative emotionalisation rests on four sub-processes: (1) the prioritisation of emotion-based knowledge; (2) the suppression of the variety and complexity of emotional experience; (3) the enforcement of strict emotions rules and sanctions; and (4) the consistent performance of emotions across narrative occurrences. Combined, these four sub-processes amount to all objects and events of a narrative—in all its occurrences—being systematically wrapped in emotional meanings.

Such a process should not be equated with a mere intensification of emotion words in the quantitative sense. Emotions are not merely, or even primarily, made accessible to an audience because they are directly named as such ("we are angry"), but rather because the meaning of objects and events become systematically linked to strong emotional meaning. Consider the sentence "There is no doubt that the perpetrators of this terrorist attack must be punished"—is it a lesser expression of anger than "we are angry" simply because the word "anger" is not explicitly named? Strong performances of emotions do not build on the precision of a statement either, but rather on what is implied in recounting the story.

The first sub-process of narrative emotionalisation refers to emotional meanings becoming progressively the only legitimate form of knowledge within a narrative. Knowledge can be individual (known by one person) or collective (regarded as general). Most scholars consider that there are four basic sources of knowledge: perception, consciousness, reason, and memory (Audi, 2009)—most of which draw on a mix of affective-cognitive processes (Bless, 2000). A piece of knowledge can be defined as the understanding of a subject or a situation through experience or study.

Knowledge can thus take many forms: it can, but need not, be factual, conceptual, procedural or moral, etc. The focus here is on knowledge rooted in (constructed) collective emotional experience. In this process, all other forms of knowledge are increasingly perceived as *illegitimate* and discarded as ways of making sense of the social world.

Second, narrative emotionalisation is characterised by the gradual reduction of emotion expressions' variety and complexity. In this second sub-process, conflicting emotional meanings tend to disappear and a recognisable emotional tone crystallises within the narrative. Nuanced emotion expressions, such as "we are angry, although we partly understand why they did what they did", are gradually silenced. Mixed emotions, such as "we were angry and worried about the implications for the future" are also suppressed. In this sub-process, the events of the narrative become wrapped in clear-cut, unequivocal emotional meanings. Eschewing potentially conflicting emotional meanings reduces a narrative's dialogic character, thereby confining the interpretation of the story. This most coherent performance of emotions—erasing asperities—endows the narrative with a distinctive tone (e.g. sense of urgency).

The third sub-process of narrative emotionalisation refers to the emotion rules that the social actors purporting the narrative (leaders of a political party, government, militant organisation, etc.) expect all those who see themselves as part of the collective to follow. Emotion rules—or "feeling rules" in Hochschild's seminal work (1979)—consist of the norms shared within a group about appropriate ways of feeling and expressing—performing, really—these feelings. While all social organisations have implicit emotion rules which aim towards appropriate performances of emotion, some set up more explicit and exclusive rules than others to ensure conformity, group cohesion and, ultimately, regulate collective attitudes and behaviour. In the third sub-process of narrative emotionalisation, exclusive emotion rules and sanctions for deviance are enforced. An example would be the rule "reserving feelings of sympathy for the in-group only": experiencing sympathy for an individual from an out-group would be illegitimate and failure to conform may bring symbolic sanctions (e.g. status, mistrust, etc.). At its fullest, the emotions enforced within the in-group are distinct from the emotions attributed to outgroups, said to feel differently. Multiple self-identities are downplayed, as are the common qualities and imperfections shared with outgroups.[11] Nuance and differentiation in the presentation of others (or, outgroups), as well as the Self (or, in-group), are erased. This, in turn, limits the attitudes and actions that are considered appropriate for members, as well as the behaviour expected of out-groups.

---

[11] This sub-process is not identical to "othering", i.e. the antagonistic identity construction of *other* subjects. While it implies that out-groups are constructed as dissimilar to the in-group, it goes much further than the identity politics implied in "othering". First, the group-appropriate performance of emotions means that all group members have to *feel* the same way—a particularly illiberal practice targeted at the *in-group*. Second, this process implies that out-groups are constructed as homogeneous affective collectives, i.e. they are objectified based on their (alleged) collective emotions.

Finally, the fourth sub-process posits that narrative emotionalisation builds up through repetition. It refers to the necessary consistency of the performance across the various texts and visuals pertaining to the narrative. Each occurrence *adds* to the others and has the potential to validate the performance of emotions. Their repetition reinforces the emotional meanings and expressions constructed in previous texts or images. It calls to conceive narrative emotionalisation as a continued process—instead of an instantaneous one—which largely builds on intertextuality. Understood here as encompassing verbal *and* visual texts, intertextuality is the character of a text of being surrounded by "the web of meaning" created by other texts (Kristeva, 1980; Fairclough, 1992, 2013). A narrative occurrence (text or visual) becomes intertextual either when it *explicitly* refers to another occurrence (i.e. "as fellow leader XY said last February"), or when the same emotional meanings are re-articulated across the narrative occurrences (i.e. "the invasion of Iraq is a war on Islam"; "this is the beginning of the decay of the White race"). Through intertextuality, the performance of collective emotions is consistent and validated. In sum, the emotional meanings constituted through the other three sub-processes become all the more potent when political actors tell/write/picture a given narrative in a similar way and across time. This consistent repetition and circulation of narrative occurrences ties past, present and future emotional experiences together and pictures the political issues addressed across occurrences as of existential importance.

Narrative emotionalisation impacts the collective attitudes and behaviour of an accepting audience in profound ways. As both narrative and the experience of emotions are potent forms of knowledge, emotionalisation in narrative form affects not only what we 'know' happened (and why it did), but also what we perceive as im/moral and consider right/legitimate or wrong/illegitimate. Narrative emotionalisation further restricts the possibilities of (alternative) knowledge and, hence, the range of imaginable collective actions. It delegitimises, silences and sanctions those emotional experiences/meanings that might disrupt the collective orientation towards specific political goals and strategies. When narrative emotionalisation works to restrict the imaginable courses of action to the use of individual and/or collective violence, it plays a crucial role in mobilisation and militancy.

4 Radicalisation and Militancy as Narrative Activity

Circling back to the critique of the literature on radicalisation, a romantic narrative does not merely construct enemy images or make the gist of an ideology accessible. More fundamentally, it provides emotion-based justifications of and incentives for violent action. Romance is the genre that a wide range of state and non-state actors calling for profound political transformation and/or radical action draw upon. Specifically, radicalising organisations and militant groups deploy *contesting* romantic narratives. As the passage quoted in the introduction shows, each narrative occurrence inserts itself into a larger narrative deployment—here, that of a "war against Islam and Muslims". This narrative attributes responsibilities for wrongdoings while dispensing with details, as much remains implied. It calls on the audience to fill in the blanks with their own emotional experiences (e.g. experiences of discrimination, abuse, rejection, repression, etc.) and draw the necessary conclusions. The romantic narrative mediates collective emotions and engenders the belief that something is not as it should be, yet can be changed. It provides "subjects to identify with and others to reject, motivation to assist the former and punish the latter"; in short, it presents collective action as desirable, makes it "feel right" (Clément, 2023, p. 100).

Further, by reducing narrative's multi-voiced character, narrative emotionalisation restricts the choices available for action. Narrative emotionalisation is bent on raising and maintaining collective action. Organisations mobilising for political violence will draw extensively on narrative emotionalisation, demanding from members a corresponding emotion performance and individual/collective action. In the quote in the introduction, *Millatu Ibrahim* expects its followers to feel affection towards "Muslim brothers and sisters" in all circumstances and hatred towards disbelieving Germans (and Westerners more broadly) without exception.[12] In this respect, an intensely emotionalised narrative is both the stage of intergroup conflict and the *locus* of social control within an organisation.

Nevertheless, the capacity of political actors to shape the narratives that they reproduce varies strongly. As much as they create the stories that become part of a narrative, a narrative which endures over time cannot be reduced to their strategies alone (Krebs, 2015, p. 826). Because narratives rely so much on the known and familiar, yet transcend the particular, they can go beyond the purpose of their creation. To some extent, established narratives have a life of their own and are partly independent from their creators. Narratives that enjoy some success are relayed, reinterpreted and transformed by their audiences and other political actors. However, relatively small, hierarchised collectives organised around selective membership can maintain a high degree of control on narrative production and, to some extent, narrative reception by members. In militant groups, the collective tends to have a large "value-setting power" (McCauley & Moskalenko, 2010, p. 89) as membership in the group precedes—even, excludes—other attachments.

Indeed, the contextual-organisational dynamics specific to radicalising and militant groups expands the potential for narrative resonance with members and followers. Within such groups, the degree of identification and cohesion demanded of members is much stronger than in less hierarchical and/or majority groups. Groups engaging in high-risk activism expect the strong identification of all members with the cause, strong attachment to the group's minority identity, and undivided loyalty in order to withstand potential implosion and/or repression (Goodwin & Pfaff, 2001; Smith, 2017; Clément, 2023). Such organisational dynamics incentivise the conformed performance of collective emotions. Such performance requires work on members' parts, especially if the emotion rules it draws upon run opposite to society's dominant rules. Such "emotion work" or "emotional labor" (Hochschild, 1979, 2016; von Scheve, 2012) implies working towards actively suppressing

---

[12] For an in-depth account of *narrative emotionalisation* in the case of *Millatu Ibrahim* and other Western European Islamist organisations, see Clément (2023).

certain emotions and inducing others. Emotion work can unfold consciously or non-consciously, at the individual as well as at the collective level (Goodwin & Pfaff, 2001, p. 284). Leaders who engage members in narrative form expect them to work on their emotions to fit in, maintain high levels of commitment over time and engage in high-risk/violent activism.

In conclusion, while narratives imply the active interpretation of an audience, the context of activism and organisational dynamics of radicalising and militant groups impact deeply on members' possibilities of interpretation and, hence, collective action. Such narrative effects are not exclusive to radicalising and militant groups either. Similar dynamics are to be expected in non-state organisations operating in a context of repression and/or in other hierarchically organised collectives exacting loyalty and a high degree of commitment from their members, be they insurgent groups, paramilitary militias, or state military forces. The proposed concept of *narrative emotionalisation* offers an alternative way to account for the organisation of political violence in a variety of contexts and actor constellations.

References

Aly, A. (2016). Brothers, believers, brave Mujahideen: Focusing attention on the audience of violent jihadist preachers. In A. Aly, S. Macdonald, L. Jarvis, & T. Chen (Eds.), *Violent extremism online: New perspectives on terrorism and the internet* (pp. 106–122). Routledge.

Andrews, M., Kinnvall, C., & Monroe, K. (2015). Narratives of (in)security: Nationhood, culture, religion, and gender. *Political Psychology, 36*(2), 141–149. https://doi.org/10.1111/pops.12224

Andrews, M., Sclater, S. D., Squire, C., & Treacher, A. (2000). *Lines of narrative: Psychosocial perspectives*. Routledge.

Andrews, M., Squire, C., & Tamboukou, M. (2013). *Doing narrative research* (2nd ed.). Sage.

Audi, R. (2009). The sources of knowledge. In P. K. Moser (Ed.), *The Oxford handbook of epistemology*. Oxford: Oxford University Press. http://www.oxfordhandbooks.com/view/10.1093/oxfordhb/9780195301700.001.0001/oxfordhb-9780195301700-e-3.

Austin, J. L. (1975). *How to do things with words*. Oxford University Press.

Awan, A., Hoskins, A., & O'Loughlin, B. (2011). *Radicalisation and the Media: Connectivity and terrorism in the new media ecology*. Routledge.

Belli, S., & Harré, R. (2010). What is love? Discourse about emotions in social sciences. *Human Affairs, 20*(3), 249–270. https://doi.org/10.2478/v10023-010-0026-8

Berntzen, L. E., & Sandberg, S. (2014). The collective nature of lone wolf terrorism: Anders Behring Breivik and the anti-Islamic social movement. *Terrorism and Political Violence, 26*(5), 759–779. https://doi.org/10.1080/09546553.2013.767245

Bially Mattern, J. (2011). A practice theory of emotion for international relations. In E. Adler & V. Pouliot (Eds.), *International practices* (pp. 63–86). Cambridge University Press.

Bleiker, R., & Hutchison, E. (2018). Conclusion: Methods and methodologies for the study of emotions in world politics. In M. Clément & E. Sangar (Eds.), *Researching emotions in international relations* (pp. 337–338). Palgrave Macmillan.

Bless, H. (2000). The interplay of affect and cognition: The mediating role of general knowledge structures. In J. P. Forgas (Ed.), *Feeling and thinking: The role of affect in social cognition* (pp. 201–222). Cambridge University Press.

Boltanski, L. (1999). *Distant suffering: Morality, media, and politics*. Cambridge University Press.

Borum, R. (2003). Understanding the terrorist mindset. *FBI Law Enforcement Bulletin, 72*(7), 7–10.

Borum, R. (2011). Radicalization into violent extremism I: A review of social science theories. *Journal of Strategic Security, 4*(4), 7–36. https://doi.org/10.5038/1944-0472.4.4.1

Braddock, K. H. (2012). *Fighting words: The persuasive effect of online extremist narratives on the radicalization process* [Doctoral thesis]. The Pennsylvania State University. https://etda.libraries.psu.edu/catalog/15349

Braddock, K., & Horgan, J. (2016). Towards a guide for constructing and disseminating counter-narratives to reduce support for terrorism. *Studies in Conflict and Terrorism, 39*(5), 381–404. https://doi.org/10.1080/1057610X.2015.1116277

Butler, J. (1993). *Bodies that matter on the discursive limits of "Sex"*. Routledge.

Calhoun, C. (2001). Putting emotions in their place. In J. Goodwin, J. M. Jasper, & F. Polletta (Eds.), *Passionate politics: Emotions and social movements* (pp. 45–47). University of Chicago Press. https://doi.org/10.7208/chicago/9780226304007.003.0003

Clément, M. (2019). *Islamist organizations in Western Europe. The role of collective emotions in group radicalization processes* [Doctoral thesis], Goethe University Frankfurt.

Clément, M. (2021). Emotions and affect in terrorism research: Epistemological shift and ways ahead. *Critical Studies on Terrorism, 14*(2), 247–270. https://doi.org/10.1080/17539153.2021.1902611

Clément, M. (2023). *Collective emotions and political violence. Narratives of Islamist organisations in Western Europe*. Manchester University Press.

Clément, M., Lindemann, T., & Sangar, E. (2017). The "hero-protector narrative": Manufacturing emotional consent for the use of force. *Political Psychology, 38*(6), 991–1008. https://doi.org/10.1111/pops.12385

Clément, M., & Sangar, E. (2018). *Researching emotions in international relations. Methodological perspectives on the emotional turn*. Palgrave Macmillan.

Copeland, S. (2019). Telling stories of terrorism: A framework for applying narrative approaches to the study of militant's self-accounts. *Behavioral Sciences of Terrorism and Political Aggression, 11*(3), 232–253. https://doi.org/10.1080/19434472.2018.1525417

Cottee, S., & Hayward, K. (2011). Terrorist (e)motives: The existential attractions of terrorism. *Studies in Conflict & Terrorism, 34*(12), 963–986. https://doi.org/10.1080/1057610X.2011.621116

da Silva, R. (2018). *Narratives of political violence: Life stories of former militants*. Routledge.

Elliott, J. (2005). *Using narrative in social research: Qualitative and quantitative approaches*. Sage.

Fairclough, N. (1992). Discourse and text: Linguistic and intertextual analysis within discourse analysis. *Discourse & Society, 3*(2), 193–217. https://doi.org/10.1177/0957926592003002004

Fairclough, N. (2013). *Critical discourse analysis: The critical study of language* (2nd ed.). London: Routledge. (Original edition, 1995).

Fattah, K., & Fierke, K. M. (2009). A clash of emotions: The politics of humiliation and political violence in the Middle East. *European Journal of International Relations, 15*(1), 67–93. https://doi.org/10.1177/1354066108100053

Fierke, K. M. (2012). *Political self-sacrifice: Agency, body and emotion in international relations*. Cambridge University Press.

Fisher, W. R. (1984). Narration as a human communication paradigm: The case of public moral argument. *Communications Monographs, 51*(1), 1–22. https://doi.org/10.1080/03637758409390180

Fisher, W. R. (1987). *Human communication as narration: Toward a philosophy of reason, value, and action*. University of South Carolina Press.

Franzosi, R. (1998). Narrative analysis—or why (and how) sociologists should be interested in narrative. *Annual Review of Sociology, 24*(1), 517–554. https://doi.org/10.1146/annurev.soc.24.1.517

Gable, G., & Jackson, P. (2011). *Lone wolves: Myth or reality?* Searchlight Magazine.

Glazzard, A. (2017). Losing the plot: Narrative, counter-narrative and violent extremism. The International Centre for Counter-Terrorism – The Hague, *Research Report*, pp 1–21. https://icct.nl/app/uploads/2017/05/ICCT-Glazzard-Losing-the-Plot-May-2017.pdf

Goodwin, J., & Jasper, J. M. (2004). *Rethinking social movements: Structure, culture, and emotion*. Rowman & Littlefield.

Goodwin, J., & Pfaff, S. (2001). Emotion work in high-risk social movements: Managing fear in the US and East German civil rights movements. In J. Goodwin, J. M. Jasper, & F. Polletta

(Eds.), *Passionate politics: Emotions and social movements* (pp. 282–302). University of Chicago Press. https://doi.org/10.7208/chicago/9780226304007.003.0017

Gupta, D. K. (2010). Accounting for the waves of international terrorism. *Perspectives on Terrorism, 2*(11), 3–9. https://www.jstor.org/stable/26298382

Hammack, P. L., & Pilecki, A. (2012). Narrative as a root metaphor for political psychology. *Political Psychology, 33*(1), 75–103. https://doi.org/10.1111/j.1467-9221.2011.00859.x

Hinchman, L. P., & Hinchman, S. (1997). *Memory, identity, community: The idea of narrative in the human sciences.* State University of New York Press.

Hochschild, A. R. (1979). Emotion work, feeling rules, and social structure. *American Journal of Sociology, 85*(3), 551–575.

Hochschild, A. R. (2016). *Strangers in their own land: Anger and mourning on the American right.* New Press.

Holbrook, D., Ramsay, G., & Taylor, M. (2013). "Terroristic content": Towards a grading scale. *Terrorism and Political Violence, 25*(2), 202–223. https://doi.org/10.1080/09546553.2011.653893

Horgan, J. (2008). From profiles to pathways and roots to routes: Perspectives from psychology on radicalization into terrorism. *The Annals of the American Academy of Political and Social Science, 618*(1), 80–94. https://doi.org/10.1177/0002716208317539

Hutchison, E., & Bleiker, R. (2014). Theorizing emotions in world politics. *International Theory, 6*(3), 491–514. https://doi.org/10.1017/S1752971914000232

King, M., & Taylor, D. M. (2011). The radicalization of homegrown jihadists: A review of theoretical models and social psychological evidence. *Terrorism and Political Violence, 23*(4), 602–622. https://doi.org/10.1080/09546553.2011.587064

Koschut, S. (2015). Macht der Gefühle: Zur Bedeutung von Emotionen für die sozialkonstruktivistische Diskursforschung. *ZIB Zeitschrift für Internationale Beziehungen, 22*(2), 7–33.

Krebs, R. R. (2015). How dominant narratives rise and fall: Military conflict, politics, and the cold war consensus. *International Organization, 69*(04), 809–845. https://doi.org/10.1017/S0020818315000181

Kristeva, J. (1980). *Desire in language: A semiotic approach to literature and art.* Columbia University Press.

Kruck, A., & Spencer, A. (2014). Vom "Söldner" zum "Samariter"? Die narrativen Grenzen strategischer Imagekonstruktion von privaten Sicherheitsdienstleistern. In W. Hofmann, J. Renner, & K. Teich (Eds.), *Narrative Formen der Politik* (pp. 145–167). Springer.

Leuprecht, C., Hataley, T., Moskalenko, S., & McCauley, C. (2010). Narratives and counter-narratives for global jihad: Opinion versus action. In E. J. A. M. Kessels (Ed.), *Countering violent extremist narratives* (pp. 58–70). National Coordinator for Counterterrorism (NCTb). https://www.clingendael.org/sites/default/files/pdfs/Countering-violent-extremist-narratives.pdf.

Llanque, M. (2014). Metaphern, Metanarrative und Verbindlichkeitsnarrationen: Narrative in der Politischen Theorie. In W. Hofmann, J. Renner, & K. Teich (Eds.), *Narrative Formen der Politik* (pp. 7–29). Springer.

Lyotard, J. (1984). *The postmodern condition: A report on knowledge.* University of Minnesota Press.

Malthaner, S. (2017). Radicalization: The evolution of an analytical paradigm. *European Journal of Sociology, 58*(3), 369–401. https://doi.org/10.1017/S0003975617000182

McCauley, C., & Moskalenko, S. (2008). Mechanisms of political radicalization: Pathways toward terrorism. *Terrorism and Political Violence, 20*(3), 415–433. https://doi.org/10.1080/09546550802073367

McCauley, C., & Moskalenko, S. (2010). Individual and group mechanisms of radicalization. In L. Fenstermacher, L. Kuznar, T. Rieger, & A. Speckhard (Eds.), *Protecting the homeland from international and domestic terrorism threats: Current multi-disciplinary perspectives on root causes, the role of ideology, and programs for counter-radicalisation and disengagement* (pp. 82–91). Inter-Agency White Paper.

Millatu Ibrahim. (2012). *Liebe und Hass für Allah*, Video, first published online in October 2012.

Moghaddam, F. M. (2005). Psychological processes and "the staircase to terrorism". *American Psychologist, 60*(9), 1039–1041. https://doi.org/10.1037/0003-066X.60.2.161

Moghaddam, F. M. (2006). *From the terrorists' point of view: What they experience and why they come to destroy*. Greenwood Publishing Group.

O'Halloran, K. L., Tan, S., Wignell, P., Bateman, J. A., Pham, D., Grossman, M., & Moere, A. V. (2016). Interpreting text and image relations in violent extremist discourse: A mixed methods approach for big data analytics. *Terrorism and Political Violence, 31*(3), 454–474. https://doi.org/10.1080/09546553.2016.1233871

Pearson, B. Z., & de Villiers, P. A. (2005). Child language acquisition: Discourse, narrative, and pragmatics. *Encyclopedia of Language and Linguistics*, 686–693.

Pfeifer, H., & Spencer, A. (2019). Once upon a time: Western genres and narrative constructions of a romantic jihad. *Journal of Language and Politics, 18*(1), 21–39. https://doi.org/10.1075/jlp.18005.spe

Prince, G. (1982). *Narratology: The form and functioning of discourse*. Mouton.

Rabatel, A. (2008). *Homo narrans: Pour une analyse énonciative et interactionnelle du récit*. Éditions Lambert-Lucas.

Rice, S. K. (2009). Emotions and terrorism research: A case for a social-psychological agenda. *Journal of Criminal Justice, 37*(3), 248–255. https://doi.org/10.1016/j.jcrimjus.2009.04.012

Riessman, C. K. (2008). *Narrative methods for the human sciences*. Sage.

Ringmar, E. (2006). Inter-texual relations: The quarrel over the Iraq war as a conflict between narrative types. *Cooperation and Conflict, 41*(4), 403–421. https://doi.org/10.1177/001083670606

Sageman, M. (2008). *Leaderless jihad: Terror networks in the twenty-first century*. University of Pennsylvania Press.

Sageman, M. (2009). Confronting al-Qaeda: Understanding the threat in Afghanistan. *Perspectives on Terrorism, 3*(4), 4–25. https://www.jstor.org/stable/26298421

Sakwa, R. (2012). Conspiracy narratives as a mode of engagement in international politics: The case of the 2008 Russo-Georgian War. *The Russian Review, 71*(4), 581–609. https://doi.org/10.1111/j.1467-9434.2012.00670.x

Schlag, G. (2018). Moving images and the politics of pity: A multi-level approach to the interpretation of images and emotions. In M. Clément & E. Sangar (Eds.), *Researching emotions in international relations* (pp. 209–230). Palgrave Macmillan.

Schuurman, B., & Taylor, M. (2018). Reconsidering radicalization: Fanaticism and the link between ideas and violence. *Perspectives on Terrorism, 12*(1), 3–22. https://www.jstor.org/stable/26343743

Searle, J. R. (1992). *The rediscovery of the mind*. MIT Press.

Shenhav, S. R. (2006). Political narratives and political reality. *International Political Science Review, 27*(3), 245–262. https://doi.org/10.1177/0192512106064474

Shoshan, N. (2016). *The management of hate: Nation, affect, and the governance of right-wing extremism in Germany*. Princeton University Press.

Silber, M., & Bhatt, A. (2007). *Radicalization in the West: The homegrown threat*. U.S. Department of Justice. https://www.ojp.gov/ncjrs/virtual-library/abstracts/radicalization-west-homegrown-threat.

Smith, D. (2017). So how do you feel about that? Talking with Provos about emotion. *Studies in Conflict & Terrorism, 41*(6), 433–449. https://doi.org/10.1080/1057610X.2017.1323467

Spencer, A. (2016). *Romantic narratives in international politics: Pirates, rebels and mercenaries*. Manchester University Press.

Van Rythoven, E. (2015). Learning to feel, learning to fear? Emotions, imaginaries, and limits in the politics of securitization. *Security Dialogue, 46*(5), 458–475. https://doi.org/10.1177/0967010615574766

Van Stekelenburg, J. (2017). Radicalization and violent emotions. *PS Political Science & Politics, 50*(4), 936–939. https://doi.org/10.1017/S1049096517001020

Von Scheve, C. (2012). Emotion regulation and emotion work: Two sides of the same coin? *Frontiers in Psychology, 3*(496), 1–10. https://doi.org/10.3389/fpsyg.2012.00496

Wibben, A. T. R. (2011). *Feminist security studies: A narrative approach*. Routledge.

Wiktorowicz, Q. (2004). *Islamic activism: A social movement theory approach, Indiana series in Middle East studies*. Indiana University Press.

Wittgenstein, L. (1958). *Philosophical investigations* (G. E. M. Anscombe, Trans.). New York: Macmillan.
Wolf, R. (2012). Der 'emotional turn' in den IB: Plädoyer für eine theoretische Überwindung methodischer Engführung. *Zeitschrift für Außen- und Sicherheitspolitik, 5*(4), 605–624. https://doi.org/10.1007/s12399-012-0288-x

Making Sense of Terrorism and Violence: A Case Study

Ramzi Merhej and Ziad Fahed

1   Introduction

This chapter[1] approaches radicalization through the conflict transformation lenses (Lederach, 2015). The case study aims to understand how individuals adapt or abandon political violence, and to identify the root and motivational factors of these processes. It explores, in total, the experiences of 23 individuals who were violently engaged in the Lebanese civil war (1975–1990), through seven semi-structured in-depth personal interviews, and a focus group with 20 participants (four interviewees also participated in the focus group). In the past, the correspondents had engaged in political violence, extremism, and/or terrorism, but are currently living their "civil life" away from physical, political violence. Some of them are even currently engaged in peacebuilding and dialogue initiatives.

In this chapter, we wish to explore political violence, including violent extremism and terrorism, which we see as possible results of a radicalization process. In addition, we aim to study de-radicalization, the reverse process of radicalization, as the objective of our research is to advance knowledge in how to prevent and mitigate political violence. Approaching political violence and terrorism through the conflict's lenses aims to link violence and its consequences to the context. Advancing knowledge on how to understand and react to political violence is the cornerstone of

---

[1] This chapter is a modified and expanded version of our published chapter in Pesquisas em Teologia 3, no. 6 (2020): 394–431 entitled *"Does Terrorism make sense?"*

R. Merhej (✉)
The Philipps University of Marburg, Marburg, Germany

Z. Fahed
Notre Dame University, Louaize, Lebanon
e-mail: ziadfahed@ndu.edu.lb

© The Author(s), under exclusive license to Springer Nature Switzerland AG 2023
D. Beck, J. Renner-Mugono (eds.), *Radicalization and Variations of Violence*, Contributions to International Relations,
https://doi.org/10.1007/978-3-031-27011-6_3

creating politically resilient societies and culture. In addition, we wish to strengthen the role of scholars and researchers from the conflict transformation field in the radicalization and terrorism fields to counter-balance the increased securitization of the latter fields for the last three decades.

After this introduction, we present the results of our literature review within the conceptual and theoretical frameworks. The conceptual framework presents and discusses the adopted definition for the political terms and concepts of Terrorism, Radicalization, and Extremism. The theoretical framework highlights the importance and benefits of studying terrorism from a conflict perspective to overcome some explanations, which can be criticized for their over-focus on security, legal, ideological, and (personal) psychological aspects. We, therefore, present the methodology and discuss its validity and reliability, as well as provide a summary of the case study and interviewees' backgrounds. Finally, we present two uncovered controversial mechanisms of radicalization and de-radicalization and compare them to ideology. In our conclusion, we summarize the results of this case study and draw recommendations directed mainly at preventive or interceptive programs, which aim to de-radicalize, or are part of, among others, PVE or CVE programs.

2   Conceptual Framework

Ambiguity in arguments leads to incorrect or contradictory conclusions. However, it is used, especially in political languages, to deliberately conceal bad argumentation based on glittering generalization. Political language is not neutral. Thus, it influences the perception of both sympathizers and antagonists, and the meaning of any term can change to fit the political context. Therefore, "what one calls 'things' matter" and "concepts follow politics" (Crenshaw, 1995, p. 7). This also accounts for the definition of terms used by scholars, especially when they are based on ordinary language and its value judgments (Crenshaw, 1995, p. 8) or when they serve as a tool for political systems (Said, 1978). In the radicalization discourse, greater attention is needed on the importance of the effect of political language (Crenshaw, 1995, p. 7) because of its impact on the lives of many around the globe, and its threat to open societies[2] (Doosje et al., 2016, p. 79).

As a result, an important challenge for researchers on radicalization is, to a certain extent, a definitional one (Powers, 2014). What is terrorism? What is extremism? What is radicalization? These questions are unlikely to have answers that are generally agreed upon (Shafritz et al., 1991). "The correct definition would be the one which is constantly used by all users" (Grob-Fitzgibbon, 2005, p. 234). In this field, however, there is no agreement on any definition (ibid) due to their political meaning (Crenshaw, 1995, p. 7). For the purpose of this chapter, we are not going

---

[2] The induction of fear can have further deleterious effects increasing polarization along between in-groups and out-groups (ethnic, religious, and national), escalating conflict within the same society.

to repeat the extensive political and academic debate about the definitions, which is, at a general level, "familiar to the point of tedium" (Freedman, 2002, p. 46).

Nevertheless, most of the radicalization discourse, especially after 9/11, was bound by the needs of governments' security establishments aiming to create immediate solutions for counter-terrorism policymakers, and to find a clear profile of the terrorist (Doosje et al., 2016; Hafez & Mullins, 2015; Kundnani, 2012). Consequently, terrorism, or more precisely, non-western private or non-state actors' terrorism, became the center of the discussion about de-radicalization in most of the literature (Fitz-Gibbon, 2016).

On the one hand, the academic discourse of terrorism included problematic "conceptual, rather than empirical" oversimplifications of the complex realities (Borum, 2011, p. 37). On the other hand, researchers have depoliticized radicalization and terrorism's driving factors and presented them as isolated individual phenomena, neglecting the role of the contexts and the emerging conflicts (McCauley & Moskalenko, 2011, p. 17). This oversimplification and de-politicization have led, for example, to a problematic presentation of Islamic ideology as an essential cause or driver of terrorism, for which Crenshaw (1995, p. 7) has coined the term "drama of terrorism." Thus, the focus in most of the research has been on them- the Muslims, the terrorists, the radicals, the crazy, immoral, evil ones, etc., rather than on the situations that these people were or are actually living in, or that they perceive themselves to be in (McCauley & Moskalenko, 2011, p.17).

In this chapter, we aim to balance the focus between *"them and us"*- and to study the dynamics in between, i.e., the conflict, since radicalization works not only on radicals and terrorists (i.e., *them*), but also on those who react to radicals and terrorists (i.e., *us*), because "[t]he friction of conflict heats both sides" (McCauley & Moskalenko, 2011, p. 223).

3 Radicalization and Terrorism

Radicalization and terrorism are inseparable (Veldhuis & Bakker, 2007): the latter is one of the many results of the former (Schmid, 2013). To avoid any ambiguity, by radicalization, we mean a non-linear process of "development of beliefs, feelings, and actions in support of any group or cause in conflict" (McCauley & Moskalenko, 2011, p. 4), with increased motivation "to use violent means against members of an out-group or symbolic targets" (Doosje et al., 2016, p. 79).

Radicalization can be identified in non-state groups, as well as in governments and/or state-sponsored agents (McCauley & Moskalenko, 2011, p. 223), although many governments and agents are reluctant to admit it (Fitz-Gibbon, 2016, p. 21). The only ostensible difference is that governments have agents with a specific uniform and insignia (ibid). Democratic and developed states are also not immune; radicalization can be demonstrated, for example, by resorting to the practice of torture, which does not conform to international human rights standards (Schmid, 2013, p. 18), by hardening foreign policies and, for example, having a more conservative borders policy. Moreover, by de-radicalization, we mean the reverse process of radicalization, i.e., "the process of becoming less radical" (Demant et al., 2008, p. 13), thus, less violent.

4 Theoretical Framework

Every phenomenon can be studied from different perspectives, and the immensely diverse body of literature around radicalization is proving this (Luiten & De Graaf, 2016; Young et al., 2015). The current radicalization discourse can be criticized for the fact that the majority of scholars have ignored the peace and conflict studies perspective, while focusing mainly on security, legal and psychological aspects. Therefore, we chose to study the radicalization phenomena using the peace and conflict studies perspective and, in particular, through the conflict transformation lenses (Lederach, 2015); studying radicalization as a conflict. Slavoj Zizek argued there are not only wrong answers but also most crucial wrong questions, because the way the problem is perceived is part of the problem (Big Think, 2016). On the one hand, the multidisciplinary approach of the conflict transformation lenses provides an inclusive understanding of the problem, avoiding narrow and wrong questions. On the other hand, it results in a variety of prerequisite steps (Lederach, 2015, pp. 7–11) to describe the processes of radicalization and to understand why it happens.

The conflict transformation lenses are based on a fundamental element: i.e., *every social conflict should make sense* (Lederach, 2003, webpage). This element is a revelation of a key aspect in the understanding of radicalization: although it might not be comforting for some, radicalization and its results, including violence, extremism, and terrorism, *should make sense*. Thus, radicalization can occur for either good or bad causes and is not about being *right* or *wrong* (McCauley & Moskalenko, 2011, p. 13). Hence, moral outrage can be a driving factor for violence. Therefore, terrorists can also be fighting for social justice, at least from their *perceived* reality (Hafez & Mullins, 2015, p. 965). Similarly, the philosopher Karl Popper wrote, "All things living are in search of a better world. Men, animals, plants, even unicellular organisms are constantly active" (Popper, 2012, p. vii). The former undercover CIA officer Amaryllis Fox, who worked on counter-terrorism for almost ten years, described it as well by arguing that "we all think that we are the good guys" (AJ+, 2016).

Making sense does not mean excusing, accepting, or justifying in any way the use of violence by any party, but only means understanding the root causes behind the violent behavior. These violent acts were, are, and will always be considered horrific and amoral; familiarity with them does not make them any more acceptable or justifiable (Powell, 2014, p. 11), "it just makes them more (psycho-) logical" (Doosje et al., 2016, p. 82) because normalizing violence hurts everyone (Fahs, 2015, p. 53). Nevertheless, making sense of radicalization also means the application of another fundamental element in conflict transformation, which is the re-humanization of the enemy by differentiating between the evil and the evildoers (ibid). "Put simply, something you've done doesn't have to constitute the sum of who you are" (Elva & Stranger, 2017).

The re-humanization process breaks the monster myth by realizing that these evildoers also have personal and positive human needs, because "how will we understand what it is in human societies that produces violence if we refuse to recognize the humanity of those who commit it?" (ibid). To prevent, discourage, and stop people from turning to violence, we first have to understand why they are doing it. Otherwise, it is impossible to mitigate its effects, which will most likely always tend to become more violent (McCauley & Moskalenko, 2011, p. 4).

Additionally, acknowledging the survival goal of the extremist and terrorist (groups) by not limiting their goals into fighting states and terrorizing their citizens is another important step after the re-humanization element. Extremist and terrorist organizations, like any other organizations, have further goals, such as consensus building and recruitment (Della Porta, 1995, p. 126). This step further helps to understand the problem of radicalization, thus providing the opportunity to create the means to deal with it (McCauley & Moskalenko, 2011, p. 4).

5 Methodology

This chapter aims to find a way of identifying mechanisms of radicalization by understanding political violence from peace and conflict studies perspectives. The empirical data that inform this chapter are drawn from a case study that examined the radicalization and de-radicalization processes of 23 ex-combatants from Lebanon. The participants are 19 males and 4 females from diverse religious, sectarian, social, economic, regional, and educational backgrounds, self-selecting as ex-combatants who were (partly) involved in the *so-called* Lebanese Civil War (1975–1990) and its preceding and subsequent related fighting, and who are currently living *"civil lives"* as relatively integrated members of their societies. It should be noted that all names have been changed to protect their identities.

The case study was conducted in 2017 and 2018, in-person through seven in-depth, semi-structured interviews and one focus group discussion (FGD) with 20 participants. The data were collected and analyzed using the Interpretative Phenomenological Analysis (IPA) method.

During the personal interviews, participants had the opportunity and time to tell their stories and to disclose more sensitive and intimate information. Moreover, the focus group discussions offered a platform for attendees to discuss their experiences, form a dialogue about issues important to them, and challenge each other's opinions. Nevertheless, the participants encouraged each other, directly and indirectly, to share more personal, specific stories, just as focus group discussions are intended, by offering "an opportunity to observe the process of collective sense-making" (Wilkinson, 1998, p. 193).

The framework for the data collection was the Interpretative Phenomenological Analysis (IPA). The participants were chosen using purposive sampling (not randomized), where a small number of participants were chosen precisely because of their experiences (Reid et al., 2005, pp. 20–23). Initially, contact was established with individuals who had previously published about, or publicly shared, their de-radicalization stories, while later on, a few civil society and non-governmental organizations working on de-radicalization, reconciliation and dialogue, and peacebuilding in Lebanon were also contacted. Potential interviewees were listed, and five pilot meetings were conducted.

Interviews were held at any location chosen by the participants. The Lebanese dialect of Arabic was always used. The interview times ranged between one and four hours, while the focus group time was four hours, with a break in between.

The collected raw data consisted of the transcribed data from the interviews and focus group discussion in the Lebanese dialect of Arabic. Back in 2017, qualitative analysis computer programs did not support a user-friendly Arabic language analysis. Therefore, the analysis of the collected data was conducted manually. Complete translation and later data entry would make the analysis even more complicated.

The Interpretative Phenomenological Analysis (IPA) (Smith & Osborn, 2007) approach was chosen for this case study because it focuses on the *meaning-making activity*[3] and helps the researchers "to explore in detail how participants are making sense of their personal and social world" (ibid, p. 53), as they are the experts of their world's perspectives (Gilbert, 2002, p. 232).

For the analysis, the authors followed the IPA's two-stage interpretation process for the *meaning-making activity*, where "the participants are trying to make sense of their world; the researcher is trying to make sense of the participants trying to make sense of their world" (Smith & Osborn, 2007, p. 53).

6 Validity and Reliability

Every study is impeded by various limitations caused by the chosen methods of research. Besides the critiques of the interrelated issues of methodological rigor and the researchers' subjectivity, single-case studies, using mainly qualitative methodologies, are often questionable when it comes to reliability and validity, both internal and external. On one hand, the subjective nature of qualitative studies often makes reliability difficult (Daymon & Holloway, 2010, p. 222), while on the other hand, Lincoln and Guba (1985) argue that the replicability criterion is a naïve concept, especially when studying complex phenomena. The authors sought to increase the reliability of this study through conceptualizing the main concepts and terms, both theoretically and in the field, and by applying Creswell's (2017) criteria of creating, following, and disclosing the framework of procedures for the field study and analysis. Hence, the resulting clear definitions, methods, and contexts would enable a second researcher to understand and apply a similar strategy. The internal validity of this study, which concerns the relationship of causes and effects of radicalization, is maintained by accurately reflecting upon "the social world of those

---

[3] The meaning-making activity is "the process of how individuals make sense of knowledge, experience, relationships, and the self" (Ignelzi, 2000, p. 5).

participating in the study" (Daymon & Holloway, 2010, p. 79) through building the analysis on the personal words and perceptions of interviewees, not only on the interpretations of the authors. The external validity, i.e., generalizability, determines whether the results and findings are socially representative and academically relevant (Daymon & Holloway, 2010, p. 91). Even though the interviewees come from a relatively wide variety of backgrounds, to verify if the results of this research have a strong external validity, inside or outside Lebanon, can only be done through further comparative research. However, the results of the discussions with the participants about the generalizability of their experiences by comparing their cases with other previous or current "extremists or terrorists," inside or outside Lebanon, increased the possibility of generalization.

7   Case Background

The case study respondents come from a society that experienced vast political developments and violence (Maalouf, 2008). Simply put, different crises and wars occurred during and after Lebanese independence from French colonization in 1943 (Salibi, 1976) and in parallel to the pan-Arab movements, Israeli-Arab conflicts, and the Cold War. The peak period was between 1975 and 1990, which was called the Lebanese Civil War. Besides this war, which welcomed a lot of international interferences and local and foreign fighters, crises continued to emerge parallel to the old, unsolved ones (Khalaf, 2002, pp. 15–55). During their lifetime (since the 1950s), the interviewees faced a variety of political, cultural, religious and social issues, which the region and the world are (still) facing today. This made them feel the need to adopt violence for different reasons and causes (political, social, economic and existential), and to join or establish radical and military groups that appealed to this need (Salibi, 1990; Kassir, 2013).

At the age of seven, one participant was getting his first military training at school. Another joined a militia at 22 years old. Their average age of being involved with political violence is around sixteen years old. All of the partakers had passed through different de-radicalization processes, and currently, they are relatively integrated into their society. Finally, the contributors come from diverse religious, sectarian, social, economic, regional and educational backgrounds. The reality of their diverse backgrounds enriches the collected data and gives the opportunity to advance knowledge in the theoretical discourse, too (Smith & Osborn, 2007, pp. 53–80).

8   Analysis

In our previously published paper (Fahed & Merhej, 2020), we described in detail the analysis process of the empirically collected data. The making-sense narratives of the interviewees' radicalization and de-radicalization processes were analyzed using the conflict transformation lenses, highlighting relations between each process and its causes and effects. The results of the analysis widely correspond with various radicalization models, mechanisms and/or driving factors that scholars, in general, reached a consensus about.

In this paper, we adopted an explorative approach, and we aimed to delve deeper into two controversial novel radicalization mechanisms that were fundamental in the radicalization processes of the 23 participants in this case study. These two mechanisms were relatively weak in the literature, but fundamental driving factors of the participants' radicalization and de-radicalization processes. Obviously, not solely responsible. Other mechanisms, upon which there is a general consensus in the literature, also played a vital role in the de-radicalization processes. We present below the two outstanding mechanisms and discuss some of their controversial aspects.

8.1 I Did Not know: I Did Not Trust (Access and Trust)

Various participants (FGD and PIs)[4] identified two double-edged de-radicalization mechanisms. We refer to the first one as *I did not know—I did not trust*. Although weak in the literature, our analysis shows that *perceived access to violent means* is an indispensable mechanism for radicalization, and *perceived access to nonviolent means* is an indispensable mechanism for de-radicalization as well as preventing radicalization.

"I did not know that there is an alternative to violence. Today, after I joined Fighter for Peace (FfP),[5] I have learned about a variety of nonviolent approaches… I wish, I knew these means before, so that maybe I would not have joined the war" (FGD, 28 May 2017). One respondent explained, "I was ignorant about conflict transformation approaches and the nonviolent and peaceful culture. Our parents, schools, and society did not teach us because, maybe, violence was an international culture and approach; they were unaware of an effective alternative." Another added, "We were children, [parents, social environment, political and religious leaders] taught us to use violence. I believed and I was totally convinced that violence is the only means and way of protecting our existence and identity to make a good change."

Access to and *trust* in alternative nonviolent means are highly dependent on the culture and norms of the respective society and social group of each individual. In the diverse context of our interviewees, one of the very few common social factors was the overwhelming presence of the culture of violence and heroism within their patriarchal societies. "We inherited a culture of power and patriarchy; the culture of

---

[4] Although all the participants accepted to disclose their real names and identities, we decided to follow the recommendation of Corti et al. (2000), who suggested replacing identifying details, i.e., interviewees' names, with pseudonyms. In this way, the data is anonymized but remain authentic (Corti et al., 2000). Therefore, the analyzed data is referred to, using the following codes: focus group discussions with the ex-fighters (FGD, Date); personal interview with an ex-fighter (PI, Alias, Date), and all the 23 participants (FGD and PIs).

[5] Fighters for Peace (FfP) is an organization in the Middle East that brings ex-fighters and ex-combatants from different backgrounds together, to support them to become fighters for peace. http://fightersforpeace.org/

you are a man. Our parents, religion, political parties, and society gave us violent role models, such as Salah Eddine, Hercules, St. Georges, and other historic heroes," explained one female participant (FGD, 28 May 2017), stressing on the indirect role of culture in supporting the use of violence by creating heroes who were violent.

Violence, in general, and political violence, in particular, could be advantageous and effective, at least in the short term. Although *access* to nonviolent means could be achieved or taught, it is similarly essential to have effective and trustworthy nonviolent means in both short and long terms. One participant pointed out that it is not only the access to violent or nonviolent means, but also the lack of *effectiveness* of and *trust* in those means: "we did not trust the nonviolent or peaceful means or believe in the effectiveness of any alternative means other than violence. Because you could use nonviolent means for seven hundred thousand years, but the occupation would remain." Finally, one participant added, "it was not only about learning alternative means to violence, but it was also about how we perceived violence and the double standards that might overcome our rationality… I used to think that our revolutionary violence was good, but their reactionary and traditional violence was bad." The protagonists' perceptions of their violence in comparison to their opponents add to the complexity of trust and access. To simplify this complexity, we discuss below the advantages of political violence and how it is used as a means to an end, i.e., peace.

8.1.1 Advantages of Political Violence

Identifying the advantages of political violence does not aim to show the *goodness* of violence, but to stress the reality of people who use it and the advantages that they get, shedding light on the complex mixture between the absurd and the reasonable aspects of violence. This theme could help Fighter for Peace (FfP) and other organizations to know what to tackle when they are approaching new generations (FGD, 28 May 2017).

The goal of discussing the advantages of violence is to point out what issues are to be addressed in any de-radicalization program. It clarifies what is to be done to create alternative paths for individuals to dismiss violence and to instead use alternative nonviolent means when they are trying to realize their motives and interests. Although one participant (FGD, 28 May 2017) claimed at first that, "It is not easy to find them," the group discussed a variety of benefits, advantages, and gains, which the authors then ordered into five categories of advantages: (1) existential, survival, and becoming; (2) skills and competencies; (3) belonging and intimate relationships; (4) status, power, and fame; and (5) political, social and cultural.

"Political violence saved my existence," claimed one participant (FGD, 28 May 2017). Another added, "[participating] in the war created [for me] a valuable goal worth living and fighting for. It made me feel proud and strong." Many participants affirmed that the war gave meaning to their life and a perceived change to become a better person. Daniel (PI, 25 May 2017) and Elena (PI, 27 May 2017) elaborated on the meaning of life that the war gave them and stressed the importance of the combatants' reintegration when they dropped their weapons, since "after the war, many fighters committed suicide because they lost their life's meaning. The only thing that they knew was fighting" (PI, 27 May 2017).

FGD participants talked about various skills and competencies that they gained during their participation in political violence (28 May 2017). They claim to have learned about such life and survival skills as how to communicate, how to convince, how to survive, and how to manage. They were also empowered in other skills and competencies, such as leadership, adaptability, and cultural awareness, among other personal and public skills.

Belonging and the establishment of intimate relationships are two main advantages of radicalization. The participants (FGD and PIs) affirmed the deep and close relationships and friendships within their closed social environment that the war offered them: "my relations with my comrades were stronger than my relationship with my family" (FGD, 28 May 2017). This spirit of identity and belonging, coupled with high levels of trust, honesty, cooperation, and love permeated the relationships among the comrades. "There is no better name than a comrade." The isolation that they had experienced due to political violence provided the fighters with an alternative family, where they had the chance to meet with different people "with whom we shared the same goals and objectives, and a similar understanding of life." Political violence also offered a lot of sexual benefits and intimate relationships. Elena (PI, 27 May 2017) explained, "In wartime, love relationships follow more of a survivor approach because sex means creation and war means death. You compensate for your need for life through sex, especially because the social boundaries are completely broken; thus, casual sex becomes easier and more meaningful. Sex becomes the opposite of death." Thus, women had more relationships with men, and vice-versa (FGD, 28 May 2017).

Status, power, and fame, combined with the advantages of the relationship, made political violence very attractive, (FGD and PIs). "I had the feeling that I was 'the man'" (FGD, 28 May 2017). The feeling and practice of power, higher self-confidence, independence, respect, pride, and the sense of being needed and useful were the main outcomes of the status, power, and fame level, where "You feel you are strong and that people have to respect you and ask your help; you feel needed." One participant called these advantages "social and political capital." "I had a lot of social capital; I was accepted and respected because I defended our group and killed the enemy, and did what had to be done."

On the political, social, and cultural level, violence offered the fighters opportunities to make social, political, and economic changes to suit their interests. If the change was not possible or easy to make, violence at least empowered their political presence and status, making them a strong party in the conflict. In addition, one woman argued that the war proved the capability of women, enabling them to participate and lead in politics. Some kind of gender equality, or at least a better gender balance, was created. Moreover, one participant claimed, "in the war, the level of higher education among the poor was raised [through the financial support and scholarships offered by the empathizers and allies, mainly the Soviet Union]." However, one participant objected because he believed these things were done for political interests and not for the sake of the poor, reminding everybody that political violence can only provide temporary perceived advantages. One woman concluded, "When you meet people's needs and tackle the reasons which drive people to behave violently, then the violence will stop. If what we got as advantages from our engagement in the war can be provided for new generations by nonviolent means, then, no one will adopt violence."

8.1.2 Violence: The Means of Achieving Peace

The relationship between political violence and its advantages shifted "the focus group discussions" (FGD, 28 May 2017) toward a central question: does political violence ultimately aim to achieve peace? Most of the ex-fighters did not think a lot about their highest goals during the daily fighting, "I used to live day by day, trying to perform my duties, and my only concern was to survive and help my group to conquer." All of them agreed that, at some point during their fighting, they took peace for granted as the ultimate objective of the political violence that they were engaged in. "Everything we were doing was, supposedly, leading to peace... Our party's slogan, which we repeated almost every day, was 'Free Nation—Happy People,' and we thought that we were fighting to achieve this slogan." Their end goal of peace seemed to justify their violent means: "Through the violence, I was building peace for my people and my society." Moreover, their missions of building peace were organically dependent on, and affiliated with, those who held authority and power. Thus, they considered peace as the ultimate result of the victory: "By conquering, you think you are building peace because you believe that if you rule, peace and love will also rule naturally."

In addition, security, protection, and liberation were considered as the major steps in their pursuit of peace. For example, one participant explained, "When you conquer a region or you protect your people, this is also partly building peace, despite the use of violence." Another added, "By freeing my country from the occupier and conquering my enemies, for sure I was building peace," and a third elaborated, "The occupation was the reason for people's problems. When you free the people from the occupation, then peace will come back accordingly."

The discussion developed further, and one FDG participant asked, "are violence and war indispensable for the development of humanity?" All participants agreed that violence always leads to destruction, but only a few believed that nothing should justify it. The majority argued, "The only occasion in which you can use violence is when you are defending yourself." The idea of self-defense was expanded to include achieving political goals: "I built my peace by achieving my goals." As a reaction, a participant speculated, "Every ideology aims ultimately to achieve peace, at least this is the belief of the ideology's followers. Violence is only a temporary means, and sometimes it is indispensable," while a second elaborated, "We believed that we had the perfect project and solution, you can call it Ideology. We thought if through violence we can achieve it, so let it be; because only through our project peace will be possible."

Some participants meant that violence was indispensable. One ex-fighter stressed, "Violence is the only means of preserving your existence if you are threatened, and existence is a part of peace." A second person added, "How do you fight an occupation- with flowers? No- with a gun, with explosives, with any power that you have," and a third quoted a famous line of Renatus, "If you want peace, prepare for war," and continued, "Peace can only be protected or achieved through war. Power should be faced with power. Violence should be faced with greater violence." One participant concluded, "Listening to the opinion of different ex-fighters on the relationship between violence and peace gives us an understanding of how radical groups recruit new members. Then, we [FfP] have to see how we can counter these narratives."

8.2 Normality of Violence

The second double-edged de-radicalization mechanism is what we refer to as *Normality of Violence*. While the previous identified mechanism, *I did not know—I did not trust,* depends completely on the individual knowledge and skills related to day-to-day conflict management, the *Normality of Violence* mechanism is a contextual mechanism that affects indirectly the individual by setting or blurring the borders of violence. In other words, a person could individually improve his conflict management styles and learn *"non-violent"* transformation approaches. However, the border of *"violence"* and *"non-violence"* is always set by the relative *Normality of Violence*.

The relative *Normality of Violence* played a major role in the 23 studied de-radicalization processes. The authors suggest that this relativity, which could be ostensibly understood as the inability to find a specific definition of violence, is an indispensable mechanism of radicalization *and* de-radicalization. This inability to reach a specific definition of violence is an integral part of the human condition, as the relation between the subject (human) and the object (violence) is always ambiguous (De Beauvoir, 1962, pp. 21–65). Our analysis led us to conclude that one of the main challenges of the terrorism and radicalization fields is the need to grapple with ambiguity as long as there are some scholars and political institutions who try to mask this ambiguity of violence, thus its normality, and give it clear definition that suits their political agenda.

Therefore, to explain the *Normality of Violence*, it is important to explain what is meant by violence. For this study, the definition of violence was based on the understanding of the participants from their own contexts. The participants (FGD, 28 May 2017) defined violence as a variety of verbal, physical, social, psychological, structural, and cultural behaviors or attitudes. One participant explained, "When dialogue stops, violence starts," another elaborated, "Violence is when we don't dialogue about our daily life's problems and conflicts," and a third clarified, "Violence is the culture of 'me or no one else'…" Other participants gave more specific examples: "Any practice of obedience or giving orders is violence, especially when it disrespects and blocks the development of other human beings and their innovative life." Power, force, authority, preached hatred, enforcement of behavior or attitude, inequality, infringement, injustice, deprivation, and humiliation of human dignity were central in their definitions of violence. For example, violence was considered making change by power or force; stealing another's decision, life, material, or spiritual properties; and using any means against others obliging them to behave, believe, or adopt one's own truth, values, and views: "Violence is any coercion or murder, and everything in between."

Normality, the first part of the term, represents what the society considered, from the above definitions of violence, to be *Normal*, and what rewards are offered for committing any of these acts of violence. In other words, the *Normality of Violence* is the combination of what in a society is considered to be violence and what is not, plus how the society would appeal to the person who takes, or does not take, violent actions. For example, society might categorize killing as violence, but might treat the killer as a hero in specific situations. Tim (PI, 1 June 2017) explained, "In the war, social pressure played a big role in me choosing between being either a coward [i.e. not fighting] or a hero [i.e. killing the enemy]." Therefore, what is *normal* is shaped by context, time, and place, i.e., what is normal in wartime is different during ceasefires, partially clarifying why wartime or political instability catalyzes and initiates more radicalization processes. Nowadays, the influence of instability is not limited to the local (unstable) society, but has a worldwide influence due to globalization, as discussed by Hafez and Mullins (2015, p. 959).

As a mechanism of radicalization, we consider a *Lower Normality of Violence*,[6] which means fewer actions are considered violent with promised positive rewards—i.e., a relatively easier radicalization path. A *Lower Normality of Violence* offers enough reasoning and rewards for committed political violence. It is like diving in the water: the deeper you go, the higher the pressure. A *Lower Normality of Violence* normalizes and justifies almost any violent actions. Elena (PI, 27 May 2017) explained, "Back then, I did not see myself as an extremist, but as a responsible person. However, if I were to judge myself today, I could clearly say I was an extremist." Similarly, armies create a conditioned, justified, and moralized *Lower Normality of Violence,* radicalizing their soldiers and preparing them for violence whenever it is "needed."

As a mechanism of de-radicalization, we consider a *Higher Normality of Violence*, which means more actions are categorized as violent with negative rewards for the perpetrators—i.e., a relatively more difficult radicalization path. Lesser practices of dehumanization and more practices of living together and dialogue, even if it is "obligatory"—i.e. under the rule of law, or ostensibly created, the *Higher Normality of Violence* played a major role in the de-radicalization of several of our case study participants. Although Julian (PI, 11 June 2017) kept his weapon after the end of the war, he never dared to use it again due to the obligatory practice of humanization and living together.

8.2.1 Ideology Versus Normality of Violence

Talking about *Normality of Violence* might be seen as an attempt to create another variation of Ideology, which is often considered in various academic debates to be a major driver and/or motive for political radicalization and violence. It is important

---
[6] The comparative adjective is essential here to stress on the relativity of the normality of violence.

to mention that most of the academic discussions around ideology have been based on understanding non-western terrorism, foreign fighters, the homegrown terrorist phenomenon, or terrorists attacking the Western world (see: i.e., Hafez & Mullins, 2015). This creates a biased understanding of the relationship between ideology and violence. In this same biased understanding, some of the participants of the study did consider ideology as a driving factor for their radicalization (i.e., PI, Luca, 24 May 2017; PI, Daniel, 25 May 2017; and PI, Elena, 27 May 2017). A deeper analysis of Luca's, Daniel's, and Elena's processes supports the role of ideology in the rationalization and justification of their decision to join the violence, as described by McCauley and Moskalenko (2011, p. 220). In other words, ideology is the tool which activates the meaning-making process; it is the umbrella under which a new violent life gains its sense. While the *Normality of Violence* offers enough relative reasoning and rewards for committed political violence (relative to time and space), *Ideology* offers justification and bigger meaning to these violent actions (in a certain sense, forever). Therefore, the authors believe that there is a difference between *Ideology* and the *Normality of Violence* mechanisms. While the latter is deeply contextual and always relative—thus changeable—Ideology is usually a defined set of beliefs circulating around a defined set of answers to life's biggest questions and purposes.

Luca, Daniel, and Elena, similarly to all the other participants (FGD; PIs), claimed that their very existence and survival were important factors in their radicalization process and their decision to join the war. This analysis is not limited to the Lebanese case study; Christian Picciolini, a former extremist, shares a similar opinion, "I think ultimately people become extremists not necessarily because of the ideology. I think that ideology is simply a vehicle to be violent. I believe that people become radicalized, or extremist because they're searching for three very fundamental human needs: identity, community and a sense of purpose" (Upworthy, 2017).

Nevertheless, three crucial questions arise here:

(1) Is ideology only a justification for the past, or also for current actions/behavior which aim to fulfill certain human needs, or can it also trigger people to behave violently in the future? The case study findings revealed that ideologies also offer dreams for a better future, where the underlying problems of the previous unfulfilled needs are perceptively solved. As Daniel (PI, 25 May 2017) elaborated, "What drove me to violence was fear and self-defense as defensive mechanisms, as well as the goal of building a Christian nationalist nation as an offensive mechanism. The Christian nation as a political ambition is offensive because the idea is not only to protect ourselves, but also to annihilate the other. We wanted to have power and to purify the land." An FGD participant added, "Violence is usually perceived to be used as a defensive means, but it ends being an offensive one geared at achieving different interests." This understanding fits Glasl's (2002) conflict escalation model, where ideologies start to play a role in the middle of the escalation, i.e., at the fifth stage: "Loss of Face," in which parties lose their moral credibility, and the conflict moves to the win-lose situation. Hannah Arendt explained, from a philosophical perspective, "The need of reason is not inspired by the quest for truth but by the quest for meaning" (1981, p. 15).

(2) How much do ideologies influence actions? There is consensus in the political discourse that diverges between beliefs and actions (McCauley & Moskalenko, 2011, p. 220). Equally, overwhelming evidence in social psychology confirms that beliefs alone are weak predictors of actions. Ideology and actions are only sometimes connected, but not always (Borum, 2011, p. 9), because a very small number of people who follow a specific violent ideology move all the way to violence, extremism, and/or terrorism (Doosje et al., 2016, p. 79). McCauley and Moskalenko (2011, pp. 219–220) argue that ideology is too simple and too broad a mechanism to be considered in understanding radicalization. They purport that many radicalization pathways to extremism do not involve ideology, similar to the cases of Stefan (PI, 28 May 2017), Tim (PI, 1 June 2017), and Julian (PI, 11 June 2017).

Dissonance Theory supports this argument, proposing that humans tend to change their opinions to fit their behavior to reduce the inconsistency between their desired positive self-image and their perceived bad behavior (Festinger, 1957). People come up with reasons to justify or excuse their bad behavior because it is easier than acting only according to what is reasonable, or what is according to their ideology (ibid).

(3) If it is true that ideology is only a rationalization/justification, how should de-radicalization programs or authorities deal with it? A study by Norman and Mikhael (2017, p. 12) stressed that policymakers should not focus on "the intricacies or appeal of the ideology itself," but on the process of radicalization, especially because similarities can be found in a variety of "radicalization processes across different ideologies and contexts."

The discussion above suggests that the only way to overcome ideologies is through actions, which, in turn, can create a counter-reality to overcome ideologies. Therefore, identifying ideology as a mechanism of radicalization is a deviation from the focus and the goal, because understanding radicalization from the lenses of ideology creates opposite ideologies. These are, in turn, a wrong perception of reality, for even though they address real problems, they end up mystifying the solutions (Video: Zizek, 2012). Simply put, the importance and ranking of ideology in de-radicalization studies should neither be exaggerated nor reduced, but instead taken seriously.

9 Conclusion

The findings of the case study point out clearly that, although the main factors that initiate or serve as a catalyst in the de-radicalization processes might be common between different individuals, the radicalization process of each individual is unique, personal, and nonlinear. Moreover, the participants perceived adopting and using violent means, including terrorism and violent extremism measures, as a normal, natural, and essential decision taken within their context. Nevertheless, the role of the group was indispensable and fundamental in the radicalization processes of the 23 participants.

Studying (de)radicalization from the peace and conflict studies perspectives uncovers two new mechanisms, *I did not know—I did not trust* and the *Normality of Violence* mechanisms, which are fundamental driving and rewarding factors in the radicalization processes of the case study participants. Likewise, the results of this case study support the opinion that suggests a minimal role of ideology in radicalization processes and political violence.

The results of this case study also display that, besides the noncontroversial mechanisms and root causes of radicalization, extremism, and terrorism, the *I did not know—I did not trust* mechanism, i.e., the lack of familiarity, access, and trust in nonviolent means, is a fundamental mechanism for radicalization processes. Similarly, familiarity, access, and trust in nonviolent means are fundamental mechanisms of de-radicalization.

Furthermore, the political context provided opportunities for the normalization of violent or nonviolent behavior and attitudes. The personal, the group, and the mass levels of the participants were interdependent, and their connections were multi-layered. Based on the results of this study, we conclude that any preventive or interceptive programs which aim at de-radicalization or are part of, among others, PVE or CVE programs must, and for most, focus on creating a *Higher Normality of Violence*, i.e., work on further de-normalization of violent action and reduce their social and culturally rewards.

Investing in creating *access* to nonviolent means, strengthening their *effectiveness*, and building *trust* in these means, as well as working on creating a *Higher Normality of Violence,* is the best that can be done for de-radicalization.

We realize the importance of further advancing knowledge on how to manage the *Normality of Violence*. This study, however, suggests a *Higher Normality of Violence* could be achieved by working on sustainable improvement of society's resilience to political violence through addressing the root causes of *structural* and *cultural* violence.

References

AJ+. (2016, June 14). *Former undercover CIA officer talks war and peace* [Video]. Youtube. https://www.youtube.com/watch?v=7WEd34oW9BI

Arendt, H. (1981). *The life of the mind: The groundbreaking investigation on how we think*. HMH.

Big Think. (2016, September 21). *There are not only wrong answers, but also wrong questions Philosopher Slavoj Zizek on the importance of asking the right questions* [Video]. Facebook. Retrieved September 22, 2016, from https://www.facebook.com/BigThinkdotcom/videos/10153934720643527/?video_source=pages_finch_main_video.

Borum, R. (2011). Radicalization into violent extremism I: A review of social science theories. *Journal of Strategic Security, 4*(4), 7–36. https://doi.org/10.5038/1944-0472.4.4.1

Corti, L., Day, A., & Backhouse, G. (2000). Confidentiality and informed consent: Issues for consideration in the preservation of and provision of access to qualitative data archives. *Forum Qualitative Sozialforschung/Forum: Qualitative Social Research, 1*(3).

Crenshaw, M. (1995). Thoughts on relating terrorism to historical contexts. In M. Crenshaw (Ed.), *Terrorism in context*. Pennsylvania State University Press.

Creswell, J. W., & Creswell, D. J. (2017). *Research design: Qualitative, quantitative, and mixed methods approaches*. Sage.

Daymon, C., & Holloway, I. (2010). *Qualitative research methods in public relations and marketing communications*. Routledge.

De Beauvoir, S. (1962). *The ethics of ambiguity, tr.* Citadel Press.

Della Porta, D. (1995). Left-wing terrorism in Italy. In M. Crenshaw (Ed.), *Terrorism in context* (pp. 105–159). Pennsylvania State University Press.

Demant, F., Slootman, M., Buijs, F., & Tillie, J. (2008). *Decline and disengagement: An analysis of processes of deradicalisation*. Institute for Migration and Ethnic Studies. https://pure.uva.nl/ws/files/1079141/64714_Demant_Slootman_2008_Decline_and_Disengagement.pdf

Doosje, B., de Wolf, A. B., Mann, L., & Feddes, A. R. (2016). Radicalisering en de-radicalisering. In P. J. Van Koppen, M. Jelicic, J. W. De Keijser, & R. Horselenberg (Eds.), *Routes van het Recht. Over de rechtspsychologie*. Boom Juridisch.

Elva, T., & Stranger, T. (2017, February). Our *story of rape and reconciliation* [Video]. TED Conferences. https://www.ted.com/talks/thordis_elva_tom_stranger_our_story_of_rape_and_reconciliation

Fahed, Z., & Merhej, R. (2020). Does "Terrorism" make sense? *Pesquisas em Teologia, 3*(6), 394–431. https://doi.org/10.46859/PUCRio.Acad.PqTeo.2595-9409.2020v3n6p394

Fahs, H. (2015). بعلي مسؤليت. Voix Du Liban, Beirut, Lebanon.

Festinger, L. (1957). *A theory of cognitive dissonance* (Vol. 2). Stanford University Press.

Fitz-Gibbon, A. (2016). *Talking to terrorists, non-violence, and counter-terrorism: Lessons for Gaza from Northern Ireland*. Springer.

Freedman, L. (2002). The coming war on terrorism. *The Political Quarterly, 73*, 40–56. https://doi.org/10.1111/1467-923X.73.s1.5

Gilbert, K. R. (2002). Taking a narrative approach to grief research: Finding meaning in stories. *Death Studies, 26*(3), 223–239. https://doi.org/10.1080/07481180211274

Glasl, F. (2002). *Konfliktmanagement. Ein Handbuch für Führungskräfte, Beraterinnen und Berater*. Verlag Freies Geistesleben, Stuttgart.

Grob-Fitzgibbon, B. (2005). What is terrorism? Redefining a phenomenon in time of war. *Peace and Change, 30*(2), 231–246. https://doi.org/10.1111/j.0149-0508.2005.00318.x

Hafez, M., & Mullins, C. (2015). The radicalization puzzle: A theoretical synthesis of empirical approaches to homegrown extremism. *Studies in Conflict and Terrorism, 38*(11), 958–975. https://doi.org/10.1080/1057610X.2015.1051375

Ignelzi, M. (2000). Meaning-making in the learning and teaching process. *New Directions for Teaching and Learning, 82*, 5–14. https://doi.org/10.1002/tl.8201

Kassir, S. (2013). *Being Arab*. Verso Books.

Khalaf, S. (2002). *Civil and uncivil violence in Lebanon*. Columbia University Press.

Kundnani, A. (2012). Radicalisation: The journey of a concept. *Race and Class, 54*(2), 3–25. https://doi.org/10.1177/0306396812454984

Lederach, J. P. (2003). *Conflict transformation. Beyond intractability*. In Burgess, G., & Burgess, H. (Eds.), Conflict information consortium. University of Colorado, Boulder. Posted: October (2003). Retrieved January 22, 2017, from http://www.beyondintractability.org/essay/transformation.

Lederach, J. (2015). *Little book of conflict transformation: Clear articulation of the guiding principles by a pioneer in the field*. Simon and Schuster.

Lincoln, Y., & Guba, Y. (1985). *Naturalistic inquiry* (Vol. 75). Sage.

Luiten, H., & De Graaf, S. (2016). *Begrijp jij het Midden-Oosten nog?* Amsterdam University Press.

Maalouf, A. (2008). *Origins: A memoir*. Farrar, Straus and Giroux.

McCauley, C., & Moskalenko, S. (2011). *Friction: How radicalization happens to them and us*. Oxford University Press. https://doi.org/10.5038/1944-0472.4.4.10

Norman, J., & Mikhael, D. (2017, August 28). Youth radicalization is on the rise. Here's what we know about why. *The Washington Post*. https://www.washingtonpost.com/news/monkey-cage/wp/2017/08/25/youth-radicalization-is-on-the-rise-heres-what-we-know-about-why/

Popper, K. (2012). *In search of a better world: Lectures and essays from thirty years*. Routledge.

Powell, J. (2014). *Talking to terrorists: How to end armed conflicts*. Random House.

Powers, S. M. (2014). Conceptualizing radicalization in a market for loyalties. *Media, War and Conflict, 7*(2), 233–249. https://doi.org/10.1177/1750635214538620

Reid, K., Flowers, P., & Larkin, M. (2005). Interpretative phenomenological analysis: An overview and methodological review. *The Psychologist, 18*(1), 20–23.

Said, E. (1978). *Orientalism: Western concepts of the Orient*. Pantheon.

Salibi, K. S. (1976). *Crossroads to Civil War: Lebanon, 1958-1976*. Ithaca Press.

Salibi, K. (1990). *A house of many mansions: The history of Lebanon reconsidered*. University of California Press.

Schmid, A. P. (2013). Radicalisation, de-radicalisation, counter-radicalisation: A conceptual discussion and literature review. *ICCT Research Paper* 97, no. 1, 22.

Shafritz, J. M., Gibbons, E. F., & Scott, G. E. (1991). *Almanac of modern terrorism*. Facts on File.

Smith, J. A., & Osborn, M. (2007). Pain as an assault on the self: An interpretative phenomenological analysis of the psychological impact of chronic benign low back pain. *Psychology and Health, 22*(5), 517–534. https://doi.org/10.1080/14768320600941756

Upworthy. (2017, August 14). *This reformed white supremacist believes racism is learned – and it can be unlearned* [Video]. Facebook. Retrieved September 5, 2017, from https://www.facebook.com/Upworthy/videos/vb.354522044588660/1919104821463700/?type=2andtheater.

Veldhuis, T., & Bakker, B. (2007). Causale factoren van radicalisering en hun onderlinge samenhang. *Vrede en veiligheid, 36*(4), 447–470.

Wilkinson, S. (1998). Focus group methodology: A review. *International Journal of Social Research Methodology, 1*(3), 181–203. https://doi.org/10.1080/13645579.1998.10846874

Young, H. F., Rooze, M., & Holsappel, J. (2015). Translating conceptualizations into practical suggestions: What the literature on radicalization can offer to practitioners. *Peace and Conflict: Journal of Peace Psychology, 21*(2), 212–225. https://doi.org/10.1037/pac0000065

Zizek, S. (Ed.). (2012). *Mapping ideology*. Verso Books.

Correlates for Foreign Fighters in Tunisia

Protest and Marginalization as Predictors for Foreign Fighter Mobilization?

Julius Strunk

1 Introduction

Although research on the topic of foreign fighters (FF)[1] often notes that it is not a phenomenon, especially when considering fighters like the volunteers in the Spanish Civil War of the 1930s, Hegghammer nevertheless stresses that it "[…] remains notoriously understudied" (2011, p. 54). However, there has been an observable rise in interest on the topic since the start of the civil war in Syria, the massive influx of foreign fighters thereafter, and the establishment of the self-proclaimed "Islamic State."[2] While this interest is mostly driven by the large number of FF stemming from Western countries and related security concerns for their countries of origin once they return, there has also been a growing interest in the Tunisian case. Despite its small size, Tunisia is the fourth highest supplier of foreign fighters to Syria and Iraq when measured by country population (Barrett, 2017). Consequently, several experts have asked about the reasons why Tunisia "produce[d] so many terrorists" (Caryl, 2016).

At first glance, this fact seems puzzling, since the country has undergone a democratization process following the ousting of long-term ruler Ben Ali in the wake of the so-called Arab Uprisings (Alexander, 2016, pp. 83–99). This period was accompanied by extensive protests (Jöst & Vatthauer, 2019, pp. 77–79), voicing a

---

[1] Following Malet, a foreign fighter (FF) is, in this paper, broadly defined as "[a] non-citizen of a state experiencing civil conflict who arrives from an external state to join an insurgency" (Malet, 2015, p. 459).

[2] In the following, the author will refer to the so-called Islamic State by using the Arabic acronym, *Daesh*. For further information. See Dearden (2014).

J. Strunk (✉)
Goethe University Frankfurt, Frankfurt, Germany

© The Author(s), under exclusive license to Springer Nature Switzerland AG 2023
D. Beck, J. Renner-Mugono (eds.), *Radicalization and Variations of Violence*, Contributions to International Relations,
https://doi.org/10.1007/978-3-031-27011-6_4

wide range of political and socio-economic issues and demands (Vatthauer & Weipert-Fenner, 2017, pp. 14–15). During the context of this transition, until the end of 2014, it is estimated that around 2560 Tunisian fighters left to fight in Syria and Iraq, with many joining *Daesh* and an additional 9000 who were prevented from traveling, as well as an unknown number leaving to fight in Libya (Zelin, 2018b, p. 5).

Researchers stress that this radicalization[3] is happening not despite, but because of the transformation process. While some point to the open atmosphere following the overthrow of Tunisia's long-term ruler Ben Ali, in which Tunisians could be recruited for the fight in Syria, and later Iraq without state interference (e.g., Corneau-Tremblay, 2015; Zelin, 2020), others specifically highlight the disillusionment and discontent with the Tunisian state, especially after the revolution did not deliver on its promise of economic improvement (Macdonald & Waggoner, 2018). In this regard, Sterman and Rosenblatt (2018) are the only researchers thus far to claim a direct positive link between discontent towards the Tunisian government and foreign fighter mobilization in Tunisia on a wide empirical basis. The authors connect the two phenomena, stating that *Daesh* "[…] was drawing upon populations that were already rebelling against the status quo conditions in Tunisia" (Sterman & Rosenblatt, 2018, p. 39). This claim is based on their finding that regions with a high mobilization rate were also characterized by an elevated protest rate. Their explanation is that, be it protesting or joining *Daesh* in Syria, both are possible expressions of discontent towards the government, concluding that *Daesh* "[…] built upon a growing anger in Tunisia that found multiple expressions—of which ISIS was only the latest" (Sterman & Rosenblatt, 2018, p. 41). While their findings are compelling, their analysis remains descriptive and lacks rigorous testing of their results. Yet, considering the nature of their paper as a policy paper, verification is crucial to understanding the phenomenon and developing appropriate counter policies.

Following Sterman and Rosenblatt's methodological approach of a spatial analysis, this paper intends to further investigate and test their claim as to how far discontent—expressed via protest—and underlying marginalization are strong predictors for foreign fighter mobilization. To this end, not only will their outcomes be inserted into a comprehensive model, but they will also be applied on the more localized sub-administrative level of delegations rather than governorates, as Sterman and Rosenblatt did, thus testing the robustness of their findings. Thereby, the effect of protest, in particular, and marginalization, in general, on foreign fighter mobilization in Tunisia will be assessed. Sterman and Rosenblatt's clear preference for push factors which go against the current state of the art gives this paper an interesting

---

[3] Radicalization is broadly defined here as "the process by which an individual acquires the motivation to use violence" (Hegghammer, 2013, p. 2); Mobilizing to fight as an FF can thus clearly be interpreted as a sign of being radicalized. Still, the term foreign fighter mobilization, rather than radicalization, is used predominantly in this paper, as it is focused on this topic specifically and does not aim to make broader claims on the radicalization process as such.

angle. This paper thus adds to the small number of quantitative studies as well as to the theoretical discussion on the topic of foreign fighter mobilization.

This paper is structured as follows: First, theoretic approaches and empirical studies on the topic of FF in Tunisia are discussed. Subsequently, the possible factors contributing to foreign fighter mobilization in Tunisia are analyzed. After presenting and discussing the analytical results, possible future research fields are proposed.

2 State of the Art

So far, attempts to build a foreign fighter theory have highlighted pull factors as the most potent explanation for FF mobilization. Arguing from a contentious politics perspective, Malet acknowledges the importance of social ties and interpersonal networks for the quantitative success of mobilizing foreign fighters. However, he stresses that the most important piece is the framing of a shared transnational identity and a severe threat to this community, which is not dealt with by any other government (2013, pp. 207–209). Malet states "[t]he constant casus belli used to recruit foreign fighters […] [is] the necessary defense of their transnational identity communities" (2013, p. 198). Similarly, Hegghammer, also arguing from a social movement perspective, identifies two factors that are central to explaining foreign fighter mobilization: an "[…] ideology stressing solidarity within an imagined transnational community […] [and] a strong cadre of transnational activists" (2011, p. 90). Summarized, these factors include grievances of a suffering people, an identity in some way shared with those people, an ideology that contains the logic to help, and a subculture that spreads and intensifies this ideology (Ahmed & Pisoiu, 2014, pp. 9-11).

Sterman and Rosenblatt, on the other hand, assume that focusing mainly on ideology as an explanandum for mobilization of foreign fighters is not sufficient, but that the local conditions offer a more potent explanation (2018, pp. 28, 33), as "[…] 75 percent of IS foreign fighters were recruited from areas that constituted 11 percent of the [MENA] region's total population" (Rosenblatt, 2021, p. 2). These hotbeds share a common characteristic: they are marginalized, both economically as well as politically, and exhibit high numbers of political unrest (Rosenblatt, 2021). Although these claims were debated academically (e.g., Ben Arab, 2016; Colombo, 2016; Macdonald & Waggoner, 2018), Sterman and Rosenblatt make this claim on a wider empirical base provided by the leaked *Daesh* entry files.[4] Respective observations regarding marginalization on similar empirical bases have been made about FF from Sweden (Gustafsson & Ranstorp, 2017, 83–85) or Belgium (van Vlierden, 2016). Yet, those studies are of a descriptive and exploratory nature and not made on

---

[4] These files were leaked by a supposed *Daesh* defector and acquired by several news outlets. They were filled out by individuals that crossed into territory held by *Daesh* and contained, among other things, information on the individual's place of origin. For more information, see Dodwell et al. (2016).

a statistical basis, as Sterman and Rosenblatt state explicitly for their paper (2018, p. 9). Even though data is scarce,[5] there has been a small number of empirical/statistical studies approaching the link between FF mobilization and marginalization from a cross-country perspective. While they could not corroborate the positive association between marginalization and FF (Benmelech & Klor, 2016), they find a positive effect of political instability (Schraeder & Schumacher, 2020) or the activity of Al-Qaida (Pokalova, 2019). So far, only Rosenblatt (2021) offers a subnational analysis for the MENA region, albeit excluding protest rates and utilizing a rather broad regional conception, thereby disabling a detailed analysis of inter-country variance.

While the factor of marginalization has been tested at least on a cross-country level with inconclusive results, the Sterman and Rosenblatt central topic of discontent, understood, for example, through protest, remains unchecked. As for Tunisia specifically, there exists an article in the Washington Post that contradicts Sterman and Rosenblatt's findings, however, it only covers protest events between 2010 and 2012 (Barrie & Ketchley, 2018). Other studies do not focus on spatial aggregation, but rather on the mobilized individual and their recruitment processes, drawing on case studies of foreign fighters (Ben Arab et al., 2018; Corneau-Tremblay, 2015; Orozobekova, 2016). While those studies provide interesting findings regarding the mobilization process in Tunisia, their explanatory power is restricted due to the small number of cases. One must highlight Zelin (2020), who offers a thorough account of the evolution of the Jihadi movement in Tunisia, but does not focus on the spatial aggregation of foreign fighters specifically.

3   Factors for Foreign Fighter Mobilization in Tunisia

In their paper, Sterman and Rosenblatt (2018) present three factors that are spatially associated with foreign fighter mobilization in Tunisia: Protest events, marginalization, and mobilization structures. In the following section, these three factors are discussed in greater detail. How do Sterman and Rosenblatt describe the mechanisms that link these empirical findings with FF mobilization, and how are these mechanisms discussed in the literature? Are they sound, and what competing or additional explanations are offered? Of course, most of these factors are all somewhat interrelated, hence, discussing them in isolation is almost impossible. Still, they will be separated as much as possible before hypotheses, corresponding to each factor, are formulated at the end of this chapter.

The primary focus of this paper is to analyze the positive connection between protest and FF mobilization that was found by Sterman and Rosenberg (2018)—a connection that, they explain, is based on discontent towards the government, for which protest is an indicator. They describe them as rebellious areas that *Daesh* could tap into (2018, pp. 18–19, 39). However, how far would anger against one's

---

[5] See, for example, Dawson (2021) for a non-systematic, yet thorough, review of the empirical literature on (Western) foreign fighters.

government fuel FF mobilization? While protesting can be broadly understood as a tactic of claim-making towards one's government (Tilly & Tarrow, 2015, p. 7), fighting in a foreign theater of war is clearly not. Rather than focusing on one's own government, the concern is directed outwards to a threatened transnational community. In the case of *Daesh*, this community included the people suffering under Bashar Al Assad. Voicing support was, at least in the beginning, tolerated by the Tunisian government, especially under Ennahda (Ben Arab et al., 2018, p. 10). Taken further, if discontent towards the Tunisian government really was the primary reason for FF mobilization and taking up arms was a valid option, then why fight in a foreign theater and not join one of the then-active local organizations? One explanation for foreign rather than domestic fighting is based on norms, which favor the former rather than the latter (Hegghammer, 2013). This might be apparent in Ansar al-Sharia in Tunisia (AST) strategically labeling Tunisia "a land of *Dawa*, not jihad" (Zelin, 2020, p. 114). Yet, they violated this norm themselves, for example, with the attack on the US embassy, and later officially abandoned it once outlawed in 2013 (Zelin, 2020). One could also argue that it was safer to travel to Syria to train and then return to Tunisia. However, one would not have to look further than neighboring Libya, which already housed multiple training camps, out of which attacks in Tunisia were planned and carried out, such as the infamous failed Ben Gardane takeover in 2016 (Zelin, 2018a). Even if discontent towards the government was the primary reason, then why should mobilization be higher in regions, where people chose a democratic way to express it? In fact, there is some evidence that political activism reduces the threat of FF mobilization, which Marcusa (2019) claims for union activism based on a case study on Sidi Bouzid, and Metlaoui and Barrie and Ketchley (2018) also find regarding protest on the delegation[6] level. So, a direct association between protest and foreign fighter mobilization based on discontent towards one's government is theoretically weak.

An alternative explanation as to why protest events are spatially linked to FF mobilization is if those protests were by a movement that aimed at establishing an Islamic State in Tunisia, but left when their goal did not materialize. In the context of Tunisia, this would relate, for example, to AST, who advocated for an Islamic state in Tunisia. After they were outlawed, a great number of their members were pushed to leave (Zelin, 2018b, p. 6). In this case, protest events, in general, should not be a potent predictor for FF mobilization, but rather specific protest events or AST activity in general. Furthermore, Weipert-Fenner and Wolff conclude regarding the herein analyzed protest cycle in Tunisia that "[i]slamists did not play any role in any of the socio-economic protests and social movements [...]" (2019, p. 24). Hence, this explanation can be excluded as well.

However, what if protest was correlated to foreign fighter mobilization simply because both were fueled by similar underlying grievances, thus leading to a spurious correlation? This is a point that Sterman and Rosenblatt touch upon themselves when stating that the anger caused by economic and political marginalization fueled both the Arab Uprising, as well as FF mobilization (2018, p. 41). According to

---

[6] Delegation refers to an administrative unit in Tunisia subordinate to a governorate.

Sterman and Rosenblatt, fighters were disproportionately mobilized in poorer regions that were characterized by a high unemployment rate and have been neglected by the central state politically (Sterman & Rosenblatt, 2018, pp. 36-39). A similar argument is made by Colombo, who claims "[u]nemployment [...] together with social and geographical marginalization, are a factor of radicalization leading to jihadism." (Colombo, 2016, p. 116) The same reasons of economic and political marginalization, especially of young people, have been stated as the main reasons for protests in Tunisia as well (e.g., Honwana, 2013). Indeed, unemployed youth were the main actors of the protests (Vatthauer & Weipert-Fenner, 2017, p. 17). Almost mirroring Rosenblatt, Boughzala describes them as "[y]outh, especially angry and unemployed youth and those who have been ignored and least integrated [...]" (2016, p. 175).

But, how would marginalization lead to foreign fighting? Rosenblatt proposes a direct effect through economic incentives when generally stating regarding hotbeds, in that "[...] many joined so as to abandon their home countries to pursue a better life elsewhere" (2021, p. 7). Even though some reports highlight economic incentives in the mobilizing efforts of *Daesh* (Zelin, 2018b, p. 12), it is unclear how widespread they actually were, and whether those were more than just a welcomed, but otherwise insignificant, positive side effect. Malet (2013) and Hegghammer (2011) generally reject the significance of local grievances or marginalization in the fighters' place of origin, which might directly push the individual to leave his or her country and fight in the sense of a greed- and grievances-based approach, as described beforehand, because the historically, financial reward was low if not inexistent. Furthermore, highlighting economic incentives would make foreign fighting somewhat equivalent to migration. That stands in stark contrast to past experiences as, from a historical perspective, fighters were never motivated by settlement (Malet, 2013, pp. 208–209). One can see, however, how the establishment of a caliphate changes the picture and is indeed cited as an important factor explaining mobilization (Zelin, 2020, 219). Even if, in the case of *Daesh,* migration could be a valid argument for FF mobilization, one has to keep in mind that only after mid-2014, with the declaration of the self-proclaimed "caliphate," does *Daesh* begin to be a state-building project and adapt its recruiting message in this regard (Stern & Berger, 2015, pp. 85–89; Vidino & Hughes, 2015, p. 15). Since the fighter in this analysis crossed into *Daesh* territory before this declaration, the argument does not hold up.

So, while a direct effect of marginalization is rather unlikely, an indirect one can be imagined. Malet acknowledges the marginalized background of foreign fighters in the sense that they "[...] tended to be [...] economically marginalized and [...] not active as citizens within their broader national polities." (2013, p. 208) In this regard, marginalization, politically as well as economically, would lead to a feeling of not belonging to a state and, hence, those persons or their communities might be more vulnerable to the perception of an ideology that substitutes for their sense of belonging. In their study of returnees, Ben Arab et al., for example, found that they expressed a weak connection to Tunisia as a nation (2018, pp. 52–54), thus supporting this assumption. This is also mirrored in the disillusionment with the outcomes of the Arab Uprising in Tunisia, which is cited as a reason for FF mobilization

(Macdonald & Waggoner, 2018; Zelin, 2020, p. 218). Frustrated that the situation neither economically nor politically improved, individuals moved away from the society and were open for the perception of an FF ideology. A study on marginalized communities in Tunisia emphasized that disillusionment with the outcomes of the Arab Uprising led to turning away from the state but strengthening of bounds in the community (Lamloum, 2016). Even though at first glance, this would run contra to foreign fighting, as the focus is on internal bounding, one can imagine how turning to a community beyond the nation-state is substituted internationally instead of locally, a theme AST displayed in their message (Zelin, 2020, pp. 154–156). If marginalization and disillusionment were important for FF mobilization, then one should expect mobilization in marginalized areas in general and not just those that display protest events. Yet, one could also expect a stronger effect in regions that displayed protests, as the disillusionment might be higher there because democratic attempts for change did not pay off.

The last factor stressed by Sterman and Rosenberg is the relatively open atmosphere in the aftermath of the Arab Uprising that allowed extremist groups to recruit openly, and which is an often-cited reason for the quantitative success of the FF mobilization in Tunisia compared to other countries (Corneau-Tremblay, 2015, p. 6; Sterman & Rosenblatt, 2018, pp. 30–33). Calls for the support of the Syrian people were made openly and were even somewhat supported officially (Ben Arab et al., 2018, p. 10). Furthermore, the state lost control of a large number of mosques that are believed to have facilitated jihadist thought in Tunisia (Wolf, 2014). Additionally, a large number of prisoners of the Ben Ali era were released, many of which were part of Islamist organizations, had fought abroad in previous theaters, or were radicalized in prison. AST in particular, which was founded in those prison structures, was able to exploit this situation. It was one of, if not the central, actor for mobilizing foreign fighters to fight in Syria and Iraq, as well as Libya and elsewhere, as the organization provided a vast network to facilitate recruits by providing contacts, assurances, and training (Sterman & Rosenblatt, 2018, pp. 30–32; Zelin et al., 2013, p. 5; Zelin, 2020, pp. 178–187). Theories on FF point to the crucial role of mobilization structures for the quantitative success of recruitment through interpersonal networks (Malet, 2013) and transnational activists (Hegghammer, 2011). Therefore, mobilization structures grasped through AST activities might explain mobilization variance between delegations in Tunisia.

The spatial connection of protest and FF mobilization based on discontent towards the Tunisian government is unlikely. However, a connection based on disillusionment might be possible. Hence, even though the mechanisms as to how protest would be positively associated with FF mobilization are theoretically rather thin, this article follows Sterman and Rosenblatt's findings for closer replication. Therefore, the first hypothesis is: *The number of foreign fighters is positively correlated to the number of protests.*

However, protests can take very different forms. The protest cycle to which Sterman and Rosenblatt allude was characterized by a wide variety of actors and claims (Vatthauer & Weipert-Fenner, 2017). But, if protest itself was associated with foreign fighter mobilization, then the number of foreign fighters should be correlated to protest, regardless of its claim. Therefore, to check the robustness of this paper's potential findings, the second hypothesis is: *The number of foreign fighter mobilization is positively correlated to protest, regardless of its demands.*

As both protests and FF mobilization might be caused by the same marginalizing structures, a moderating effect due to a spurious correlation could be expected. Hence, the third hypothesis is: *The number of foreign fighters is positively correlated to marginalization, moderating a possible association between mobilization and protest events.*

As most researchers agree upon the crucial role played by mobilization structures, a strong positive effect is expected. Thus, the fourth hypothesis is: *The number of foreign fighters is positively correlated to AST activities.*

4 Research Design and Data Sample

This paper will, in a replicative style, test Sterman and Rosenblatt's analysis of factors that correlate with the flow of foreign fighters in Tunisia. Besides integrating their variables in a comprehensive model and testing for protests separated by their claims, the analysis will be taken one step down the administrative ladder to the level of delegations in order to evaluate the robustness of their findings. Tunisia consists of 264 delegations that form a sub-administrative division subordinate to governorates. A negative binomial regression will be utilized for the following three reasons: The data used represent a count variable, a constant mobilization rate cannot be assumed because most fighters crossed into the territory in a rather small time window (Dodwell et al., 2016, pp. 6-7), and individual cases of foreign fighter mobilization cannot be expected to be independent.

The dependent variable will be the number of Tunisians that left to fight in Syria and crossed into *Daesh*'s territory between 2011 and 2014 by delegation. Unfortunately, Sterman and Rosenblatt provide their data only at the administrative level of governorates. Therefore, the number of foreign fighters that will form the dependent variable will be drawn from Zelin (2018b). While both are based on the same raw data, it is noteworthy that, for an unknown reason, their data differ slightly (Zelin, 2018b, p. 7), even though the overall trends align (Sterman, 2018). While this poses the problem that this paper cannot replicate Sterman and Rosenblatt's study in detail, it also encompasses the possibility to assess whether their paper is biased based on the fighters' distribution.

Zelin (2018b) reported on city and governorate levels and was manually designated to its respected delegation. While this was rather straightforward in most cases, three cases posed a problem. For the cities Kebili (11 FF) and Medenine (8 FF), this was not possible because the two cities stretch across two delegations. As for the government of Tunis, there were 54 FF that were only assigned to the city of Tunis, instead of one of the 15 delegations of which it consists, like in the other cases, due to inaccuracy in the original data files. Hence, a definite assignment in those cases was not possible. Therefore, for each case, the number of fighters was assigned to the disputed delegations randomly. This, of course, limits the validity of this paper, especially when fighters are assigned to delegations that did not previously display mobilization, which was the case for seven delegations. However, as evident in Table 3, the effects do not differ substantially when using the number of FF with or without the randomized distribution. In addition, there are other obvious limitations due to the nature of the data, as no information on the entire Tunisian FF population is available. Thus, the results have to be interpreted in the context of these pitfalls.

The protest data that will form this paper's independent variable are drawn from Vatthauer and Weipert-Fenner (2017). They utilize the same ACLED[7] data as Sterman and Rosenblatt, but further distinguish the claims of protest between socio-economic and other protests.[8] In both papers, ACLED data was reduced to demonstration events and their subcategories.[9] Corresponding to Sterman and Rosenblatt, the data was further reduced to the time span of 2011 until 2014. Even though the time dimension is neglected here, one cannot expect a bias based on time variance in the distribution, as socio-economic and other protests have always accompanied each other (Vatthauer & Weipert-Fenner, 2017, p. 15).

Corresponding to Sterman and Rosenblatt, all other variables were drawn from the 2014 census in Tunisia but regarding delegations. The average unemployment rate in percent will capture the degree of economic marginalization. In order to take into account the central role played by unemployed youth, the share of unemployed young people (25-29 years) and the percentage of young people were included. To capture the lack of service provision, this paper includes the rate of households that are connected to the sewing systems provided by the *Office National de l'Assainissement* (ONAS)[10] as a proxy. Additionally, this paper includes the internal migration rate, measured between 2009 and 2014 as an indicator for a delegation's attractiveness. The internal migration rate is included as a dichotomy variable in accordance with being positive or negative. To control for mobilization structures, this paper utilizes data on AST activities, including mosques, protest events, neighborhood committees, and so on, provided by Zelin.[11]

---

[7] The Armed Conflict Location and Event Data (ACLED) Project provides comprehensive conflict data worldwide, encompassing wars as well as demonstrations. For more information see: https://acleddata.com/#/dashboard_last checked: 06/05/2021.

[8] For the exact definition of socioeconomic and other protests, see Vatthauer and Weipert-Fenner (2017, p. 9).

[9] For more information, see the ACLED codebook https://acleddata.com/resources/general-guides/_last checked: 03/13/2020.

[10] ONAS is responsible for sewerage system in Tunisia, as well as the protection of the water environment and fight against water pollution: http://www.onas.nat.tn/Fr/index.php?code=3_last checked:01/05/2020.

[11] Aaron Y. Zelin's Ansar al-Sharia in Tunisia Full Activities Database, last updated August 26, 2016; It is important to note that Zelin does not claim exhaustiveness regarding AST activity.

5 Analysis

5.1 Descriptive Analysis

The following descriptive analysis will be narrowly focused on FF mobilization and protest. Additional descriptive statistics are provided in Tables 1 and 2. In 139 out of 264 Tunisian delegations, no reported FF mobilization could be observed, and in approximately 16% (41) of the delegations, the departure of only one individual was reported. Around 75% of all delegations do not exhibit more than two fighters and in only about 5%, the rate is higher than ten. The highest number of FF was 37, and the second highest was 34, which can be observed in Bizerte Nord and Sousse Medina, respectively.

When looking at protest events between 2011 and 2014 in Tunisia, one can also observe an unequal distribution, as depicted in Fig. 1. In 167 delegations (ca. 63%), no protest was witnessed, and in 34 delegations (ca. 13%), only one protest event was reported. In total, in approximately 91% of all delegations, no more than five protest events could be observed. The highest number of protests was 300, followed by 51, observed in Bab Souika and Sidi Bouzid Est, respectively. When separating the protest events based on their claims, the distribution differs slightly. Looking at socio-economic protests, in 211 delegations (ca. 80%), no protest event was reported, and in 27 delegations (ca. 10%), there was only one event. The highest and second-highest number of events can be found in Bab Souika and Sidi Bouzid Est, with 42 and 19 events, respectively. When looking at non-socio-economic protests, in 178 delegations (ca. 67%), no event was reported, and in 28 delegations (ca. 11%), only one event was reported. Around 91% of all delegations do not exhibit more than four non-socio-economic protest events. By far, the highest number of protest events with 258 can be observed in Bab Souika, and the second highest with 27 in Sidi Bouzid Est.

Be it socio-economic or non-socio-economic protests, the highest number of protest events is exhibited in Bab Souika, and the second highest in Sidi Bouzid Est. Even though non-socio-economic protests occurred in slightly more delegations, the occurrence of socio-economic-based protests does not differ substantively, which is also evident by their strong correlation coefficient.[12] This could imply that differentiating the protest based on its claim might not improve the analysis. Regarding protest and FF mobilization, there is some geographic congruence, but the whole picture remains unclear.

Figure 1 depicts the spatial distribution of FF in Tunisia, as well as protest, both total and separated by claim. At least at first glance, it does not seem that there is a clear geographical concentration of FF mobilization. Fifty-six delegations display protest events and FF mobilization, while 51 delegations display only protests, 69 only mobilizations, and 98 neither. This further underlines the supposition that protest events and FF mobilization might not be connected.

---

[12] Pearson's r is approximately 0.586.

Table 1 Descriptive statistics I

	Mean	sd	min	max	p25	Median	p75
Foreign fighter	2.420	4.943	0.000	37.000	0.000	0.000	2.000
Reduced FF	2.129	4.834	0.000	37.000	0.000	0.000	2.000
Total protest	3.269	19.244	0.000	300.000	0.000	0.000	1.000
Socio-economic Protest	0.697	3.172	0.000	42.000	0.000	0.000	0.000
Other protest	2.572	16.382	0.000	258.000	0.000	0.000	1.000
Unemployment in %	16.312	6.689	5.812	42.400	10.844	15.593	20.101
Unemployed Youth	60.013	5.140	45.403	74.809	56.718	59.871	63.099
Unemployed academics	26.050	10.084	5.474	56.061	18.111	25.430	33.139
Youth in %	24.871	2.172	19.042	32.433	23.297	24.734	26.315
ONAS in %	49.447	34.789	0.000	98.926	15.546	50.373	84.823
Analphabet rate in %	21.943	10.320	4.400	55.708	13.665	19.802	30.003
Population	41600.288	25918.491	4295.000	129693.000	23287.000	34624.500	54704.500
Observations	264						

Source: Own estimations

Table 2 Descriptive statistics II

	Negative migration rate	AST activity
Yes	147	130
No	117	134
Total	264	264
Observations	264	264

Source: Own estimations

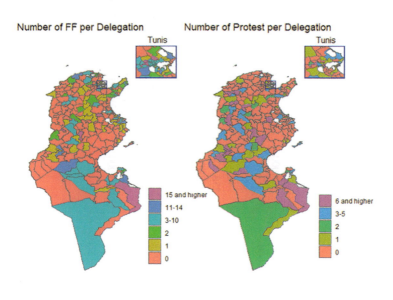

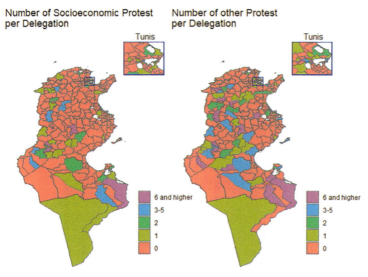

Fig. 1 FF mobilization and protest per delegation

Correlates for Foreign Fighters in Tunisia

Table 3 Coefficient table

	Model 1	Model 2	Model 3	Model 4	Model 5	Model 6
Protest	1.028*** (1.016–1.040)		1.000 (0.991–1.009)		1.001 (0.991–1.010)	0.998 (0.988–1.009)
Socio-economic Protest		1.023 (0.874–1.198)		1.070 (0.939–1.219)		
Other Protest		1.030 (0.999–1.062)		0.987 (0.963–1.012)		
Migration Rate (negative)			2.637*** (1.646–4.223)	2.711*** (1.694–4.340)	3.075*** (1.894–4.994)	2.688*** (1.632–4.425)
Unemployment (%)			1.002 (0.969–1.037)	0.998 (0.964–1.033)		0.995 (0.959–1.031)
ONAS (%)			1.017*** (1.010–1.025)	1.018*** (1.011–1.025)	1.013* (1.003–1.023)	1.016*** (1.008–1.024)
Unemployed Youth (%)					1.033 (0.989–1.079)	
Unemployed University (%)					1.016 (0.990–1.043)	
Youth (%)			1.138* (1.027–1.261)	1.127* (1.017–1.249)		1.135* (1.018–1.266)
AST Activity (yes)			3.444*** (2.129–5.573)	3.240*** (2.002–5.243)	3.090*** (1.911–4.995)	3.409*** (2.050–5.671)
N	264	264	264	264	264	264
AIC	982.681	984.675	920.912	921.375	919.878	868.053
BIC	993.409	998.979	949.520	953.559	952.062	896.661
Pseudo R² (Cragg-Uhler)	0.011	0.011	0.252	0.257	0.261	0.227

Exponentiated coefficients; 95% confidence intervals in brackets
***$p < 0.001$; **$p < 0.01$; *$p < 0.05$
Results of the negative binomial regressions. Independent variable: total number of foreign fighters per delegation. Model 1 and 3 depict the results using the total protest as a dependent variable, Model 2 and 4 protests separated by claims. Model 5 depicts the result using the reduced number of foreign fighters excluding the randomly assigned as a dependent variable

5.2 Regression Analysis

Table 3 depicts the result of the negative binomial regression models. Instead of coefficients, the exponential coefficients are reported. A coefficient above one indicates a positive relationship, and conversely below one a negative. Model 1 and Model 2 each display the effect of the dependent variable, protest in total numbers as well as separated by claim, respectively. Model 3 and Model 4 present the whole model, including the control variables. As is evident by the low pseudo-R^2 value, protest events alone, neither combined nor separated by claim, have a strong explanatory power. When including the control variables, the value increases from 0.011 to 0.252 in both cases.

Looking at Model 1 and Model 2, one can observe that the effect of protest is marginal. Given the model and the data, each additional protest event, regardless of its claim, would increase the predicted number of FF in any given delegation by the factor 1.028, ceteris paribus. However, once the control variables are included, the effect decreases to 1.000 and becomes statistically insignificant. When one separates the protest events based on their claim into socio-economic protests and non-socio-economic protests, the effect remains roughly the same. As depicted in Model 2, each additional protest event would increase the number of FF by the factor of 1.023 and 1.030 keeping all other variables constant, respectively. Once integrated into the full model, the explanatory power of socio-economic protest increases slightly to 1.070, while the effect of non-socio-economic protest turns negative to 0.987. None of the exponentiated coefficients are statistically significant. Moreover, as all the 95%-confidence intervals reach into values below and above one, translated into a negative and a positive effect, one cannot even conclude a clear trend. Based on this model and the data, protest events do not seem to have a substantive effect on the mobilization of FF.

When looking at the marginalization indicators, some interesting effects can be found. While the overall employment rate is insignificant, the ONAS rate, as well as the share of young people in a delegation, display positive statistically significant effects. The positive effect of ONAS runs, however, is contrary to the marginalization hypothesis, as a larger number of ONAS indicates more houses with access to sewerage systems. The migration rate of a delegation on the one hand and the AST activity on the other are by far the most potent predictors in this model. Given the data and the model, experiencing a negative migration rate increases the number of FF by a factor of around 2.6/2.7 in both models, as opposed to those delegations that display a positive national migration rate, ceteris paribus. A delegation that experienced any form of AST activity, including AST mosques, demonstrations, neighborhood watches or charity events, increases the likelihood of FF mobilization by the factor of ca. 3.4/3.2 compared to those delegations which do not, ceteris paribus. Unemployment was an indicator that was predicted to have a strong effect, however, it did not. Yet, it could be assumed that it is not unemployment in general, but rather unemployment of specific parts of society that drives FF mobilization. Barrie and Ketchley (2018), for example, test for unemployed university graduates, as they seem to be making up a large share of the Tunisian FF (Sterman & Rosenblatt, 2018), and Colombo (2016) points to unemployed youth, who are the most vulnerable segment of society to be recruited. Model 5 shows the result for the percentage of unemployed university graduates, as well as the share of the unemployed youth. The percentage of youth was omitted to reduce the risk of multicollinearity. Yet, both fail to show a strong and statistically significant effect. Hence, neither unemployment in general, nor of supposed vulnerable parts of society, display a strong explanatory power.

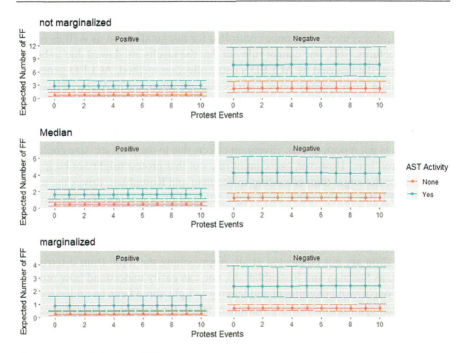

Fig. 2 Expected Number of FF

For a more intuitive interpretation, as put forward by King et al. (2000), the expected number of FF fighters is calculated. As there does not seem to be a substantive difference between the effect of protest in general or protest separated on the basis of its claim, the following estimations are based on Model 3. To capture the marginalization effect, ONAS and the unemployment rate were calculated using their respective 25th percentile, the median, as well as the 75th percentile. The estimation is further subset by AST activity, as well as the migration rate, as those were the most powerful predictor variables in this model. The share of young people is kept at its median. As evident in Fig. 2, the number of protest events does not influence FF mobilization at all. The negative effect of the marginalization predictors is also evident. As expected, FF increase somewhat moving from a marginalized to a wealthier delegation. However, what is very clear is that FF mobilization is mainly driven by AST activity as well as the negative migration rate. AST activity increases the expected number of FF by roughly 0.6, 1.2, 2.0 fighters in a delegation with a positive migration rate, and by additionally 1.6, 3, 5.3 fighters in delegations with a negative internal migration rate, corresponding to a marginalized, a median, and a wealthier hypothetical delegation.

6 Discussion

The first and most important takeaway from this analysis is that, based on the data and the model, protest events are not able to predict FF mobilization, neither generally nor separated by their claim. Therefore, the first hypothesis has to be rejected.

Even though protest events did display a positive and statistically significant, yet weak effect, it was moderated once controlled for marginalization as well as mobilization structures. Still, one cannot rule out that the results are flawed due to biases of the utilized data caused by ACLED's data collection method. ACLED generates its protest data from various news sources that are often not in Arabic. However, smaller protests or protests in smaller areas might not gain the attention of the media at all, or at least not from foreign language outlets, thus resulting in an underreporting bias that cannot be controlled for (Weipert-Fenner, 2021, p. 14). In addition, the protest size is not reported, thus, divergent effects due to the protests' size could not be considered here. However, one cannot rule out that protest might not be a good indicator for the anger that, according to Sterman and Rosenblatt, drives the mobilization of FF due to a possible local aggregation of protest at specific, meaningful locations, such as the capital Tunis, squares and so forth. The delegation Bab Souika, which displayed by far the most protest events, might be a hint to that.

However, there is also a strong theoretical reason to believe that discontent and FF mobilization are not connected at all. Approaching the topic from a terrorism perspective, as Sterman and Rosenblatt do, one can easily understand how protesting against one's own government and leaving to fight abroad can be understood as a political act against one's own government since, for example, a potential attack by a returnee is already anticipated. However, there are strong analytical reasons to treat FF and domestic or transnational terrorism as distinct phenomena. Even though they are closely aligned, Hegghammer points out their differences regarding al-Qaida (2011, p. 89), and so does Corneau-Tremblay in respect to organizations in Tunisia (2015, pp. 16–17). Specifically, Hegghammer points to the fact that foreign fighters participate in a theater of war fighting against combatants, whereas (inter)-national terrorists "[…] specialize in out-of-area violence against non-combatants" (2011, p. 58). Furthermore, only a small number of FF return to their place of origin to perpetrate an attack, even if it might not have been their original intention when leaving (Hegghammer, 2013). Hence, while protest might be driven by discontent towards one's own government, and domestic terrorism as well, foreign fighting is most likely not. Fighting voluntarily in a foreign theater of war is not a substitute for political activism, violent or not, in one's home country. This is also evident because moderating effects of protest events as put forward by Barrie and Ketchley (2018) could not be reproduced. This also questions the negative effect of the availability of political participation opportunities and FF as claimed by Marcusa (2019), at least when looking at the spatial aggregation of protest events.

This is also evident when we look at the marginalization predictors used in this paper. If discontent was elicited by marginalization, then a clear effect should have been observed between delegations exhibiting different socio-economic statuses. Even though an effect was observed, it was reversed. Contrary to the expectations, delegations with higher socio-economic status exhibited a higher number of FF. Thus, hypothesis three has to be rejected as well. That does, of course, not eliminate the role marginalization might play in the process of FF recruitment, but rather points to a more complex relationship not adequately captured through this kind of objective proxies, as individually perceived marginalization might very well be a factor for radicalization in Tunisia (Süß & Aakhunzzada, 2019). This perceived marginalization might even be stronger in wealthier regions, as Sterman and Rosenblatt stress that even when fighters are not mobilized in marginalized regions, they themselves seem to be marginalized (2018, pp. 36–39). The strong effect of the migration rate might be a hint to that.

However, the negative migration rate could also be an indicator for loosening community ties, possibly due to disillusionment with the outcomes of the Arab Uprising. In this regard, turning away not just from the state, but also the community, leaves one vulnerable to an ideology promoting foreign fighting. Especially in conjunction with respective mobilization structures, the effect could be elevated. This might explain the different effects of AST activity in delegations with a positive and negative migration rate, as depicted in Fig. 1. What speaks against this disillusionment argument, however, is that one could not observe an interaction between marginalization, protest and FF mobilization, as the estimated number of FF remains untouched by the number of protest events. If disillusionment and frustration with the outcomes of the Arab Uprising in Tunisia was a major driving force for FF mobilization, one would have expected higher numbers of FF in marginalized regions with a higher number of protest events. Still, the link between migration and FF mobilization is worth further investigation, as Ben Arab et al. find a similar connection between external migration and foreign fighter mobilization (2018, p. 57), and some researchers even see "[...] illegal migration and foreign fighting as substitutes for each other" (Rosenblatt, 2021, p. 12) a point also highlighted by Zelin (2020, p. 218). This is delicate, since the willingness for migration is widespread among the Tunisian youth (Dihstelhoff, 2018, pp. 14–15).

The last point to be discussed here is the strong effect of AST activity. The fact that mobilization structures are the most potent explanatory variable is not surprising. Hegghammer (2011) and Malet (2013) both emphasize that the quantitative success of FF mobilization mainly relies on mobilization structures or structures that spread an ideology. This, then, runs somewhat contrary to Sterman and Rosenberg's claim that ideology on its own is not sufficient enough to explain FF mobilization. Unfortunately, this paper can only speculate as to whether the effect of AST activity was due to their recruitment success or was caused by the crackdown on AST after its outlawing in 2013, like Zelin (2018b, p. 6) stresses, because only the arrival date into *Daesh*'s territory somewhere between mid-2013 and late-2014 is known, but not their departure date from Tunisia. Still, this falls in line with other studies that highlight the importance of mobilization structures rather than socio-economic factors, regardless of the ostensibly marginalized areas FF originated from, for example, in Georgia (Clifford, 2018) or in Belgium (van Vlierden, 2016).

7 Conclusion

This paper aimed to assess the factors responsible for the mobilization of FF in Tunisia based on the fighter's delegations of origin, as reported in the *Daesh*-Files. To this end, it followed the results made by Sterman and Rosenblatt (2018) and set out to verify them in a replicative approach. However, their findings could not be reproduced. Protest events failed to be a strong predictor for FF mobilization, and so did the marginalization indicators. Only the internal migration rate, as well as AST activities, proved to be potent predictors. While the transformation period might very well be enhancing FF mobilization in Tunisia, a direct link between marginalization or anger voiced via protest and radicalization cannot be concluded, or at least not via a spatial analysis given the currently available data.

A topic that was only touched upon here briefly, but which is of great importance, is the separation of domestic terrorism and foreign fighting. Often, researchers implicitly or explicitly mix both phenomena, as Sterman and Rosenblatt do, which might have driven the discontent-based explanation of FF mobilization in Tunisia. While both phenomena are, of course, closely connected, the question remains as to which individuals decide to fight abroad and why, whereas others decide to fight in the domestic scene, such as in the case of Tunisia. Are there competing recruitment networks scrambling for the same pool of potential recruits? Does one find spatial patterns? Further research is needed to investigate this connection through cross-country, as well as inter-country comparison. For example, in Tunisia, a comparison with individuals charged on the basis of terror-related crimes Data (CTRET, 2016) holds great potential. Another focus should be on the differences between fighters who left before and after the declaration of the "Caliphate" when *Daesh* changed their recruiting message, and whether they appeal to and mobilize different people. In the case of Germany, there is some evidence for this hypothesis (BKA et al., 2016, pp. 32–33).

Following the result of this analysis, the focus should be on mobilization structures and migration, as they were the most potent predictors for mobilization. As AST activity is unequally distributed throughout Tunisia (Zelin, 2020), the question is whether spatial aggregation follows patterns that can be explained: Was activity set up, or was it more successful in specific areas? If yes, why? The proximity with other Islamist movements would be especially interesting, such as whether one is more likely to observe AST activity in regions that are more supportive of Islamist parties than others. Is there an overlap with activities of other violent extremist groups such as Al-Qaida? As for migration, the question is whether factors conducive to migration also enabled radicalization and recruitment to jihadist organization, such as loosening community ties or a possible stronger relative (perceived) marginalization.

As Rosenblatt points to the importance of "local politics" (2016, p. 2) to explain mobilization, the question is how far those politics are actually reflected in the recruitment message. For instance, does *Daesh* appeal and thus enhance those push factors or do they use play pull factors, such as highlighting a duty to fight, which may be the more potent explanation?

This analysis showed that spatial analysis can yield valuable results in discovering patterns in FF mobilization in Tunisia. Still, these findings do not support a complete shift to push factors and objective marginalization indicators, as proposed by Sterman and Rosenblatt (2018). Rather, the focus should be on mobilization structures, ideology and recruitment messages, as well as their interaction with local conditions conducive to, for example, migration.

Acknowledgments The author would like to thank Constantin Ruhe for his technical feedback, the participants of the PRIF-Colloquium, and the two anonymous reviewers for their critical and valuable input, as well as Aaron Zelin for generously sharing his data. A special gratitude is reserved for Clara Süß for her strong encouragement and invaluable feedback.

References

Ahmed, R., & Pisoiu, D. (2014). *Foreign fighters: An overview of existing research and a comparative study of British and German foreign fighters*. ZEUS IFSH Working Paper 8.

Alexander, C. (2016). *Tunisia: From stability to revolution in the Maghreb*. Routledge.

Barrett, R. (2017). Beyond the caliphate: Foreign fighters and the threat of returnees. *The Soufan Center and The Global Strategy Network*. https://thesoufancenter.org/research/beyond-caliphate/.

Barrie, C., & Ketchley, N. (2018, December 10). *Is protest a safety valve against ISIS in Tunisia?* The Washington Post. Retrieved May 7, 2020, from https://www.washingtonpost.com/news/monkey-cage/wp/2018/12/10/is-protest-a-safety-valve-against-isis-in-tunisia/

Ben Arab, E. (2016). The making of a FTF: Tunisia as a case study. In S. Zeiger (Ed.), *Expanding research on violent extremism* (pp. 41–54). Hedayah.

Ben Arab, E., Maalej, F., & Elloumi, M. I. (2018). *Assessing the threat posed by Tunisian foreign fighters*. Tunisian Institute for Strategic Studies.

Benmelech, E., & Klor, E. F. (2016). *What explains the flow of foreign fighters to ISIS?* NBER Working Paper Series 22190, National Bureau of Economic Research.

BKA, BfV & HKE. (2016). *Analyse der Radikalisierungshintergründe und -verläufe der Personen, die aus islamistischer Motivation aus Deutschland in Richtung Syrien oder Irak ausgereist sind: Fortschreibung 2016*. Bundeskriminalamt, Bundesamt für Verfassungsschutz and Hessisches Informations- und Kompetenzzentrum gegen Extremismus. Retrieved May 9, 2020, from https://www.verfassungsschutz.de/de/download-manager/_analyse-der-radikalisierungshintergruende-fortschreibung-2016.pdf

Boughzala, M. (2016). Youth employment and economic transition in Tunisia. In H. Ghanem (Ed.), *The Arab spring five years later: Case studies* (pp. 153–176). Brookings Institution Press.

Caryl, C. (2016). *Why does Tunisia produce so many terrorists? The success story of the Arab Spring has made room for moderate secularists to flourish. But that's a double-edged sword*. Foreign Policy, Retrieved May 25, 2018, from http://foreignpolicy.com/2016/07/15/why-does-tunisia-produce-so-many-terrorists-nice-france-truck-terrorist-attack/

Clifford, B. (2018). Georgian foreign fighter deaths in Syria and Iraq: What can they tell us about foreign fighter mobilization and recruitment? *Caucasus Survey*, 6(1), 62–80.

Colombo, V. (2016). Multiple layers of marginalization as a paradigm of Tunisian Hotbeds of Jihadism. In A. Varvelli (Ed.), *Jihadist hotbeds: Understanding local radicalization processes* (1st ed., pp. 107–120). ISPI.

Corneau-Tremblay, G. (2015). Tunisian fighters joining the war in Syria (and Iraq): A comparative study. *The Researcher: The Canadian Journal for Middle East Studies*, 1(1), 1–28.

CTRET. (2016). الإرهاب في تونس: من خلال الملفات القضائية . .Centre tunisien de la recherche et des études sur le terrorisme. Retrieved April 29, 2020, from https://ftdes.net/ar/etude-terrorisme-en-tunisie/

Dawson, L. L. (2021). *A comparative analysis of the data on western foreing fighters in Syria and Iraq: Who went and why?* ICCT Research Paper, International Centre for Counter-Terrorism – The Hague.

Dearden, L. (2014, November 23). Isis vs Islamic State vs Isil vs Daesh: What do the different names mean – and why does it matter? France has changed the name it uses to avoid legitimising terrorists. *The Independent*.

Dihstelhoff, J. (2018). *Umgang mit Frustration: Eine Selbsteinschätzung der tunesischen Jugend: FES MENA-Jugendstudie: Länderanalyse Tunesien*. Friedricht Ebert Stiftung, Naher/Mittlerer Osten und Nordafrika.

Dodwell, B., Milton, D., & Rassler, D. (2016). *The Caliphate's global workforce: An inside look at the Islamic state's foreign fighter paper trail*. Combating Terrorism Center.

Gustafsson, L., & Ranstorp, M. (2017). *Swedish foreign fighters in Syria and Iraq: An analysis of open-source intelligence and statistical data*. Swedish Defence University.

Hegghammer, T. (2011). The rise of Muslim foreign fighters: Islam and the globalization of Jihad. *International Security, 35*(3), 53–94.

Hegghammer, T. (2013). Should I stay or should I go? Explaining variation in Western Jihadists' choice between domestic and foreign fighting. *American Political Science Review, 107*(1), 1–15.

Honwana, A. (2013). *Youth and revolution in Tunisia*. Zed Books.

Jöst, P., & Vatthauer, J.-P. (2019). Socioeconomic contention in post-2011 Egypt and Tunisia: A comparison. In I. Weipert-Fenner & J. Wolff (Eds.), *Socioeconomic protests in MENA and Latin America: Egypt and Tunisia in interregional comparison* (pp. 71–103). Palgrave Macmillan.

King, G., Tomz, M., & Wittenberg, J. (2000). Making the most of statistical analyses: Improving interpretation and presentation. *American Journal of Political Science, 44*(2), 341–355.

Lamloum, O. (2016). *Politics on the margins in Tunisia: Vulnerable young people in Douar Hicher and Ettadhamen*. International Alert.

Macdonald, G., & Waggoner, L. (2018). Dashed hopes and extremism in Tunisia. *Journal of Democracy, 29*(1), 126–140.

Malet, D. (2013). *Foreign fighters: Transnational identity in civil conflict*. Oxford University Press.

Malet, D. (2015). Foreign fighter mobilization and persistence in a global context. *Terrorism and Political Violence, 27*(3), 454–473.

Marcusa, M. (2019). Radicalism on the periphery. *Comparative Politics, 51*(2), 177–197.

Orozobekova, A. (2016). The mobilization and recruitment of foreign fighters: The case of Islamic State, 2012–2014. *Connections: The Quarterly Journal, 15*(3), 83–100.

Pokalova, E. (2019). Driving factors behind foreign fighters in Syria and Iraq. *Studies in Conflict & Terrorism, 42*(9), 798–818.

Rosenblatt, N. (2016). All Jihad is local: What ISIS' files us about its fighters. .

Rosenblatt, N. (2021). *'A Caliphate that Gathered': Addressing the challenge of Jihadist Foreign Fighter Hubs'*. Policy Note 104, The Washington Institute for Near East Policy.

Schraeder, P. J., & Schumacher, M. J. (2020). Collective action, foreign fighting, and the global struggle for the Islamic State. *Democracy and Security, 16*(3), 234–259.

Sterman, D. (2018). *Re-examining the local roots of Tunisia's foreign fighter mobilization: A return to all Jihad is local*. New America, Washington, DC. Retrieved August 22, 2021, from https://www.newamerica.org/international-security/blog/re-examining-the-local-roots-of-tunisias-foreign-fighter-mobilization/

Sterman, D., & Rosenblatt, N. (2018). *All Jihad is local, Volume 2: ISIS in North Africa and the Arabian Peninsula*. New America, Washington, DC.

Stern, J., & Berger, J. M. (2015). *ISIS: The state of terror*. HarperCollins Publishers.

Süß, C.-A., & Aakhunzzada, A. N. (2019). *The socioeconomic dimension of Islamist radicalization in Egypt and Tunisia*. PRIF Working Paper 45.

Tilly, C., & Tarrow, S. (2015). *Contentious politics*. Oxford University Press.

Van Vlierden, G. (2016). Molenbeek and beyond: The Brussels-Antwerp Axis as Hotbed of Belgian Jihad. In Varvelli, A. (Ed.), *Jihadist hotbeds: Understanding local radicalization processes* (1st ed., pp. 49–61).

Vatthauer, J.-P., & Weipert-Fenner, I. (2017). *Die soziale Frage in Tunesien: Sozioökonomische Proteste und politische Demokratisierung nach* 2011. HSFK-Report 3, HSFK, Frankfurt am Main.

Vidino, L., & Hughes, S. (2015). *ISIS in America: From Retweets to Raqqa*. Program on Extremism The George Washington University.

Weipert-Fenner, I. (2021). Go local, go global: Studying popular protests in the MENA post-2011. *Mediterranean Politics, 26*(5), 1–23.

Weipert-Fenner, I., & Wolff, J. (2019). Introduction: Socioeconomic protests in times of political change: Studying Egypt and Tunisia from a comparative perspective. In I. Weipert-Fenner & J. Wolff (Eds.), *Socioeconomic protests in MENA and Latin America: Egypt and Tunisia in interregional comparison* (pp. 1–40). Palgrave Macmillan.

Wolf, A. (2014). The radicalization of Tunisia's Mosques. *CTC Sentinel, 7*(6), 17–20.

Zelin, A. Y. (2018a). *The others: Foreign fighters in Libya*. Policy Note 45, The Washington Institute for Near East Policy.

Zelin, A. Y. (2018b). *Tunisian foreign fighters in Iraq and Syria*. Policy Note 55, The Washington Institute for Near East Policy.

Zelin, A. Y. (2020). *Your sons are at your service: Tunisia's Missionaries of Jihad*. Columbia University Press.

Zelin, A. Y., Kohlmann, E. F. & al-Khouri, L. (2013). Convoy of Martyrs in the Levant: A joint study charting the evolving role of Sunni Foreign fighters in the Armed uprising against the assad regime in Syria. Flashpoint Global Partners.

Part II

Approaches to Prognosis, De-radicalization and Prevention

Radicalization and Public Discourse

Government Narratives in Reaction to Terrorist Attacks and Their Relevance in Addressing and Preventing Violent Extremism

Mareike Tichatschke

1 Introduction: Why Narratives Matter

When talking about narratives and their role in preventing and countering violent extremism and terrorism, the literature usually discusses the construction of targeted communication interventions directed towards a certain audience that might be at risk of radicalization, or is perceived as such. Recent years have seen many valuable scientific analyses and practical approaches.[1] When looking at the broader public discourse, however, it is less the specific interventions towards individuals that prove relevant for the perception of the wider public on violent extremism, as well as the overall political climate. Rather, it is narratives that are widely disseminated by key players such as governments, political parties, or even extremist organizations and perpetuated via both traditional and social media that impact the general public (Schmitt et al., 2017, p. 15). Words or whole narratives might be "loaded pistols," as Braddock and Horgan (2016, p. 400) quote Sartre when looking at how terrorist groups use strategic communication. The question here is how they might also work as a shield to provide resilience against polarization and radicalization efforts. This chapter will analyze narratives by governments that hold special relevance in this regard, as they are part of the crisis management in the direct aftermath of terrorist attacks, providing the government with an amplified position of attention and opportunity to shape discourse. The central question of this chapter will be: How do narratives used in reaction to terrorist attacks pose a risk or hold

---

[1] See, for example, the European Commission's Radicalisation Awareness Network (RAN) (Russel, 2019), Braddock and Horgan (2016) or Frischlich et al. (2018).

M. Tichatschke (✉)
Mainz, Rheinland-Pfalz, Deutschland

© The Author(s), under exclusive license to Springer Nature Switzerland AG 2023
D. Beck, J. Renner-Mugono (eds.), *Radicalization and Variations of Violence*, Contributions to International Relations,
https://doi.org/10.1007/978-3-031-27011-6_5

potential for publicly and politically countering and preventing the spread of violent extremism? The role of such narratives has been discussed in some approaches, especially using the example of the US *War on Terror*[2]-narrative and the public relations campaigns that surrounded it (see, for example, Corman et al., 2008). One point of criticism is that, by using the *war*-narrative to describe the situation, the US government had, on the one hand, validated the interpretation perpetuated by jihadist narratives who legitimize their actions as part of a *cosmic war of good against evil*. On the other hand, declaring a war on a relatively small organization (or terrorism as a whole) and the measures that came with this narrative might also help achieve the terrorist goal of unmasking the US government as less democratic and peaceful as they usually narrate themselves to be (McCauley, 2017, p. 86). It is against this backdrop that this chapter seeks to draw attention to the narratives coined in public discourse and their role with regard to furthering or restraining the radicalization of public discourse, polarization of the political debate and shaping policies and perceptions (see Lyons-Padilla et al., 2015 for an empirical argument). It will take the example of narratives used by European governments in reaction to jihadist terrorist attacks to discuss how those might contribute to strengthening democracy and pluralism in societies or confirm extremist narratives, or how they might be taken up by extremist organizations in their radicalization efforts, or even worsen polarization in societies (see Ravndal, 2018, p. 846; Pfeil, 2016, p. 16).

The narratives analyzed are of a special prominence and relevance for several reasons. When an event is publicly narrated as a terrorist attack, its significance is extended beyond the direct tragedy of the lives lost and scattered and towards the state itself, giving the act of violence a symbolic and political component (Hegemann & Kahl, 2018, p. 12; Stampnitzky, 2017, p. 11). In many cases, the government puts itself in the place of representing one of the entities attacked, the "democratic system" or "way of life" as you might hear it in the respective narrative (Martin, 2018, p. 44). The second reason is their timing. Focusing on the first five days after an attack, they are coined in a situation where the attention of the media, as well as the public, is focused on the government, as information is scarce and they speak for the entity under attack (Rogers & Pearce, 2016, p. 35). This moment of crisis gives the government an opportunity to set the stage for the discourse, as well as policy decisions that follow (Boin et al., 2017, p. 87). Others that join the discussions are likely to use it as a point of reference, agreeing, opposing to it, or using it for legitimacy. Lastly, such narratives are constructed in a particular environment. They tap into existing meanings and narratives but at the time of crisis may also include an opportunity for transformation and lay the discursive ground for a shift in policy (Russel, 2019, p. 10). Even if they are constructed in times of crisis, urgency and a desperate need for communication, they may be prepared beforehand by government agencies specialized on such crises. Thus, it will be valuable to reflect upon their possible implications for addressing and preventing violent extremisms and consider these in crisis preparedness efforts (Russel, 2019), as is the intention of this chapter.

---

[2] These terms do not represent an assessment by the author, but are very much to be seen within the narratives referred to. They will be written in italics to highlight their constructed nature.

The following pages will discuss some core assumptions underlying the argument and perspective used here, before presenting three examples of Germany, France, and Great Britain. It will go on to discuss the approaches in light of current literature on terrorism and the prevention of violent extremism before concluding with the discussion of ways to shape such narratives in a way that does justice to their prominence in public discourse, and make use of their transformational potential to create an environment that is more resilient to the efforts of violent extremist organizations.

2 Core Theoretical Assumptions

2.1 On Meaning-Making and Narratives

The research on which this chapter is based was conducted from a pragmatist point of view.[3] Pragmatism postulates that (1) human experience is grounded in the physical world but shaped by perception. Perception is in turn shaped by sets and structures of beliefs that are constantly being shaped and renewed by new experiences (Ralston, 2011, p. 75). The belief systems might be renewed and changed especially in times of crisis when they are called into question (Hellmann, 2017, p. 364). (2) Belief is made up of intersubjectively shared and constructed systems of meaning and value relations (Friedrichs & Kratochwil, 2009, p. 704) and form more or less consistent rules for action (Friedrichs & Kratochwil, 2009, p. 703). How objects or events are perceived is thus shaped by intersubjectively constructed sets of ascribed meanings and beliefs as are the reactions to an event (see Dewey, 2004, p. 231). (3) These meanings in turn can be reconstructed using the methods of reconstructive social science from any documentation of action (Roos, 2013, p. 316). In this chapter, the speeches of government and other executive officials serve as such documented actions from which the underlying meaning and belief systems have been reconstructed to uncover the narratives used (see Jasper, 2013 for a similar approach).

The function of a narrative, simply put, is to connect events, actants, and consequences into a compelling story line and to ascribe a meaning to them. They are central to making sense of acts of terrorist violence and activating or altering systems of beliefs (Braddock & Horgan, 2016, p. 382; Viehöver, 2006, p. 181). As there are many sets of terminology available, this chapter will use the vocabulary coined by Viehöver to relate to the typical structures of narratives consisting of: (1) a plot that gives the backdrop for the events, links it to other events and creates the general meaning of the story being told (Viehöver, 2014, p. 85), (2) actants that are put into relationships with one another by the plot and drive the events of the story towards its resolution. These might be actual people, groups or even objects and concepts (Viehöver, 2006, p. 198). Events tend to evolve around a central set of opposing

---

[3] The empirical argument presented in the next subsection is based on the author's original research that was accepted as her master's thesis at the University of Augsburg in July 2019. The corresponding reference is Edler (2019), mirroring a change in legal name.

values that drive the actions (Keller, 2011, p. 111) and to result (3) in a resolution of some sorts which Viehöver refers to as the objective as it is what is to be gained by the central positive actant or *hero* (Viehöver, 2006, p. 198; see also Braddock & Horgan, 2016, p. 382 for a similar definition). Thinking about what members of a government might say in their statements after a terrorist attack, the narratives might be analyzed to show an array of configurations of reality within them, depending on: who is depicted as the *hero* in the narrative, who is blamed and what motivation is ascribed to the attacker. Is a group in society constructed as linked to either of them? Is the plot a battle of *good* against *evil* that can only end in destruction? Or an act of political violence that is to be condemned, but might be tackled by policy measures or negotiation? Narratives used to give meaning to an act of political violence will open an array of options to act upon in policy and discourse (Boin et al., 2017, p. 15), making some reactions more and others less likely to be coherent with the narrative (Jasper, 2013, p. 33).

2.2 On Extremism, Terrorist Violence and Communication

The relationship between the narratives used by a government to react to a terrorist attack and the development of public discourse, let alone the radicalization of groups towards violent extremism or the motivation of any individual to commit acts of terrorism, is by no means a simple causal one. Starting from the most visible element, terrorist violence, this subsection will attempt to clarify the understanding of these concepts and their relationships in the analysis.

As previously mentioned, identifying an act of violence as terrorism is in and of itself a political act, as well as an act of narrative construction (Stampnitzky, 2017, p. 11). It tends to signal a symbolic and political dimension of the event (Waldmann, 2011, p. 14). What is important is the observation that different understandings of acts of terrorist violence (or plot configurations in the narrative sense) as a military or security problem, as acts of madmen[4] or a result of political grievances result in different approaches to try and counter or prevent such violence (Hegemann & Kahl, 2018, p. 113). One thing most definitions include is the notion that the significance extends beyond the immediate victims and the communicative dimension of terrorism itself (Waldmann, 2011, p. 16). Three types of audiences can be conceptualized: first, the side of the victims and the political or social institutions they represent, second, the group the terrorist organization attempts to represent, especially to convince them to join their cause, and third, other organizations the perpetrators think of as competitors or allies (Waldmann, 2011, p. 17, see also Henke, 2018, p. 37). What mediates between the physical attack and the way it is interpreted by these groups are narratives communicated by all the involved parties to give meaning to the event.

For the sake of looking at the public discourse more generally, a fourth audience might be added: extremist groups that see themselves as representatives of those

---

[4] A highly problematic narrative, as will be pointed out later.

attacked by an initial act of terrorist violence and position themselves on the opposing end of the political spectrum. In the case of jihadist terrorism in Europe, right-wing extremists might be the most obvious example for such groups. These dynamics are important for the argument of this chapter, as empirical evidence suggests that they might have edged each other on: following the series of jihadist attacks in Europe around the years 2014 to 2017, the EU law enforcement agency Europol found an increase in right-wing and anti-Muslim activity (see e.g. Europol, 2019, p. 9). It suggests that such events and the subsequent narratives and reactions might play a role in the radicalization of other groups. Ravndal (2018) suggests that a highly polarized conflict between right-wing extremist groups and their *enemies* might be a necessary condition for right-wing extremist violence to occur. His description of such *enemies* focuses on the extreme left (pp. 861–862), but given the discourse surrounding Muslim migration to Europe and Jihadism, this pairing should not be overlooked. When concepts of *enemies* and threats are activated in public discourse, polarization within society may increase, and more extreme groups might find more points to attach their narratives to (Pfeil, 2016, p. 16; Hargie & Irving, 2016, p. 91; Hegemann & Kahl, 2018, p. 172).[5] Such a discursive environment provides a ground that may facilitate radicalization and extremism. This is the dynamic of polarization this chapter has in mind.

Radicalization and extremism are two concepts that are not without their problems in their use for scientific reflection. Defining what is extreme also is a political act of intersubjective construction that might be influenced by a changing and evolving norm of what is the middle ground (Arzheimer, 2020). And, in a democratic society, following a set of beliefs that deviates from the norm must be permissible as it is a signal of a pluralistic society (Neumann, 2013, p. 886). Radicalization, as the process of a person to alienate themselves from the majority, then holds the same challenge (Githens-Mazer, 2012, p. 556). The path from holding a view outside the mainstream to agreeing with or even committing violence against a constructed group of *enemies* is a gradual and very individual process, and many stop at one of the early stages, while for others, it happens in a very short time (see Jukschat & Leimbach, 2020). As previously mentioned, this chapter will not focus on individual stories of radicalization into extremism that might have a variation of triggers, but on narratives in public discourse and how easy extremist groups that already position themselves against democratic principles might find it to use them for their cause. Discourses and narratives may have different functions in these efforts, shaping belief as a rule for action in the pragmatist sense: for example, by perpetuating a certain *permission to hate*, as van Meeteren and van Oostendorp (2019, p. 538) aptly put it, that legitimizes discrimination against members of a group, or by offering narratives that legitimize violence as a political means and constructing an *enemy* and threat that necessitates such armed struggle (Englund et al., 2017, p. 229). It has been documented in research concerning radicalization that the presence and perception of discrimination or depreciation might make a

---

[5] See also Köhler and Ebner (2019, p. 18), who analyze how strategic manuals of both jihadist and right-wing extremist organizations state this as a goal in their communication.

group more vulnerable to efforts of extremist organizations to win over people to join their cause (Lyons-Padilla et al., 2015). Other studies point out that anti-Muslim prejudice becomes more activated after jihadist attacks (Frindte et al., 2016, p. 207; von Sikorski et al., 2018). Narratives also play a part in these efforts, as they are used to give new recruits a compelling set of reasons as to why they are doing the right thing by joining a cause (Frischlich et al., 2018). Extremist organizations also try to strategically further their agenda by promoting polarization in public discourses, as Köhler and Ebner (2019) show by analyzing both jihadist and right-wing extremist handbooks on strategic communication. The aim is to shift what is socially acceptable to the general audience (p. 18).

All these narratives are not isolated stories. They tap into sets of meanings and beliefs present in wider public discourse, connecting new meaning and new possible reactions to for example perceived acts of discrimination or injustice.

One thing that needs to be kept in mind is that narrative configurations that provide reasons to hate and legitimize violence can be found in narratives by all kinds of authors. It is not useful here to limit one's analysis to the analysis of narratives by groups that are already labeled extremist organizations. One of the core interests of this chapter is to analyze the narratives of governments and see if, and how, they might provide such narrative configurations to public discourse, thus providing legitimization to violence by the state or others, furthering polarization and lending legitimacy to what extremist groups of any political orientation might see as their struggle and goal (van Meeteren & van Oostendorp, 2019, p. 538). The narrative a government holds towards extremist groups of different orientation might even influence their ability to mobilize for violence, as Ravndal's (2018, p. 861) analysis suggests, with a negative framing from a government they oppose correlating with higher violent activity of right-wing groups. Herein lies the potential the prominent narratives after terrorist attacks hold for the prevention of violent extremism: if successful, they might help construct a discursive environment in which hate and violence find less fertile ground and do not find plausible arguments to connect to people's beliefs.

3 Narratives on Cases of Terrorist Violence

The following subsection will provide a brief overview of narratives used by European governments in reaction to jihadist attacks. For a detailed analysis and the complete data set used, see Edler, 2019. The incidents selected present a sample of similar cases along a range of factors concerning the incidents and their political environment, despite the particularities of each act committed and the national political contexts. In the tradition of Grounded Theory, they also represent maximally contrasting cases to compare with each other, starting from the strikingly different styles of narratives initially observed between the communication by the French, German, and British government. To focus on a comparable set of narratives, only attacks by persons affiliated with IS were selected within the time of its highest activity in Europe. Incidents with a comparatively high number of victims were selected to ensure their relevance within the public discourse. The sample was restricted to EU member states (at the time of the attack) to achieve some level of comparability between the political systems and tools available to democratic governments, while making use of the broad base of research about their counter-terrorism histories. Relevant statements by core members of government were then sampled from official websites or social media channels, as well as from YouTube via video transcription. The texts were analyzed using the Grounded Theory toolkit (Strübing, 2014, p. 10), informed by the reconstructive epistemology (Franke & Roos, 2013, p. 12).

The three cases used here shall be introduced briefly in the following section before the three core elements of their narratives (plot, actants, and objects) are analyzed for their challenges and potential to tackle dynamics of radicalization in public discourse.

3.1   The French Narrative: An Act of War

The attacks in Paris on November 13, 2015, claimed over 130 lives and were the first of this design in Europe (Goertz, 2017, pp. 106, 110). The French government was quick to offer a narrative of what happened during the night of the events: an act of war, committed by a foreign jihadist army, had struck, and attacked not only innocent people enjoying their night out in Paris, but an idealized national way of life, as well as the French Republic and the ideas of liberalism (and laicism) it represents (Kempf, 2017, p. 14).

Stressing the national unity and values of France on the one hand, with the citizens returning to their normal lives and the institutions protecting them as *heroes* (Hollande, 2015b), the *enemy* is constructed in terms that are absolute. The motive of barbarism dominates the narrative to describe IS[6] separating the perpetrators and the organization they represent from all culture and almost humanity (Stampnitzky, 2017, p. 16; Laqueur, 1987, p. 19). To resolve the situation, the French government assured the public that the Republic will win the war against terrorism as a way to end the conflict that caused the crisis.

3.2   The German Narrative: A Tragedy the System Can Handle

The narrative used by the German government following the attack at Breitscheidplatz in Berlin shortly before Christmas 2016 uses a fundamentally different plot. The central interpretation given is that of tragedy and grief for the lives lost.

---

[6] The question of how to refer to the entity that calls itself the Islamic State is a complicated one. This chapter will use the abbreviation of this name in order to avoid associations with Islam, as this is a perception the IS tries to create. The abbreviation also avoids assessing the question whether the organziation ever did or will resemble the state it attempted to create (see Manne, 2017, p. 7).

(…) [D]ies ist ein sehr schwerer Tag. Ich bin wie Millionen von Menschen in Deutschland entsetzt, erschüttert und tieftraurig über das, was gestern Abend am Berliner Breitscheidplatz geschehen ist (Merkel, 2016).[7]

Across the statements by members of government, no state of emergency or war is declared, and the narrative puts the police and security institutions in the center of the resolution.

When it comes to the definition of what is attacked and who is the perpetrator, members of the German government are careful to emphasize that hate and division cannot be the answer, but rather, pluralism and being united in solidarity with the victims (Merkel, 2016). The perpetrator is less singled out for the aim to disrupt a constructed national way of life as in the French case, but associated with a more general interest of dividing and polarizing society.

3.3 The UK Narrative: An Atrocity

The narrative used by the British government in the aftermath of the suicide attack at Manchester Arena in May 2017 evolves around the central framing of the act as an atrocity, especially targeting children and teenagers attending the Ariana Grande concert and the depiction of the attacker as a despicable coward.

Pluralism and communities coming together are then depicted as one of the central mechanisms to resist against terrorism (Edler, 2019, p. 89). A "liberal, pluralistic" Britain (May, 2017a) is set against the "hateful ideology of the terrorists" (May, 2017a).

The focus of the reaction is on the work of security forces and, as in the German case, it is stressed that a well-established plan, called Operation Temperer, will now take effect, and the increased presence of armed personnel on the streets is unusual, but not exceptional, as it is within the scope of such emergency plans (May, 2017a,b). The objective of the measures is twofold: on the one hand, the pluralist society is called upon to resist hate and division, while on the other hand, it is to remain calm and let the security forces do their job to keep the country safe, as for the first few days, it is unknown whether the attacker might have had help from an organized cell that might still be active and at large (May, 2017b).

4 Discussion: The Challenges of Meaning-Making After Terrorist Attacks

This discussion will revolve around three complexes of issues that can be analyzed with the three narratives presented regarding the implications they might hold for countering and preventing violent extremism, shown as the columns in Table 1.

---

[7] "This is a very black day. Like millions of others in Germany, I am shocked, horrified and deeply saddened by what happened yesterday evening on Berlin's Breitscheidplatz" (Official Translation).

Table 1 Original representation

	Defining the situation: validation & disregard	Constructing actants and identities: in-groups & *enemies*	The objective of reacting: overreaction & reluctance
Narrative Element	Plot	Actants	Object & actions
Analytical Questions	Is the definition of the situation by the terrorists being shared or challenged?	How are *heroes* and *villains* defined? Who is included in which group?	What is the object(ive) to be attained by a reaction?
Examples & Variations	France: an act of war (validation) Germany: a system reacting to a tragic event (disregard) UK: a cowardly attack on innocent people (disregard)	France: the republic vs. a barbaric terrorist army Germany: democracy and her *enemies* UK: appalling cowardice and pluralist society	France: to win a war and destroy an *enemy* (overreaction) Germany: to investigate (reluctance) UK: protecting the pluralist society
Risks	Validating the definition of the situation by extremist groups as an incommensurable struggle of *good* vs. *evil*	Furthering discrimination by associating social groups with the perpetrators, delegitimizing democratic criticism of the state	(a) Overreaction by the state, setting aside democratic principles (b) Slow or ineffective reaction, failure to address the emotional component of the situation
Negative outcome	Engaging in wars that cause societies to perceive the state as the aggressor, legitimizing terrorism as a form of defense	Opposed radical groups might benefit from official legitimization of their stance against pluralism	(a) Repression & abuse of emergency powers enhance opposition to the state (b) Leaving the window of opportunity open for radical groups to set the tone
Potential	Turning the attention from the attacker the pluralist resilience of society	Preventing discrimination by stressing pluralism as an advantage	Showing an effective reaction by using regular executive mechanisms while addressing the emotional component of the events
Positive outcome	Opposition to violence as a positive point of identification across groups within society, disregarding the attack	Strengthening democracy and pluralist identities	Finding an emotional, but inclusive, narrative to condemn violence and depict paths to action all members of society can participate in

They are tied to the central structures of the narratives, concerning the way the situation is depicted in the plot, how the identities of actants are constructed in relation to society and what objective and end the devised plan to action points to. The first issue is whether to validate or to disregard the self-concept and situational definition of terrorist perpetrators and organizations in the plot. The second issue lies in the construction of groups and identities, of the question which groups are associated with the *heroes* or the v*illains* in the narrative. The issue evolving around the objective navigates the balance between reacting too heavily, or not reacting resolutely enough, both of which might play into the hands of extremist organizations. For each challenge, risks and potentials will be pointed out using the three cases as examples. With these narratives, the governments face a delicate balance between the demand for answers, meaning-making and emotional communication in a crisis situation, and the risk of overreaction (Boin et al., 2017, p. 15; McCauley, 2017, p. 84).

4.1 Defining the Situation: Validation & Disregard

The French narrative shows clear parallels to the almost classical *War on Terror*-narrative after 9/11 by using the *war*-narrative:

> C'est un acte de guerre qui a été commis par une armée terroriste, Daech, une armée djihadiste, contre la France (…): un pays libre qui parle à l'ensemble de la planète (Hollande, 2015a).[8]

It can be subjected to the same criticism, as it validates the self-concept of IS. The IS propagates the narrative of a struggle and war of the *just* and *good* against those they brand as *infidels* who, as an incomprehensible *enemy*, pose an existential threat to the *true believers* (Manne, 2017). In fact, it is precisely this narrative of an existential struggle and a chance for a *brave soldier* to defend the *innocent* that was used by IS to recruit followers in Europe (Smit & Meines, 2019, p. 3). It also uses a similar narrative to legitimize the use of force as an act of defense. By validating this image and entering narratively into the war, the French government lends legitimacy to the worldview propagated by IS. This is one of the central points Braddock and Horgan (2016, p. 389) warn against in their guide on constructing counternarratives for radicalization prevention campaigns.

Any military action by the state, especially if civilians are amongst the victims, will be used by the recruiters as an obvious example how the French state is actually fighting Muslims, thus providing recruiters with examples to convince their target groups (McCauley, 2017, 87).

In public discourse, a second problem might add to that. Right-wing and nationalist groups might take up this narrative as a call to arms and use it to legitimize what they perceive as a struggle against the *enemy* on their own soil and promote violence and hate against those they associate with the terrorist group. This could be done by agreeing with the government if the extreme right associates with the

---

[8] "An act of war committed by a terrorist army, Daesh, a jihadist army against France (…): a liberal country that speaks to the entire planet earth" (Author's translation).

government, or by criticizing that the government is not doing enough by only fighting IS on foreign soil.

Opposing the French and US narrative of war, the German Minister of the Interior, Thomas de Maizière, said a few days after the attack in Berlin:

> Aber wir wollen dieser Terrorbande nicht die Ehre antun, sie als Soldaten zu bezeichnen; das sind Mörder. (de Maizière, 2016)[9]

The same tactic has been shown for the British narrative referring to the attacker as a coward: an effort to deprecate the perpetrator and the organization that claimed an act of violence by explicitly opposing their self-image as part of a heroic struggle.

> All acts of terrorism are cowardly attacks on innocent people, but this attack stands out for its appalling, sickening cowardice (…) (May, 2017b)

Towards the majority, this can be a valuable tactic, especially if combined with the effort to turn the attention towards positive examples of resilience. The sentiment can easily be shared across all groups of society. Opposition to violence can serve as an inclusive point of identification and invite people across groups to get involved in pluralist society. It could well be combined with efforts to talk about the victims, their relatives and the communities affected by both the event and the fact that a terrorist claimed to represent them, and how resilience and recovery can be achieved. This could be part of an attempt to reduce the reaction to the communicative element of terrorism (see Juergensmeyer, 2017, p. 68; Mueller & Stewart, 2017, p. 32) by giving less focus (and screen time) to the message and acts of the attackers.

If the attacker, however, claims to represent a minority in the country, caution might be advised not to create or further the perception of proximity between the two in public discourse when depreciating or even dehumanizing the attacker. It is thus a fine line the British government navigates in the narrative, all the while overlooking that depicting the perpetrator as a despicable and disturbed person following a hateful ideology misses the point of radicalization towards violent extremism being a complex problem in which society as a whole plays a part (Englund et al., 2017, p. 228). The narrative would be alluding to the fact that the attacker might not be in his right mind, targeting children. In her seminal work, Richardson (2006) tested this hypothesis, concluding that not only are mental illnesses not more common in terrorist organizations than anywhere else, but this narrative might be used as an easy way out to avoid the difficult question of what factors in society might bring a person to a point where they kill themselves with a bomb in a concert hall (Richardson, 2006, 40; Schanzer, 2017, 48).

---

[9] "We won't give this bunch of terrorists the honour of calling them soldiers, they are murderers" (Author's translation).

4.2 Constructing Actants and Identities: In-Groups and Enemies

Within the construction of narratives, all governments face the challenge of navigating the constructions of actants and their identities, *heroes* and *villains*, in their narratives. This is crucial because, as discussed before, an act of terrorist violence is usually committed with an audience in mind and for strategic reasons (Waldmann, 2011, p. 14). One of them is to provoke. Polarization in public discourse and victimization of a group the perpetrators seek to recruit. They might use this when communicating to potential recruits, narrating their vision of society as a positive alternative to living in a country where one's group is being marginalized and discriminated against (Köhler & Ebner, 2019, p. 19; Pfeil, 2016, p. 16). None of the narratives analyzed establishes a direct connection between the IS and Islam. On the contrary, all narratives analyzed make explicit efforts to stress that the perpetrator and the terrorist organization have nothing in common with groups identifiable in society. However, the activation of one identity bears a risk of excluding others (Hargie & Irving, 2016, p. 92). France provides the example here.

The French narrative contrasts the citizens, the institutions and the values of the French Republic as the *heroes* in the narrative, while contrasting their innocence and civility with an *enemy* constructed as *barbaric* and almost outside of humanity (Hollande, 2015b; Stampnitzky, 2017, p. 16; Laqueur, 1987, p. 19). By constructing such unbridgeable differences, the government might be doing much to reassure the population in general. However, evoking the strong republican identity as in the French narrative might make it difficult for some to associate with the Republic, having experienced the ban of certain religious clothing and symbols under the argument of republican values (Lyons-Padilla et al., 2015, p. 10). Stressing a pluralist identity might be the preferable way, as, for example, Lyons-Padilla et al. (2015, p. 9) explain that integration, including religious customs, might increase resilience to radicalization efforts (see also Smit & Meines, 2019, p. 4). The UK case can serve as an example here with the government explicitly stressing the resilience of pluralist communities against hatred:

> Terrorists attempt to disrupt our lives and create distrust and fear in communities. We have a long history in Greater Manchester of communities standing together during difficult times. In the coming days we will be working closely with community leaders to address any issues (Greater Manchester Police, 2017).

This is coupled with a call to the population to be vigilant of any further suspicious activities, and a lot of attention is given to relating practical acts of kindness and the heroism of first responders (May, 2017b). This provides a positive and open point of identification and pointing out possible ways to participate in a response instead of feeling helpless.

On the other hand, the British strategy to work closely with community leaders in mosques to report radicalization of individuals has been criticized to construct

Muslims as a "suspect community" (van Meeteren & van Oostendorp, 2019, p. 525)—so it is this discourse the crisis-narrative falls into.

When it comes to the definition of what is attacked and who is the perpetrator, members of the German government are also careful to emphasize that hate and division cannot be the answer, but pluralism and being united in solidarity with the victims can (Merkel, 2016). It is the liberal and pluralistic way of life in the center of Berlin that is constructed as under attack (Müller, 2016). This way of life is generally referred to by a vocabulary of intentionality, thus providing it with the legitimacy of being chosen by those following it (Arnold, 2012, p. 27). The perpetrator is less singled out for the aim to disrupt that way of life, but associated with a more general interest of dividing and polarizing society.

> Hass kann und darf nicht unsere Antwort auf Hass sein. (…) Wir werden uns nicht aufhetzen und gegeneinander ausspielen lassen (Müller, 2016).[10]

This aligns with communication attempts by the German government to discern the attacker, who had abused the German refugee system by registering under multiple identities, from those who peacefully seek asylum in Germany (Merkel, 2016). On the other hand, the right-wing party AfD blamed Merkel personally and her way of welcoming refugees to Germany for the attack (Presse- und Informationsamt der Bundesregierung, 2016). It can be assumed that these *enemies* that seek to divide the government mentions are not only to be found on the ideological spectrum of the attacker but also on the opposite side (Edler, 2019, p. 80).

This also goes to show that, even if the governments do not use outright anti-Muslim rhetoric, others might, as such narratives are available for reference in public discourse (Smit & Meines, 2019, p. 6). An outright anti-Muslim rhetoric might be just as counterproductive, as it increases the appeal of the IS narrative (Smit & Meines, 2019, p. 4). On the contrary, such narratives would also, following the analysis of van Meeteren and van Oostendorp (van Meeteren & van Oostendorp, 2019, 527), provide other groups in society with a *permission to hate*. As was pointed out, opinion polling shows that prejudice becomes activated after an attack (Frindte et al., 2016, p. 207; von Sikorski et al., 2018). It is thus quite likely that, even if the government does not say it explicitly, a connection will be drawn, and any construction of the *enemy* after a jihadist attack runs the risk of falling back on the Muslim members of society. These risks should be taken into account and addressed.

A second difficulty all the narratives analyzed face is the sharp dichotomy created by a certain desire to present the government and executive agencies as the *heroes* in the narrative. If the narrative leaves no room for a middle ground for those who might be critical of the government measures or might just take an apolitical perspective, but forces anyone to unanimously support the government efforts or to be sided with the *enemy,* constructed as *evil,* it may contribute to polarization

---

[10] "Hating cannot and must not be out answer to hatred. (…) We will not allow ourselves to be incited and played off against one another" (Author's translation).

(Goertz, 2017, p. 18). As such, points of identification that are less politically burdened, such as grief and condemning attacks on children, might prove more universal than a strong national identity.

4.3 The Objective of Reacting: Overreaction and Reluctance

Narrating and planning the political steps taken in reaction to a terrorist attack is a delicate matter. Both overreactions and a failure to react might be problematic. In terms of overreaction, the French narrative and the policies that it entailed serve as the prime example.

> (…) face à la barbarie terroriste qui nous a déclaré la guerre, il n'y a pas plusieurs attitudes possibles. Il n'y en a qu'une, c'est celle que les Français ont adoptée et que le Gouvernement applique de manière inflexible: la riposte implacable de la République contre ceux qui veulent la détruire (Cazeneuve, 2015).[11]

With the *war*-narrative, extraordinary responses can be legitimized, such as the declaration of the state of emergency. It is being justified as an act of defense, with the *enemy* being responsible for any damage done to the democratic principles by forcing the government to react (Edler, 2019, p. 66; Hollande, 2015b). The French state of emergency permits a wide scope of measures by security forces, such as searches and arrests without supervision by a judge (Mbongo, 2017, p. 144). These have been widely criticized by civil society organizations for their repressive and abusive character, especially in marginalized communities of French suburbs (Mucha, 2017, p. 231). This may worsen the perception and experience of discrimination, especially amongst young French Muslims, further alienating them from the unified state identity the narrative evoked (Mucha, 2017, p. 241) and thus opening opportunities for those attempting to convince them to choose the other side of the unbridgeable gap the government narrative had described. Widening this gap between the society as a whole and their imaginary target group is exactly one of the objectives violent extremist groups try to achieve in the aftermath of an attack (Köhler & Ebner, 2019, p. 18). Political theorists would also state that, in setting aside principles of democratic procedures and giving too much power to the executive forces, the state falls into the trap of unmasking itself as discriminatory and oppressive, as might have been the intention of the attack to provoke such a response (Waldmann, 2011, p. 43). The *war*-narrative also exposes the government to a high risk of falling short in their promise. If anything, the *war on terrorism* campaign by the US has demonstrated that such a narrative of war creates expectations of victories that might not be achievable (Richardson, 2006, p. 230). Even if IS has been defeated on the ground in Iraq and Syria, it continues to exist and to operate. The absolute

---

[11] "(…) faced with the terrorist barbarism that declared war upon us, there are no two attitudes possible. There is only one, and that is the one the French have adopted, and the Government has implemented in a rigorous manner: a relentless response by the Republic against those who want to destroy her" (Author's translation).

victory as constructed by the French narrative is unlikely to happen. But, it reveals much about the belief held about the underlying conflict as being an absolute one of the *good* against an incommensurable *evil*. There are no gray areas, and every citizen must choose a side, thus also possibly subjecting groups that are not unanimously viewed as part of the French identity to being associated with the *enemy* and having to prove their allegiance (Mucha, 2017, p. 241).

A different problem can be seen in the German narrative and the political environment it works in. The German chancellor was comparatively late in making a statement. Where Theresa May and François Hollande had set the tone and offered a narrative to understand the incomprehensible events during the same night (Présidence de la République, 2015; Phipps et al., 2017), Merkel waited until almost noon on the following day. Earlier statements by the minister of the interior focused very much on the technicalities of the police operation to apprehend the fugitive, offering little interpretation that could speak to the emotional demand of the audience (Phoenix, 2016). Aided by live coverage and social media, this left a window of opportunity for those who, in contrast to the government narrative, saw political advantage in associating the perpetrator with all those who sought asylum in Germany and blaming the government for the attack. Besides this window of narrative opportunity, a second problem can be identified with narratives that focus on bureaucratic and standard operating procedures: they have a greater difficulty in satisfying the desire for action and response to what is a shocking event.

> (…) Ich habe großes Vertrauen zu den Männern und Frauen, die (…) daran arbeiten, diese unselige Tat aufzuklären. Sie wird aufgeklärt werden in jedem Detail. Und sie wird bestraft werden, so hart es unsere Gesetze verlangen (Merkel, 2016).[12]

The strength of the response in this narrative is allocated within the fact that the system works according to plan and using normal instruments of criminal prosecution, thus not falling into the trap of provocation terrorist organizations try to set to expose a perceived hypocrisy by democratic governments (de Maizière, 2016). The narrative stresses that the political system continues to function, reacting to an emergency without being in crisis itself (Boin et al., 2017, p. 87). It also detaches any later policy to counter or prevent violent extremism from the emotional situation of the attack (see Hegemann & Kahl, 2018, p. 186). Narratives focusing on grief instead of anger might be less prone to overreactions (McCauley, 2017, p. 84), but they might have a hard time answering the question of what the government is doing about the general problem. This can especially be the case when actual countermeasures are deliberately excluded from the immediate reaction, as was the case in the German narrative. This again leaves room for those who propose radical measures (Köhler & Ebner, 2019, p. 18). The challenge is thus to seize the opportunity to show that a well-constructed democratic response has been put into place and is functioning, while taking on board the emotions experienced by the public in an

---

[12] "I have great confidence in the men and women working on resolving this disastrous deed. Every detail of it will come to light. And it will be punished with the full force of our laws" (Author's translation).

inclusive narrative that points out ways in which the public may participate in furthering democratic resilience to radicalization. Educational measures and community-centered resilience building measures might be an alternative to reactions focused on securitization.

5   Conclusion

One can easily imagine how, in a situation similar to the ones presented in the examples, it might be a lot easier to resort to clear, strong, and resolute rhetoric, condemning the *enemy* and vowing revenge, than to craft differentiated, nuanced responses that take into account their long-term effects. Pointing out options for this balance within the narrative structure is the goal here. It is a challenge that governments face in crisis situations but one they should take into account and look at beforehand when planning their emergency response. There are more or less likely alternatives to be considered, as such complex issues of interpersonal construction of sets of belief have a history and tap into their current political situation. Personal and party contexts of the people presenting the narrative and their audiences also play a role to be kept in mind (Hawthorn, 1991, p. 165).

As the discussion has shown, there are good reasons for governments to strategically evaluate and shape their crisis reaction narratives for them to align with their long-term efforts to counter and prevent violent extremism. The core advice would be to ask for the potential effects and risks the narratives and measures pose in relation to a radicalization of the public discourse. The narratives analyzed here provide an array of possibilities for extremist organizations to legitimize violence or to use them as proof in their efforts to radicalize sympathizers. While it might not be easy to avoid all issues and pitfalls at the same time, some ways forward will be pointed out here. It takes careful and specific deliberation to construct such a narrative for use in crisis situations, as they are dominated by a desire for simple and reassuring answers instead of critical self-reflection (Boin et al., 2017, p. 7).

Considering good practices and learning from the risks of others, as it has been attempted here, can thus improve future reactions. This analysis has pointed out variations of how governments construct their narratives in reaction to jihadist attacks. The risks, but also potentials, have been discussed. The analysis points at the central dilemma and need to balance between a clear response that fulfils the affective needs of the audience and the risks of furthering polarization and radicalization in the process. By discussing different existing approaches, however, it becomes clear that some responses already make use of the potentials in these crisis situations. There are, especially in the UK communication, attempts to provide pluralist points of identification and use the inherent features of democracy as a response mechanism, thus strengthening them as rules for action in such a situation. This avoids the risks of overreacting and validating the extremist world view that *war*-based narratives hold. The analysis has shown various features that might be strengthened in a way forward. As seen in the German narrative, actively challenging the self- and worldview is one way. A more nuanced alternative can be promoted.[13] One interesting mechanism that can be seen in the German and British example is the separation of emotions towards the attack from the political reactions to it. They both acknowledge the pain and horror caused by the act of violence. But, the reactions are not driven by sadness or disgust. They focus on the resilience of the pluralist society and less on the *enemy*, treating violent extremism as a communicative issue that revolves around discourse and perception. These approaches have their own risks. But, they provide a way forward that holds a higher chance of reducing polarization and provides less legitimization to extremist groups on any side to continue violent struggle. This is opposed to narratives relying on anger and retaliation as the core emotion—especially war-themed ones that bare higher risks to accelerate circles of violence and legitimize radicalization.

Narratives focusing on the resilience of pluralist societies are more likely to connect to prevention and counter-terrorism measures treating it as a complex political issue rather than a military one, such as educational or community-focused programs. Together with policy measures to prevent violent extremism, they actually might be a shield against it.

Two core conclusions for the practical side of crisis reaction are: (1) plan crisis reactions with the communicative dimensions and narratives in mind, paying attention to unwanted effects or alignments with extremist narratives. (2) Consider all the different audiences when doing so. These narratives will impact radicalized groups and be used by them, so this must be considered as a long-term effect in the struggle against violent extremism. But, they will also be perceived differently by various sections of society. In particular, those targeted by recruitment efforts from extremist groups must be considered, and their possible perception of the narrative should be anticipated.

The analysis also pointed out the relevance of considering opposing sides of the extremist spectrum. With right-wing extremism on the rise in Europe, the importance of considering cross-spectrum effects cannot be stressed enough. The goal to increase resilience within society and maintain a pluralist and democratic arena of public discourse where violent extremist groups find little foothold for their arguments remains relevant, even in, or even more, in a situation where democracy seems challenged by a terrorist attack. Those in charge of reacting to such a crisis should incorporate it with their other priorities in this situation and be careful not to set it aside in case of emergency. Society and science may hold them accountable for it.

Acknowledgments The author expresses her gratitude to the participants of the workshop held at the sixth Young Conference of the German Association for Peace and Conflict Studies in 2021. Using their expertise, they reiterated the importance of well-constructed narratives in the face of violent extremism while also sharing in the experience how difficult it is to construct them and how shockingly easy it is to construct narratives to spread hate and polarization.

---

[13] See Braddock and Horgan (2016: 386, 389) for the use of this principle in deradicalization work.

References

Arnold, M. (2012). Erzählen. Ethisch-politische Funktion narrativer Diskurse. In M. Arnold, G. Dressel, & W. Viehöver (Eds.), *Erzählungen im Öffentlichen – Über die Wirkung narrativer Diskurse* (pp. 17–64). Springer VS.

Arzheimer, K. (2020). Extremismus. In T. Faas, O. W. Gabriel, & J. Maier (Eds.), *Politikwissenschaftliche Einstellungs- und Verhaltensforschung – Handbuch für Wissenschaft und Studium* (pp. 296–308). Nomos.

Boin, A., 't Hart, P., Stern, E., & Sundelius, B. (2017). The politics of crisis management – Public leadership under pressure. : Cambridge University Press.

Braddock, K., & Horgan, J. (2016). Towards a guide for constructing and disseminating counter-narratives to reduce support for terrorism. *Studies in Conflict & Terrorism, 39*(5), 381–404. https://doi.org/10.1080/1057610X.2015.1116277

Cazeneuve, B. (2015, November 16). Déclaration de M. Bernard Cazeneuve, ministre de l'intérieur, sur le bilan des mesures de lutte contre le terrorisme prises dans le cadre des lois de 2012 et de 2014 et de l'état d'urgence, à Paris le 16 novembre 2015. *Vie Publique*. Retrieved September 18, 2021, from https://www.vie-publique.fr/discours/196888-declaration-de-m-bernard-cazeneuve-ministre-de-linterieur-sur-le-bil

Corman, S. R., Trethewey, A., & Goodall, H. L. (2008). *Weapons of mass persuasion – Strategic communication to combat violent extremism*. Peter Lang Publishing.

de Maizière, T. (2016, December 21). Keine absolute Sicherheit vor Terrorismus. *Die Bundesregierung*. Retrieved September 18, 2021, from https://www.bundesregierung.de/breg-de/suche/keine-absolute-sicherheit-vor-terrorismus-353568

Dewey, J. (2004 [1938]). Die Struktur der Forschung. In J. Strübingm, & B. Schnettler (Eds,), *Methodologie interpretativer Sozialforschung – Klassische Grundlagentexte* (pp. 225–246). : UVK.

Edler, M. (2019). *Narrative zu jihadistischem Terrorismus in Europa – Rekonstruktion und kontrafaktische Analyse staatlicher Reaktionen auf terroristische Anschläge* [Masters thesis]. Universität Augsburg.

Englund, S., Stohl, M., & Burchill, R. (2017). Conclusion – Understanding how terrorism is constructed. In M. Stohl, R. Burchill, & S. Englund (Eds.), *Constructions of Terrorism – An interdisciplinary approach to research and policy* (pp. 223–230). University of California Press.

Europol. (2019). *European Union Terrorism Situation and Trend Report (TE-SAT) 2019*. European Union Agency for Law Enforcement Cooperation. https://www.europol.europa.eu/sites/default/files/documents/tesat_2019_final.pdf

Franke, U., & Roos, U. (2013). Einleitung: Zu den Begriffen "Weltpolitik" und "Rekonstruktion". In F. Ulrich & U. Roos (Eds.), *Rekonstruktive Methoden der Weltpolitikforschung* (pp. 7–30). Nomos.

Friedrichs, J., & Kratochwil, F. (2009). On acting and knowing: How pragmatism can advance international relations research and methodology. *International Organization, 63*(4), 701–731. https://doi.org/10.1017/S0020818309990142

Frindte, W., Geschke, D., & Wagner, S. (2016). Terrorism – Orchestrated staging and indicator of crisis. In A. Schwarz, M. S. Seeger, & C. Auer (Eds.), *The handbook of international crisis communication research* (pp. 200–211). Wiley.

Frischlich, L., Rieger, R., Morten, A., & Bente, G. (2018). The power of a good story: Narrative persuasion in extremist propaganda and videos against violent extremism. *International Journal of Conflict and Violence, 12*, 1–16. https://doi.org/10.4119/ijcv-3106

Githens-Mazer, J. (2012). The rhetoric and reality: Radicalization and political discourse. *International Political Science Review, 33*(5), 556–567. https://doi.org/10.1177/0192512112454416

Goertz, S. (2017). *Islamistischer Terrorismus – Analyse – Definitionen – Taktik*. C.F. Müller.

Greater Manchester Police. (2017). Latest statement on incident at Manchester Arena. *gmp.police.uk*. Retrieved May 1, 2019, from http://www.gmp.police.uk/content/TriageWebsitePages/5C071E8A3B6E6761802581290023AD7E?OpenDocument

Hargie, O., & Irving, P. (2016). Crisis communication and terrorist attacks. In A. Schwarz, M. S. Seeger, & C. Auer (Eds.), *The handbook of international crisis communication research* (pp. 85–95). Wiley.

Hawthorn, G. (1991). *Plausible worlds – Possibility and understanding in history and the social sciences*. Cambridge University Press.

Hegemann, H., & Kahl, M. (2018). *Terrorismus und Terrorismusbekämpfung – eine Einführung.* Springer VS.

Hellmann, G. (2017). Pragmatismus in den internationalen Beziehungen. In F. Sauer & C. Masala (Eds.), *Handbuch internationale Beziehungen* (pp. 359–397). Springer VS.

Henke, M. (2018). Bedrohung durch mediale Präsenz? Die Mediennutzung durch terroristische Akteure und ihre Wirkung auf die Öffentlichkeit. In T. Jäger, A. Daun, & D. Freudenberg (Eds.), *Politisches Krisenmanagement, Band 2: Reaktion – Partizipation – Resilienz* (pp. 35–51). Springer VS.

Hollande, F. (2015a, November 14). Déclaration de M. François Hollande, Président de la République, sur les attaques terroristes à Paris, le 14 novembre 2015. *Vie Publique*. Retrieved September 18, 2021, from https://www.vie-publique.fr/discours/196845-declaration-de-m-francois-hollande-president-de-la-republique-sur-les

Hollande, F. (2015b, November 16). Déclaration de M. François Hollande, Président de la République, devant le Parlement réuni en Congrès à la suite des attaques terroristes perpétrées à Paris et en Seine-Saint-Denis, Versailles le 16 novembre 2015. *Vie Publique*. Retrieved September 18, 2021, from https://www.vie-publique.fr/discours/196856-declaration-de-m-francois-hollande-president-de-la-republique-devant

Jasper, U. (2013). Eine Grounded Theory-basierte Rekonstruktion gesellschaftlicher Überzeugungen: Ursachen nuklearer Non-Poliferation in der Schweiz und Libyen. In U. Franke & U. Roos (Eds.), *Rekonstruktive Methoden der Weltpolitikforschung* (pp. 31–58). Nomos.

Juergensmeyer, M. (2017). Killing before an audience – Terrorism as performance violence. In M. Stohl, R. Burchill, & S. Englund (Eds.), *Constructions of terrorism – An interdisciplinary approach to research and policy* (pp. 67–78). University of California Press.

Jukschat, N., & Leimbach, K. (2020). Radikalisierung oder die Hegemonie eines Paradigmas – Irrititationspotenziale einer biografischen Fallstudie. *Zeitschrift für Soziologie, 49*, 335–355. https://doi.org/10.1515/zfsoz-2020-0028

Keller, R. (2011). *Diskursforschung – Eine Einführung für SozialwissenschaftlerInnen*. Springer VS.

Kempf, U. (2017). *Das politische system Frankreichs*. Springer VS.

Köhler, D., & Ebner, J. (2019). Strategies and tactics: Communication strategies of jihadists and right-wing extremists. In J. Baldauf, J. Ebner, & J. Guhl (Eds.), *Hate speech and radicalisation online – The OCCI research report* (pp. 18–26). ISD.

Laqueur, W. (1987). *Terrorismus – Die globale Herausforderung*. Frankfurt/M. [u.a.]: Ullstein.

Lyons-Padilla, S., Gelfand, M. J., Mirahmadi, H., Farooq, M., & van Egmond, M. (2015). Belonging nowhere: Marginalization & radicalization risk among Muslim immigrants. *Behavioral Science & Policy, 1*(2), 1–12. https://behavioralpolicy.org/wp-content/uploads/2017/05/BSP_vol1is2_-Lyons-Padilla.pdf

Manne, R. (2017). *The mind of the Islamic State – ISIS and the ideology of the caliphate*. Prometheus Books.

Martin, G. (2018). *Understanding terrorism – Challenges, perspectives and issues*. Sage.

May, T. (2017a). PM statement following second COBR meeting on Manchester attack: 23 May 2017. *Gov.uk*. Retrieved September 18, 2021, from https://www.gov.uk/government/speeches/pm-statement-following-second-cobr-meeting-on-manchester-attack-23-may-2017

May, T. (2017b, May 23). PM statement following terrorist attack in Manchester: 23 May 2017. *Gov.uk*. Retrieved September 18, 2021, https://www.gov.uk/government/speeches/pm-statement-following-terrorist-attack-in-manchester-23-may-2017

Mbongo, P. (2017). Die französischen Regelungen zum Ausnahmezustand. In M. Lemke (Ed.), *Ausnahmezustand – Theoriegeschichte, Anwendungen, Perspektiven* (pp. 129–166). Springer VS. https://doi.org/10.1007/978-3-658-16588-8

McCauley, C. (2017). Constructing terrorism – From Fear and Coercion to Anger and Ju-jitsu politics. In M. Stohl, R. Burchill, & S. Englund (Eds.), *Constructions of terrorism – An interdisciplinary approach to research and policy* (pp. 79–90). University of California Press.

Merkel, A. (2016, December 20). Pressestatement von Bundeskanzlerin Merkel zum mutmaßlichen Anschlag am Breitscheidplatz in Berlin. *Die Bundeskanzlerin*. Retrieved September 18, 2021, from https://www.bundeskanzlerin.de/bkin-de/aktuelles/pressestatement-von-bundeskanzlerin-merkel-zum-mutmasslichen-anschlag-am-breitscheidplatz-in-berlin-842764

Mucha, W. (2017). Polarization, stigmatization, radicalization. Counterterrorism and homeland security in France and Germany. *Journal for Deradicalization*. Nr. 10, 230–254.

Mueller, J., & Stewart, M. G. (2017). Misoverestimating terrorism. In M. Stohl, R. Burchill, & S. Englund (Eds.), *Constructions of terrorism – An interdisciplinary approach to research and policy* (pp. 21–37). University of California Press.

Müller, M. (2016, December 21). Rede des Regierenden Bürgermeisters Michael Müller zum Terroranschlag auf dem Breitscheidplatz am 19. Dezember 2016. *Berlin.de*. Retrieved September 18, 2021, from https://www.berlin.de/rbmskzl/aktuelles/pressemitteilungen/2016/pressemitteilung.545077.php

Neumann, P. R. (2013). The trouble with radicalization. *International Affairs, 89*(4), 873–893. https://doi.org/10.1111/1468-2346.12049

Pfeil, F. (2016). *Terrorismus – Wie wir uns schützen können*. Murmann.

Phipps, C., Rawlinson, K., Weaver, M., Sparrow, A., & Johnston, C. (2017, May 24). Theresa May statement. *The Guardian*. https://www.theguardian.com/uk-news/live/2017/may/22/manchester-arena-ariana-grande-concert-explosion-england?page=with:block-5923969ee4b03ddbc8d5c1b0#liveblog-navigation

Phoenix. (2016, December 20). *Breitscheidplatz Berlin: Statement von Thomas de Maizière am 19.12.2016* [Video]. Youtube. https://www.youtube.com/watch?v=UEXqNsY9Mts&fbclid=IwAR1eLv5o2yyIHdjfWAOdEnmd7mfBFC quxU4QXgC8n8fvyFvH104mQBmhJCk.

Présidence de la République. (2015). *Déclaration à la suite des attaques à Paris* [Video]. Daylimotion. Retrieved 19 September, 2021, from https://www.dailymotion.com/video/x3dpcuy

Presse- und Informationsamt der Bundesregierung. (2016). *Regierungspressekonferenz vom 21. Dezember*. Bundesregierung.de. https://www.bundesregierung.de/breg-de/suche/regierungspressekonferenz-vom-21-dezember-842950. Accessed 18 September 2021.

Ralston, S. J. (2011). Pragmatism in international relations theory and research. *Eidos, 14*, 72–105.

Ravndal, J. A. (2018). Explaining right-wing terrorism and violence in Western Europe: Grievances, opportunities and polarisation. *European Journal of Political Research, 57*(4), 845–866. https://doi.org/10.1111/1475-6765.12254

Richardson, L. (2006). *Was Terroristen wollen – Die Ursachen der Gewalt und wie wir sie bekämpfen können*. Campus Verlag.

Rogers, M. B., & Pearce, J. M. (2016). The psychology of crisis communication. In A. Schwarz, M. W. Seeger, & C. Auer (Eds.), *The handbook of international crisis communication research*, ed. Andreas Schwarz (pp. 34–44). Malden [u.a.]: Wiley.

Roos, U. (2013). Grounded theory als Instrument der Weltpolitikforschung – Die Rekonstruktion außenpolitischer Kultur als Beispiel. In U. Franke & U. Roos (Eds.), *Rekonstruktive Methoden der Weltpolitikforschung* (pp. 309–348). Nomos.

Russel, J. (2019). *Kommunikation nach einem Anschlag*. European Commission Radicalization Awareness Network. https://ec.europa.eu/home-affairs/document/download/a9f6dde3-0648-49d2-94de-ce27291f2778_en

Schanzer, D. H. (2017). Terrorism as a tactic. In M. Stohl, R. Burchill, & S. Englund (Eds.), *Constructions of terrorism – An interdisciplinary approach to research and policy* (pp. 38–52). University of California Press.

Schmitt, J. B., Ernst, J., Frischlich, L., & Rieger, D. (2017). Rechtsextreme und islamistische Propaganda im Internet: Methoden, Auswirkungen und Präventionsmöglichkeiten. In R. Altenhof, S. Bunk, & M. Piepenschneider (Eds.), *Politischer Extremismus im Vergleich* (pp. 171–210). LIT Verlag.

Smit, Q., & Meines, M. (2019). *Politik- und Praxisworkshop von RAN – Narrative und Strategien von Rechtsextremismus und islamistischem Extremismus.* European Commission Radicalization Awareness Network. https://ec.europa.eu/home-affairs/document/download/fb95fa59-318f-4ff6-a262-89885176b816_en

Stampnitzky, L. (2017). Can terrorism be defined? In M. Stohl, R. Burchill, & S. Englund (Eds.), *Constructions of terrorism – An interdisciplinary approach to research and policy* (pp. 11–20). University of California Press.

Strübing, J. (2014). *Grounded theory – Zur sozialtheoretischen und epistemologischen Fundierung eines pragmatischen Forschungsstils.* Springer VS.

van Meeteren, M. J., & van Oostendorp, L. N. (2019). Are Muslims in the Netherlands constructed as a 'suspect community'? An analysis of Dutch political discourse on terrorism in 2004–2015. *Crime Law Soc Change, 71,* 525–540. https://doi.org/10.1007/s10611-018-9802-y

Viehöver, W. (2006). Diskurse als Narrationen. In R. Keller, A. Hirseland, W. Schneider, & W. Viehöver (Eds.), *Handbuch Sozialwissenschaftliche Diskursanalyse – Band 1: Theorien und Methoden* (pp. 179–208). Springer VS.

Viehöver, W. (2014). Erzählungen im Feld der Politik, Politik durch Erzählungen – Überlegungen zur Rolle der Narrationen in den politischen Wissenschaften. In F. Gadinger, S. Jarzebski, & T. Yildiz (Eds.), *Politische Narrative: Konzepte – Analysen – Forschungspraxis* (pp. 67–91). Springer VS.

von Sikorski, C., Matthes, J., & Schmuck, J. D. (2018). The Islamic state in the news: Journalistic differentiation of islamist terrorism from islam, terror news proximity, and islamophobic attitudes. *Communication Research, 48*(2), 1–30. https://doi.org/10.1177/0093650218803276

Waldmann, P. (2011). *Terrorismus – Provokation der Macht.* Murmann Verlag.

The (Non-)escalation of Violence During the Third Act of the Yellow Vests Protests

A Critique of Interactionist Theories of Violence

Oliver Unverdorben

1 Introduction

Since its emergence in the autumn of 2018, the Yellow Vests movement in France has attracted significant attention by the media and the academic literature alike. Given the intensity of violent clashes, as well as the longevity of the movement, it has elicited a particularly keen interest of scholars in social psychology that seek to explain why individuals engage in peaceful and violent collective action (Adam-Troian et al., 2020, 2021; Mahfud & Adam-Troian, 2021; Jetten et al., 2020; Morales et al., 2020). This contribution taps into this debate by analyzing video footage of violent encounters between protesters and the police that took place during the third Act of the Yellow Vests demonstrations in Paris on December first, 2018—one of the movement's most violent anti-government protests. Thereby, it augments the existing literature on the Yellow Vests in two ways. Conceptually, it provides the first analysis of the "the situation of immediate social interaction" (Collins, 2011, p. 4), a dimension thus far ignored by social psychological accounts that have focused on structural conditions or the motivation of individuals. Methodically, it constitutes the first study that approaches collective violence during the Yellow Vests movement through the visual analysis of video recordings. The use of video footage is particularly well suited for reconstructing sequences of events and interactions, as videos contain detailed and real-time information of dynamics in a specific situation.

The type of interactional analysis employed in this contribution has recently gained increasing traction in studies on the outbreak of collective violence in situations of demonstration protests (Weenink, 2014; Gross, 2016; Tiratelli, 2018;

O. Unverdorben (✉)
Sciences Po Paris, Paris, France
e-mail: oliver.unverdorben@sciencespo.fr

Nassauer, 2015, 2016). These works are based on Randall Collins' (2008) micro-sociological interactional theory of violence, which moves away from the traditional focus on the actors committing violence and, in turn, emphasizes the importance of the dynamics and interactions in the concrete situations in which these individuals find themselves. Despite adopting Collins' framework, this contribution develops a critique of his theory by illustrating its shortcomings. It demonstrates that the scenes analyzed feature all situational conditions that, according to Collins, should result in an excessive overuse of physical force. Nonetheless, the expected escalation of violence does not materialize—an outcome that his approach cannot explain. I argue that this shortcoming is a result of Collins' exclusive focus on micro-sociological interactions that isolates these dynamics from the broader social, historical, and structural conditions in which they take place. Thereby, his theory ignores that the way individuals interpret the interactions, dynamics, and emotions in their immediate surrounding are shaped and interiorized through processes of subjectification and domination that are inscribed into one's position in the social order.

These insights in no way mean that a micro-sociological and interactionist analytical lens is futile. On the contrary, the critique developed points to the importance of integrating micro-level and macro-level approaches in order to explain when and how (collective) violence breaks out—a point already highlighted on some occasions in the literature (Tiratelli, 2018; Wieviorka, 2014). This also brings with it methodological implications. Given that a focus on the immediate situational conditions is not sufficient, visual analyses should be complemented by other quantitative and qualitative methods, such as interviews and criminal records, that give insights into the personal and collective history of the individuals that participate in collective violence. Moreover, despite their limited explanatory potential, interactionist approaches focusing on micro-situations by themselves continue to be a powerful tool to describe and compare different forms of (collective) violence.

The contribution is structured as follows. The first section outlines Collins' micro-sociological theory of violence before developing a theoretical critique of such purely interactionist approaches. Subsequently, the second section begins by providing an overview over the Yellow Vests movement and the academic literature on it. It then introduces the method of visual data analysis[1] before embarking on the empirical analysis of two scenes that took place during the Yellow Vests' third Act, referring to the movement's third round of weekly anti-government demonstrations. Finally, the conclusion reflects on the implications of my findings for future research on the Yellow Vests and on collective violence in organized protests more broadly.

---

[1] The analysis of video material is referred to in different ways in existing studies on violence. This paper follows Nassauer's (2016) term of "visual data analysis," while Klusemann (2009) calls a similar method "video-analysis" and Tiratelli (2018) merely mentions the analysis of video footage without naming a specific method.

2 Randall Collins and the Absence of the Social Order

2.1 Interactionist Approaches to Violence

Much of the scholarship on the emergence of collective violence in situations of protest demonstrations has focused on the motivations of actors as an explanatory variable (Nassauer, 2015, 2016). In turn, these works tend to analyze various factors that shape and explain the formation of these motivations, including structural issues, such as (perceived) inequality (Kawalerowicz & Biggs, 2015), ethnic tension (Olzak et al., 1996) or budget cuts and austerity measures (Ponticelli & Voth, 2020), but also individual and group-level identity processes (Klandermans, 2014; Stott et al., 2018). Consequently, these approaches tend to treat collective violence as product resulting from conditions and processes preceding its immediate outbreak (Tiratelli, 2018). More recently, a growing number of scholars has disputed the explanatory value of these accounts, arguing that the very factors purported to predict violence are all too often also present in peaceful contexts (Collins, 2008; Nassauer, 2016). Instead, they focus on the specific interactions, dynamics, and emotions within a given micro-situation in which violence breaks out (Tiratelli, 2018; Nassauer, 2015, 2016; Collins, 2008; Gross, 2016; Weenink, 2014). In doing so, these micro-sociological and interactionist approaches shift the level of analysis from individual dispositions and motivations or structural and social conditions to the concrete situation in which individuals are inserted—they are concerned not with "violent individuals, but violent situations" (Collins, 2008, p. 1). The demonstrations taking place in the context of the Yellow Vests mobilizations constitute a useful example for studying such "violent situations" during protests. Apart from the 1968 riots, the scale of violence during the Yellow Vest demonstrations is unparalleled in recent French history (Çelebi et al., 2020), while the availability of large amounts of mobile phone videos makes it feasible to reconstruct interactions in immediate situations of violence.

Recent studies analyzing demonstrations and riots from this perspective are grounded in Randall Collins' (2008) general theory of violence, which in turn is heavily influenced by Goffman's and Durkheim's micro-sociology and Katz's (1999) sociology of the emotions (Tiratelli, 2018; Wieviorka, 2014). The theory emerges from a conception of social life as constituted of a chain of interactional rituals. In normal, successful interactional rituals, people have the unconscious tendency to become focused on a mutual objective and entrained with the emotions and rhythms of one another. These interactions are very attractive and produce positive experiences for the participants, who turn toward other interactions with feelings of solidarity, confidence, and enthusiasm—what Collins refers to as emotional energy (Collins, 2004). However, in antagonistic interactions, individuals follow different objectives and rhythms, going against another person and thereby "against one's physiological hard-wiring, the human propensity to become caught up in the micro-interactional rituals of solidarity" (Collins, 2008, p. 80). This counter-intuitive dynamic of non-solidarity entrainment gives rise to tension or even fear, a feeling that is referred to by Collins (2008) as confrontational tension/fear.

It is this "emotional configuration" of confrontational tension/fear that characterizes almost all violent situations and structures the behavior of the individuals inserted in them. Based on this understanding, Collins discards common myths about violence, for instance, that it is contagious or easy. As such, the tension/fear experienced by individuals means that most people try to avoid fighting, resulting in "much bluster, little action" and in violent action being widely incompetent (Collins, 2008, p. 71). In this context, violence is understood as a technique to circumvent the distress experienced in antagonistic interactions or "a set of pathways around confrontational tension and fear" (Collins, 2008, p. 8). Consequently, violence results from a combination of situational opportunities, but can also be a question of interactional techniques that must have been acquired (Truc, 2010). Hence, the few individuals who are good at violence are those who succeed in turning the emotional situation of confrontational tension/fear to their advantage and at the expense of their opponent. However, Collins underlines that this is "a structural property of situational fields, not a property of individuals," meaning that it is the dynamics of a given situation that determine the outbreak and modalities of violence rather than factors outside or before the situation (Collins, 2008, p. 19).

Collins distinguishes between five pathways around confrontational tension/fear: audience-oriented fights, confrontation-avoiding by remote violence, deception, or absorption in technique, and finding a weak victim. It is this last technique that is of particular interest to my purpose. While there are various forms of attacking the weak, all exhibit one key characteristic: namely that an *emotionally* weak target is chosen. As such, the establishment of emotional dominance by imposing one's own rhythm on the other person precedes and makes possible physical violence (Collins, 2008). The most atrocious sub-type of this technique is found in what Collins labels forward panic. In this scenario, two sides of a conflict confront each other over a prolonged period of time in a rather passive manner, building up and intensifying the tension and fear characteristic for violent situations. When this situation changes to the overwhelming advantage of one side over another, the ease of dominating a long-sought opponent releases the confrontational tension/fear in an emotional rush—a "frenzied" attack of the many against the few. In this process, the attackers get entrained in their own adrenalin and rhythm and enter an "emotional tunnel of violence." They are carried away to conduct aggressive actions they would normally condemn, leading to a repetition of these actions and overkill—the use of force far beyond what would be necessary to dominate the other. It is this pattern of forward panic that is characteristic of the violence that breaks out during organized demonstrations (Collins, 2008).

2.2 Micro-sociological, Isolated Islands?

Collins' shift to the conditions of an immediate situation is an important innovation to the field, particularly because he is correct in arguing that theories focusing on individual motivations or structural conditions cannot predict which situations turn violent and which ones do not. However, the exclusive focus on the micro-level risks treating social life as a succession of micro-sociological islands, removed and isolated from the broader social, structural, and historical context in which they are embedded (Tiratelli, 2018; Ray, 2011; Hagedorn, 2009; Wieviorka, 2011).[2] Thereby, it depoliticizes and dehistoricizes collective violence and social life more generally. As such, it is unable to account for variations in the historical, social, and spatial patterns of violence or for the (political) meaning that perpetrators of violence may attribute to their acts (Ray, 2011; Hagedorn, 2009; Wieviorka, 2014). In fact, Collins' approach democratizes the participants in interaction, putting them on an equal footing by understanding them in a Sartrian manner as blank sheets. Yet, this means that he "entirely disregards what happens to the perpetrators, individually or collectively, before they commit an act of violence" (Wieviorka, 2014, p. 57). Consequently, it obscures from the dynamics of domination and subjectification inscribed in the social order that—according to their social position—have shaped and produced the individuals who find themselves in a certain situation at a given point in time. This is not to be understood as a sort of social determinism that predicts the behavior of individuals based on their social position. However, in the sense of the Bourdieusian *habitus*, these dynamics have the effect of interiorizing certain "structuring structures" that define the range of possible roles, behaviors, and identities that individuals perceive as intelligible in concrete interactions with one another.[3] As Eribon (2013) puts it:

> An analysis of interactions that focuses on individuals at a particular time first needs to take into consideration [the following]: each encounter between two persons entails the entire history of the social structures, the established hierarchies and the modes of domination that they establish. The present of each of us depends strongly on an individual past that itself depends on a collective and impersonal past: that of the social order and of the violences which it contains. (p. 50, my translation)

Based on this reasoning, I follow calls in the literature that advocate for an integration of micro-situational factors with social and structural conditions on the macro-level to explain when and how violence breaks out (Wieviorka, 2014; Tiratelli, 2018). After all, the way that individuals interpret the dynamics and interactions in a concrete situation—and the way they behave in these situations—is shaped by the background structures that Collins' theory is unable to account for. Following a similar reasoning, Tiratelli (2018) argues that the emotional dynamics in the 2011 London Riots were not entirely internal to the situation at stake, as emotions such as pride or indignation are shaped by individuals' expectations, for instance, vis-à-vis the police. In turn, these expectations were conditioned by demonstrators' history of negative and adversarial interactions with the police, resulting in feelings of

---

[2] In Collins defense, it needs to be added that he envisages his book *Violence* as one of a two-volume series, the second looking at the meso and macro-level. As Arsovska (2009) has remarked, he nonetheless makes very few references to macro-sociological explanations in his book and is quite critical of macro-sociological theory in general.

[3] For a less elaborate version of this argument see Arsovska (2009).

powerlessness and persecution with regard to the police that were then transcended in the riots.

Indeed, Collins himself seems aware of this shortcoming, granting some space in his theory to factors that are external to an immediate situation. More specifically, he claims that it is a combination of situational opportunities, and sometimes also a question of interactional techniques that have to be acquired, that allows violence to happen (Truc, 2010). "Violent persons" or "violent specialists," he argues, are those individuals who have acquired the techniques to overcome confrontational tension/fear and have learned to read situations of interactions, knowing which method to employ when (Collins, 2008, pp. 21–22). Patterns and historical changes in violence, in turn, are explained by changes in situational conditions and the diffusion of new techniques of violence in society (Collins, 2011). However, the purely micro-sociological approach by Collins falls short of elaborating how the circulation of these techniques is socially organized—how they are socially (re-)produced and transmitted or in which social spaces and through which institutions they are learned and taught (Magaudda, 2011). Yet, it is precisely this "more structural analysis of the material and cultural infrastructure of violence in society" (Magaudda, 2011, p. 4) that would be necessary to understand how different subjectivities—including those of "specialists of violence"—are produced dependent on one's position in the social order, and how these subjectivities shape the ways in which individuals perceive and react to situational conditions, manifested in the adoption of different techniques to manage confrontational tension/fear.

The key limitation of Collins' approach hence derives from this inconsistency between his implicit conception of the causes of violence going beyond the micro-sociological situation itself and his analytical framework that insists exclusively on this dimension—thereby being unable to capture social and structural conditions on the macro-level. Consequently, Collins' theory provides a well-founded and useful framework and vocabulary to *describe* how violence occurs in a specific time and place but, by itself, offers only limited explanatory value. A similar critique has also been put forward by Cooney (2009), who has argued that Collins offers little insight into why certain encounters, characterized by a relationship of dominance, lead to forward panic, while the majority does not. However, he goes on to propose a more granular analysis of the factors differentiating these situations as way forward. Thereby, he continues to situate the explanations for violence exclusively in the situations themselves, treating them as micro-sociological islands that exist independently from the social order. In the following, I support the theoretical reflections elaborated in this section by examining video material of outbreaks of violence during the demonstrations by the Yellow Vests movement. The scenes portrayed in the footage exhibit all situational conditions that characterize a forward panic. However, the expected excessive use of violence does not materialize, pointing to shortcomings in Collins' approach, and making the videos a useful entry point for critiquing his theory.

3 Collective Violence in the Yellow Vests Movement

3.1 Research on the Yellow Vests

The Yellow Vests movement emerged in France in the autumn of 2018 as relatively spontaneous mobilization against an increase in fuel taxes, organized through social media and without the institutional support of third parties (Royall, 2020; Paye, 2019). Swiftly, it transformed into a more general protest against social and economic inequality and the increase in the cost of living, later also demanding far-reaching institutional and political reforms (Morales et al., 2020; Adam-Troian et al., 2020). In doing so, it mainly adopted two types of protests: the occupation of roundabouts to block traffic, as well as weekly anti-government demonstration, labeled "Acts," that, since November 17, 2018, took place all over France and attracted a large number of protesters (Royall, 2020). While their total number is hard to pin down, about 300,000 people are estimated to have participated in the demonstrations in Paris at the height of the movement (Çelebi et al., 2020). The weekly demonstrations were quickly characterized by substantial outbursts of violence, with urban clashes becoming a common occurrence, especially in the capital of Paris. The movement was also met with an increasingly disproportionate violent reaction on the side of the police, sparking criticism by the United Nations High Commissioner for Human Rights and the Council of Europe, among others (Jetten et al., 2020). In fact, the violence during the Yellow Vest mobilizations is unrivaled in France since the May 1968 riots, and even surpassed them in terms of casualties (Çelebi et al., 2020).[4]

Given the magnitude of the movement, its diffuse grassroots organizational structure, and the intensity of violent clashes, the emergence and persistence of the Yellow Vests have received substantial attention in the academic literature. Among other things, studies have focused on the issue of police violence (Poupin, 2019; Adam-Troian et al., 2020; Çelebi et al., 2020), similarities with other social movements (Shultziner & Kornblit, 2020), the political causes and consequences of the Yellow Vests (Grossman, 2019; Kipfer, 2019), the socio-demographic profile of its supporters (Algan et al., 2019) or the geographic diffusion of the protests (Boyer et al., 2020). Most importantly for this contribution, a range of works in social psychology have sought to explain why individuals engaged in peaceful and violent collective action as part of the Yellow Vests. Jetten et al. (2020) highlight the importance of (perceived) socio-economic inequality and associated social discontent that fueled an increase in "us" versus "them" categorizations based on wealth. Similarly, Adam-Troian et al. (2021) emphasize the role of individuals' self-identification as members of the Yellow Vests and hence, by extension, as belonging to the marginalized and deprived as opposed to the privileged and wealthy. In turn, Mahfud and Adam-Troian (2021) and Morales et al. (2020) examine individuals' motivations to engage in collective violence, focusing on the role of feelings of anomia and the associated need to restore a sense of significance and meaning, as well as that of

---

[4] See Royall (2020) for a good overview over the key events in the Yellow Vests movement.

negative emotions toward the French government, respectively. Lastly, Adam-Troian et al. (2020) show that police violence resulted in a further radicalization of the protestors, with Jetten et al. (2020) similarly arguing that it increased protestors' belief in the legitimacy of the demonstrations.

What the existing studies have in common is that they analyze factors and processes preceding the outbreak of collective violence. As such, they look at the social and structural conditions that lead to (perceptions of) marginalization and deprivation, or at individual and inter- and intra-level group processes that mediate the path between these perceptions of unfairness and the engagement in collective violence. While these works have generated valuable insights, they fall short of examining the dynamics, interactions, and patterns in the immediate situations that turn violent. The following analysis seeks to contribute to this gap in the literature.

3.2 Data and Method

To unravel micro-sociological patterns, different sources of data have been used in the literature, including archives (Weenink, 2014), interviews (Gross, 2016) and video recordings (Nassauer, 2016; Tiratelli, 2018). Visual data is preferred in this contribution due to several reasons. Firstly, the analysis of video recordings avoids the pitfalls of relying on individuals' retrospective interpretations of their own actions in interviews or memoirs. Secondly, the use of videos has considerable practical advantages. The advent of mobile phones has resulted in a vast amount of footage from demonstrations and protests being publicly and easily available online. This makes it possible to compare different videos of the same scene to confirm what precisely happened in a specific situation and reduce potential bias. It also allows researchers to overcome limitations of ethnographic methods by broadening the scope of the analysis to cover numerous perspectives, as well as different events that happen simultaneously and whose emergence is impossible to predict (Tiratelli, 2018). Thirdly, videos contain detailed and real-time information about interactions as they happen in a particular situation (Collins, 2015; Nassauer, 2016; Klusemann, 2009).

This last characteristic makes visual analysis of videos particularly suitable for the goal of this contribution: applying Collins' analytical framework to reconstruct sequences of events, dynamics and emotions in close detail. The logic behind such approach is similar to that of causal process tracing, aiming to reveal the causal mechanisms behind a specific outcome by focusing on the interaction of various factors and processes that constitute it (Nassauer, 2016). More specifically, my analysis aims to reconstruct the situations captured in the video recordings by meticulously describing the behavior of the various actors in close detail. By repeatedly viewing the videos and reducing the playback rate, it traces, moment-by-moment, the "sequences of interaction and bodily expressions of emotional dynamics" (Malthaner, 2017, p. 5). Indeed, it has been established in the literature that emotions can be discerned through facial expressions, movements, and body language, as these are difficult to control consciously (Collins, 2015; Klusemann, 2009;

Nassauer, 2016). The subsequent analysis, however, is limited to movements and body language, as facial expressions are not recognizable due to most individuals covering their faces and the relatively bad quality of the video material. In tracing the sequences of interactions, the analysis is guided by Collins' work on the dynamics that he argues to characterize collective violence during protests.

The videos analyzed below record scenes that took place during the third Act of the Yellow Vests in Paris on December first, 2018. It was one of the most violent anti-government demonstrations by the movement and is considered as the day at which violence exploded, resulting in 412 arrests and 263 people injured (Beaulieu et al., 2018; "Gilets jaunes, scènes de guérilla urbaine à Paris," 2018). Beyond this physical harm to humans, the third Act is also considered as major turning point for the Yellow Vests, the day marking a broadening of the movement's political demands as well as a shift in the government's response toward it and the level of force employed by law enforcement agencies (Chapuis, 2019; Mahfud & Adam-Troian, 2021). Some of the most violent and, symbolically, most important scenes took place around noon at the Arc de Triomphe. At around 11:30 AM, demonstrators began occupying the monument, surrounding and "protecting" the Tomb of the Unknown Soldier. From 11:45 AM, the law enforcement authorities carried out several attempts to push back the demonstrators and eventually evacuated the Place de l'Étoile around 12:30 PM (Cloris, 2018; "Gilets jaunes, acte 3: 263 blessés et 412 interpellations à Paris," 2018). The scenes analyzed took place during this "occupation" of the Arc de Triomphe and were selected after thoroughly searching for, and viewing, videos of violence during Yellow Vest demonstrations on YouTube, Twitter, and Facebook. Selection took place on the basis of two broad criteria: the representativeness of the scenes for the kind of violence to be expected at organized protests, according to Collins, and practical issues related to the quality of the material and the availability of multiple videos capturing the same scenes.

In a first step, I rely on a video that shows clashes between the police and demonstrators under the Arc de Triomphe in the attempts of the authorities to re-take the square. It is part of a longer video uploaded to YouTube by LDC News (2018)—according to its own statements, an independent French content production agency that regularly uploaded videos about the Yellow Vests demonstrations. While it does not indicate a specific time, cross-referencing with another video of Le Parisien (2018) reveals that it depicts the events taking place between approximately 12:00 PM and 12:10 PM. This means that it took place shortly after the scene analyzed in the second step. This latter shows how demonstrators get hold of an isolated policeman, forcing him to the ground and kicking him before he manages to escape. The event has been filmed from two perspectives: the first was uploaded to YouTube by RT France (2018), the French branch of the Russian international news channel RT, while the second was uploaded to Twitter by L'Obs journalist Lucas Burel (2018) at 11.51 AM. This latter video is also listed on the L'Obs (2018) article reconstructing the day under its 11.45 AM entry, allowing us to attribute the scene to approximately this time ("Gilets jaunes, acte 3: 263 blessés et 412 interpellations à Paris," 2018). While this temporal sequence is admittedly not ideal, it arises from the practical constraints of the video material available and, ultimately, is of secondary importance. After all, similar standoffs between demonstrators and the police took place from the early morning onward, so that the first sequence can be taken as representative for the broader tensions present throughout the day, as well as in the immediate context of the Arc de Triomphe around noon (Chapuis, 2019).

3.3 The Micro-situational Dynamics of Non-escalation

3.3.1 Build-up of Confrontational Tension/Fear

The video uploaded by LDC News (2018) is almost nine minutes long and filmed under the Arc de Triomphe, showing the confrontation between law enforcement authorities and demonstrators taking place there. Most interesting for my purposes are the events shown between minutes 2:48 and 4:20, as it is there that the two sides physically clash, and the sequences of interaction in this period are reconstructed in detail in the following. The beginning of this sequence shows an organized line of policemen located under the arc of the monument and facing a large crowd of demonstrators that stand on the square outside the building. The broader crowd keeps a rather large distance to the policemen, but scattered individuals occasionally move forward, shouting at the police or making vulgar gestures toward them. Sporadically, unidentifiable objects are thrown. Afterwards, the police concertedly run toward the crowd, clashing with some few demonstrators, while the majority stays at or retreats to safe distance, and subsequently moves back to its initial position under the arc. While the police are retreating, a crowd of demonstrators runs toward them, some physically clashing with the law enforcement officers, and all demonstrators subsequently move back to their approximate initial position on the square. The rest of the sequence shows scenes similar to the beginning, with both sides facing each other, and the largest part of the crowd keeping its distance. Some individuals approach the police while shouting, making gestures and/or throwing objects, and subsequently move back again, while others stay in front of the crowd making wide and provocative gestures.

The scene is largely representative for the dynamics of violence during organized demonstrations observed by Collins. He argues that crowd violence is mainly carried out by some few individuals who stand in the front, provoking the other side, throwing stones or burning property. Conversely, most people are very cautious and oftentimes run away from potentially violent situations. However, also the "elite of ecrowd fighters" (Collins, 2008, p. 71) shows a considerable degree of tension, manifested in patterns of running forward and backward. These are precisely the dynamics and emotions that we see in the sequence analyzed. The large majority of the demonstrators stands at a safe distance from the police, and almost all run away when the police run toward them. Indeed, it seems that the only individuals physically clashing at that moment are those who are looking away and do not realize quickly enough what is happening. In turn, it is only some few individuals who come closer to the police, insulting and provoking them and throwing objects. Yet, their behavior is generally described by Collins' expression of "much bluster, little action" and characterized by a high degree of tension that is expressed through a pattern of moving forward and back. Instead, the few individuals that remain in front of the crowd, without this pattern of movement, keep a safe distance from the police.

Collins' observations are also accurate in respect to another point. He claims that violence in situations of organized demonstrations most frequently does not escalate when two organized lines collide. On the contrary, so long as the two sides keep their formation, these situations are mainly characterized by standoffs, with demonstrators taunting the authorities. When the two sides do clash physically while holding their lines, only a mild form of violence breaks out, mainly with policemen randomly hitting demonstrators that push into their formation (Collins, 2008). In our case, the clashes between the two sides may seem very violent on first sight, but this observation does not hold when analyzed more closely. In the movement of the police toward the demonstrators, they only have physical contact with two to three individuals, and it seems that they barely, if at all, hit them with their batons. Conversely, the run of the demonstrators into the police looks much more violent. However, reducing the playback rate shows that only some few policemen use their batons some few times to randomly hit those individuals crashing into their line, whereas most policemen lift the batons without using them. Moreover, of the many people who start running toward the police, the vast majority stops before colliding with them, shying away from physical confrontation.

3.3.2 The Absence of Forward Panic

The observations above are of importance beyond the specific situation in which they take place. While the interactions analyzed show a dynamic of "much bluster, little action," they are representative for a prolonged build-up of confrontational tension/fear on both sides as result of a long-standing standoff, constituting the first phase of the dynamics that lead to forward panic. Indeed, according to Collins, most harm during organized demonstrations is done when the two sides are broken up into local situations of overwhelming advantage, with a group of demonstrators beating a single policeman or vice versa (Collins, 2008). It is this kind of scenario that is depicted in the sequence I turn to in the following. While it took place shortly before the scenes analyzed above, these latter nonetheless remain representative for the broader and immediate context in which it took place.

Indeed, the 25-second-long video posted by L'Obs journalist Lucas Burel (2018) initially depicts a situation similar to the one analyzed above. We see a group of policemen standing in an ordered line and opposing a crowd of demonstrators who throw objects at them in a standoff. However, one policeman is suddenly separated from his group and is grabbed and stopped by one to two demonstrators. Quickly, a cluster of people forms around the policeman, who is seemingly forced to the ground, with more and more demonstrators assembling around him. Some individuals appear to kick him, but it is difficult to clearly identify this. Subsequently, the crowd largely disperses, and some few demonstrators help the policeman up, accompanying him away from the crowd. What precisely happened becomes clearer when complementing this observation with the 53-second-long video taken from another angle and uploaded by RT France (2018). The beginning likewise shows the standoff between demonstrators and the police outlined above. Suddenly, two demonstrators emerge together with the policeman from a cloud of tear gas, followed by a crowd forcing the policeman to the ground. While he is going down, one individual quickly approaches, kicking the policeman and falling over him. Directly afterwards, four other individuals, one shortly after another, kick the policeman lying on the ground once each, then turn around and walk away. In this very moment, two other demonstrators start shielding the policeman from the rest of the crowd that is starting to disperse and help him up. One demonstrator then accompanies him some meters away from the crowd before the policeman runs away.

While the brutality of these images should not be downplayed, the violence depicted has little in common with what we would expect from a forward panic. The individuals kicking the policeman do so only once each and almost immediately turn away and leave (apart from the one person falling to the ground). This stands in stark contrast to Collins notion of individuals getting entrained in their own rhythms and actions, entering a "tunnel of violence" and repeating them over and over again in an overuse of force. While it may seem ironic in the context of the general level of violence during the third Act, the sequence hence seems to constitute an unexpected (non-)escalation of violence relative to what we would expect from Collins' theory. Why is that so? After all, the situation described exhibits all the features of a forward panic. There is a prolonged standoff between two opponents that builds up tension, followed by an overwhelming advantage for the demonstrators who isolate one single policeman and can easily beat this long-sought enemy. Everything looks as if violence would come out in a frenzy attack, with more and more demonstrators forcing the policeman to the ground and, especially the first two attackers, hitting him very violently. But the situation does not go down this path. Why are the attackers not becoming entrained in their aggressive action? And why do some demonstrators act against this emotional rush, helping the long-sought enemy? Solely relying on Collins, these questions remain unanswered. While he provides us with a useful vocabulary to describe these situations leading to violent encounters, the analytical toolbox he offers is of little use to understand these kinds of scenarios in which violence does not break out, or only does so in a limited way.

4 Discussion

I have approached the videos on the confrontation between the police and demonstrators during the third Act of the Yellow Vests movement from a micro-sociological interactionist perspective in order to analyze the micro-dynamics in the immediate situation in which violence occurs. Despite the frequently heard claims in public discourse emphasizing the unprecedented levels of violence during the Yellow Vests protests, I have shown that the sequences under the Arc de Triomphe are in no way peculiar to this movement, but rather representative for the kind of violence we would expect in organized demonstrations. While the scale and intensity of the confrontation may be unusual, it continues to be characterized by standoffs between police and demonstrators that only exhibit relatively mild levels of violence, with acts of violence mainly being carried out by some few individuals, and the majority being cautious and keeping distance. Moreover, the second scene analyzed is also representative in the sense that it demonstrates how more severe violent acts during organized demonstrations are usually preceded by a sudden shift in the balance of power—here the overwhelming advantage of demonstrators over one policeman.

However, I have also argued that, despite the brutality of the kicks against the policeman, the scene stands in stark contrast to the phenomenon of overkill that is indicative of Collins' notion of forward panic. This relative (non-)escalation of violence is surprising, given that the scene analyzed exhibits all elements of the situations that lead to forward panic, with a prolonged build-up of tension and the sudden emergence of an overwhelming advantage for demonstrators who isolate a single policeman and have the opportunity to easily beat him. Consequently, the scene points to the insufficiency of Collins' approach to explain these kinds of instances in which violence does not escalate, substantiating my theoretical claim that Collins' theory is mainly descriptive and lacks explanatory value. Indeed, my analysis shows that the micro-situational conditions he focuses on are certainly always necessary—giving Collins' analytical lens its descriptive power—but not (always) sufficient for violence to escalate.

This shortcoming points to the necessity of integrating the sort of interactionist analysis conducted here with approaches that unravel the structural conditions and related individual and group-level processes that shape how individuals interpret the dynamics and emotions in a given micro-situation, thereby accounting for the interaction and interrelation of factors on the macro-level and micro-level. Some pointers of how such approach could look like are offered by Tiratelli (2018) who links immediate situations of violence in the 2011 London riots with their broader context by focusing on protestors' prior experience with the police and the emotional significance attributed to the places in which violence escalated. These dimensions also seem of relevance to the Yellow Vests movement. In fact, several scholars have emphasized how experiences of police violence strengthened intra-group processes of self-identification and reinforced the belief in the legitimacy of the movement and the engagement in collective violence (Poupin, 2019; Adam-Troian et al., 2020; Çelebi et al., 2020). Moreover, the Arc de Triomphe as location of escalation also appears to carry an important symbolic meaning related to French identity that plays a significant role in the self-understanding of the Yellow Vests movement. The occupation of the Arc de Triomphe could thus be interpreted as a reclaiming of French historical ideals that Yellow Vests members feel deprived of due to the perception of growing socio-economic inequalities and of political elites pursuing policies that further exacerbate this gap (see Jetten et al., 2020).

A further investigation of these leads, however, requires us to complement the visual analysis employed here with other data, including testimonies of protestors, interviews and, ideally, quantitative data sets such as criminal records. This would allow us to access individuals' interpretations of micro-situational dynamics and emotions while linking them to their position in the social order. Such an approach would offer much more promising insights into the causes of collective violence during the Yellow Vests demonstrations, as well as into possibilities to address drivers of collective violence, than interactionist theories by themselves. Indeed, the latter's exclusive focus on the immediate situation means that suggestions for violence prevention are equally limited to avoiding the emergence of "violent situations" through crowd management strategies. While this certainly constitutes an important dimension, these approaches' disregard for the individual and collective history of perpetrators of violence makes them unsuitable for understanding radicalization and for drawing lessons related to the prevention of such processes.

References

Adam-Troian, J., Çelebi, E., & Mahfud, Y. (2020). "Return of the repressed": Exposure to police violence increases protest and self-sacrifice intentions for the Yellow Vests. *Group Processes & Intergroup Relations, 23*(8), 1171–1186. https://doi.org/10.1177/2F1368430220920707

Adam-Troian, J., Mahfud, Y., Urbanska, K., & Guimond, S. (2021). The role of social identity in the explanation of collective action: An intergroup perspective on the Yellow Vests movement. *Journal of Applied Social Psychology, 51*(6), 560–576. https://doi.org/10.1111/jasp.12757

Algan, Y., Beasley, E., Cohen, D., Foucault, M., & Péron, M. (2019). *Qui sont les Gilets jaunes et leurs soutiens? CEPREMAP and CEVIPOF*. Retrieved November 11, 2021, from http://www.cepremap.fr/depot/2019/02/2019-03-Qui-sont-les-Gilets-jaunes-et-leurs-soutiens-1.pdf

Arsovska, J. (2009). Review of violence: A micro-sociological analysis by Randall Collins. *Theoretical Criminology, 13*(2), 266–269. https://doi.org/10.1177/13624806090130020504

Beaulieu, C., Maviel, N., & Perez, D. (2018, December 1). Gilets jaunes: Paris a vécu un samedi noir. *Le Parisien*. http://www.leparisien.fr/paris-75/ambiance-de-guerre-civile-a-paris-01-12-2018-7958628.php.

Boyer, P. C., Delemotte, T., Gauthier, G., Rollet, V., & Schmutz, B. (2020). Les déterminants de la mobilisation des Gilets jaunes. *Revue économique, 71*(1), 109–138. https://doi.org/10.3917/reco.711.0109

Burel, L. (2018). *Twitter*, December 1, 11:51 AM. https://twitter.com/L_heguiaphal/status/1068819851500797952. Accessed 11 November 2021.

Çelebi, E., Adam-Troian, J., & Mahfud, J. (2020). Positive links between exposure to police violence, PTSD, and depression symptoms among Yellow Vests protesters in France. *Journal of Interpersonal Violence, 0*(00), 1–22. https://doi.org/10.1177/2F0886260520935863

Chapuis, N. (2019, March 16). Gilets jaunes: Le 1er décembre, le jour où tout a basculé avec la 'prise' de l'Arc de triomphe. *Le Monde*. https://www.lemonde.fr/societe/article/2019/03/16/gilets-jaunes-le-1er-decembre-le-jour-ou-tout-a-bascule-avec-la-prise-de-l-arc-de-triomphe_5436981_3224.html, Accesed 11 October 2022.

Cloris, J. (2018, December 1). Acte III des Gilets jaunes: Revivez minute par minute le fil de cette journée agitée. *Le Parisien*. http://www.leparisien.fr/economie/gilets-jaunes-suivez-le-troisieme-samedi-de-mobilisation-en-direct-01-12-2018-7958376.php.

Collins, R. (2004). *Interaction ritual chains*. Princeton University Press.

Collins, R. (2008). *Violence: A micro-sociological theory*. Princeton University Press.

Collins, R. (2011). Reply to Kalyvas, Wieviorka, and Magaudda. *Sociologica, 13*(2). https://doi.org/10.2383/35867

Collins, R. (2015). Visual micro-sociology and the sociology of flesh and blood: Comment on wacquant. *Qualitative Sociology, 38*(1), 13–17. https://doi.org/10.1007/s11133-014-9297-5

Cooney, M. (2009). The scientific significance of Collins's violence. *The British Journal of Sociology, 60*(3), 586–594. https://doi.org/10.1111/j.1468-4446.2009.01258.x

Eribon, D. (2013). *La société comme verdict*. Flammarion.

Gilets jaunes, acte 3: 263 blessés et 412 interpellations à Paris. (2018, December 1). *L'Obs.* https://www.nouvelobs.com/politique/20181130.OBS6388/gilets-jaunes-acte-3-263-blesses-et-412-interpellations-a-paris.html. Accessed 11 October 2022.

Gilets jaunes, scènes de guérilla urbaine à Paris. (2018, December 1). *La Croix.* https://www.la-croix.com/France/Politique/Gilets-jaunes-Acte-3-2018-12-01-1200986760. Accessed 11 November 2021.

Gross, M. (2016). Vigilante violence and "forward panic" in Johannesburg's townships. *Theory and Society, 45*(3), 239–263. https://doi.org/10.1007/s11186-016-9271-1

Grossman, E. (2019). France's Yellow Vests – Symptom of a chronic disease. *Political Insight, 10*(1), 30–34. https://doi.org/10.1177/2041905819838152

Hagedorn, J. M. (2009). Collins, Randall: Violence. A micro-sociological theory. *Anthropos, 104*(1), 211–212. https://doi.org/10.5771/0257-9774-2009-1-211

Jetten, J., Mols, F., & Selvanathan, H. P. (2020). How economic inequality fuels the rise and persistence of the Yellow Vest movement. *Revue Internationale de Psychologie Sociale, 33*(1). https://doi.org/10.5334/irsp.356

Katz, J. (1999). *How emotions work.* University of Chicago Press.

Kawalerowicz, J., & Biggs, M. (2015). Anarchy in the UK: Economic deprivation, social disorganization, and political grievances in the London Riot of 2011. *Social Forces, 94*(2), 673–698. https://doi.org/10.1093/sf/sov052

Kipfer, S. (2019). What colour is your vest? Reflections on the yellow vest movement in France. *Studies in Political Economy, 100*(3), 209–231. https://doi.org/10.1080/07078552.2019.1682780

Klandermans, P. G. (2014). Identity politics and politicized identities: Identity processes and the dynamics of protest. *Political Psychology, 35*(1), 1–22. https://doi.org/10.1111/pops.12167

Klusemann, S. (2009). Atrocities and confrontational tension. *Frontiers in Behavioral Neuroscience, 3*, 1–10. https://doi.org/10.3389/neuro.08.042.2009

LDC News Agency. (2018, December 2). *Gilets jaunes: Combat urbain sur la tombe du soldat inconnu. Paris/France – 1er Décembre 2018* [Video]. YouTube. Retrieved November 11, 2021, from https://www.youtube.com/watch?v=jx8CjZv8-HA

Le Parisien. (2018, December 3). *Les affrontements autour de l'Arc de Triomphe minute par minute* [Video]. YouTube, Retrieved November 11, 2021, from https://www.youtube.com/watch?v=WHOR6vtoIDY

Magaudda, P. (2011). Comment on Randall Collins/3. The circulation of violence. Techniques and the role of materiality in Randal Collins's violence theory. *Sociologica, 13*(2). https://doi.org/10.2383/35866

Mahfud, Y., & Adam-Troian, J. (2021). "Macron demission!": Loss of significance generates violent extremism for the Yellow Vests through feelings of anomia. *Group Processes & Intergroup Relations, 24*(1), 108–124. https://doi.org/10.1177/1368430219880954

Malthaner, S. (2017). Processes of political violence and the dynamics of situational interaction. *International Journal of Conflict and Violence, 11*, 1–10. https://doi.org/10.4119/ijcv-3097

Morales, A., Ionescu, O., Guegan, J., & Tavani, J. L. (2020). The importance of negative emotions toward the French Government in the Yellow Vest movement. *Revue Internationale de Psychologie Sociale, 33*(1), 1–11. https://doi.org/10.5334/irsp.373

Nassauer, A. (2015). Theoretische Überlegungen zur Entstehung von Gewalt in Protesten: Eine situative mechanismische Erklärung. *Berliner Journal für Soziologie, 25*(4), 491–518. https://doi.org/10.1007/S11609-016-0302-6

Nassauer, A. (2016). From peaceful marches to violent clashes: A micro-situational analysis. *Social Movement Studies, 15*(5), 515–530. https://doi.org/10.1080/14742837.2016.1150161

Olzak, S., Shanahan, S., & McEneaney, E. H. (1996). Poverty, segregation, and race riots: 1960 to 1993. *American Sociological Review, 61*(4), 590–613. https://doi.org/10.2307/2096395

Paye, J.-C. (2019). The Yellow Vests in France. *Monthly Review, 71*(2), 47–57. https://doi.org/10.14452/MR-071-02-2019-06_3

Ponticelli, J., & Voth, H.-J. (2020). Austerity and anarchy: Budget cuts and social unrest in Europe, 1919–2008. *Journal of Comparative Economics, 48*(1), 1–19. https://doi.org/10.1016/j.jce.2019.09.007

Poupin, P. (2019). "We're hotter! Hotter! Hotter than tear gas!" The experience of police violence in the Yellow Vests movement. *Sociologie et sociétés, 51*(1–2), 177–200. https://doi.org/10.7202/1074734ar

Ray, L. (2011). *Violence & society*. Sage.

Royall, F. (2020). The Gilets Jaunes protests: Mobilisation without third-party support. *Modern & Contemporary France, 28*(1), 99–118. https://doi.org/10.1080/09639489.2019.1676217

RT France. (2018, December 1). *Roué de coups sous une pluie de projectiles, un CRS exfiltré par un Gilet jaune* [Video]. YouTube. Retrieved November 11, 2021, from https://www.youtube.com/watch?v=WZfffWpgM4w

Shultziner, D., & Kornblit, I. S. (2020). French Yellow Vests (Gilets Jaunes): Similarities and differences with occupy movements. *Sociological Forum, 35*(2), 535–542. https://doi.org/10.1111/socf.12593

Stott, C., Ball, R., Drury, J., Neville, F., Reicher, S., Boardman, A., & Choudhury, S. (2018). The evolving normative dimensions of 'riot': Towards an elaborated social identity explanation. *European Journal of Social Psychology, 48*(6), 834–849. https://doi.org/10.1002/ejsp.2376

Tiratelli, M. (2018). Reclaiming the everyday: The situational dynamics of the 2011 London Riots. *Social Movement Studies, 17*(1), 64–84. https://doi.org/10.1080/14742837.2017.1348942

Truc, G. (2010). La violence en situations. Entretien avec Randall Collins. *Tracés. Revue de Sciences humaines, 19*, 239–255. https://doi.org/10.4000/traces.4930

Weenink, D. (2014). Frenzied attacks. A micro-sociological analysis of the emotional dynamics of extreme youth violence. *The British Journal of Sociology, 65*(3), 411–433. https://doi.org/10.1111/1468-4446.12088

Wieviorka, M. (2011). Comment on Randall Collins/1. An approach to violence. *Sociologica, 13*(2). https://doi.org/10.2383/35864

Wieviorka, M. (2014). The sociological analysis of violence: New perspectives. *The Sociological Review, 62*(S2), 50–64. https://doi.org/10.1111/2F1467-954X.12191

Elicitive Peace Education in Polarizing Conflicts over Democracy

A Relational Perspective Complementing Prevention of Radicalization

Annalena Groppe

1   Introduction

The *"New Hambach Festival"* (NHF) has been held annually since 2018 in Neustadt, a middle-size town in Rhineland-Palatinate, Germany. Its title refers to the historic Hambach Festival of 1832,[1] a landmark of German democratic history that took place in the Hambach Castle. Today, organizers and speakers of the NHF use this symbolic place to present themselves as contemporary freedom fighters in a "dictatorship of the elites over the people." Thereby, they interpret the history of the site in a nationalistic way and reproduce authoritarian and homogenizing narratives. The propagated notions of "democracy" undermine civil liberties and pluralism and thereby endanger democracy itself (Dany, 2021). The event reaches a target group that transgresses the traditional "extreme-right": a wide audience is attracted by democratic terms, symbols and history, which at the same time are re-interpreted anti-democratically. This leads to resistance and opposition from regional, pluralistically oriented civil society and conflicts arise concerning appropriate reactions, for example, by the castle administration and politics.

Consequently, peace education, in line with political education, is called upon to analyze such conflict dynamics and to develop didactical approaches in order to

---

[1] At the end of May 1832, around 20–30.000 people from all groups of society, including international participants from France and Poland, moved up from Neustadt to the Hambach Castle, demonstrating for national unity, freedom of press and opinion and democracy, answering those day's politics of monarchist restauration. As protests were forbidden, it was declared a county fair.

A. Groppe (✉)
Rheinland-Pfälzische Technische Universität, Landau, Germany
e-mail: a.groppe@rptu.de

"strengthen societal resilience" (Herschinger et al., 2018, p. 24, translated by the author). While this matches a clear potential within peace education's core concepts (peace, violence, conflict), there is also a danger of uncritically aligning peace education with an approach of prevention of radicalization.[2] Peace education is challenged by decolonial and feminist critique by asking for reflection on its theory's onto-epistemological biases, such as the domination of individual, rational, and national understandings of peace(s) (Cremin et al., 2018). This is especially relevant for conflicting truths, e.g. over understandings of democracy, such as in the above-named instance. For example, defining peace education's purpose as prevention of radicalization narrows of the scope of its transformative potential into a modern-western perspective of peace as individual security within a nation-state. Accordingly, facilitators can unconsciously become complicit in the reproduction of structural, cultural, and epistemic forms of violence (Groppe & Hussak, 2021).

Speaking hyperbolically, prevention leads the gaze toward right-wing groups and their symbols, such as terrorists with suicide-bomb belts or black-masked demonstrators. Though, in Germany and elsewhere, radicalizing processes of the so-called political center are not seen and not addressed. Loose movements of individuals such as *PEGIDA*,[3] the *Querdenken*[4]-movement or the NHF include all classes, genders, ethnicities. For example, a collection of 65 letters[5] selected by the organizers of the NHF explicitly portrays the (upper-)middle-class conservative self-perception of participants. They highlight their high educational level, criminal inconspicuousness and non-affiliation with political parties. Participants strongly oppose the label of possible "radicals" and see illegitimate limitation of their freedom of opinion therein.

Those dynamics are rarely considered within prevention or peace education programs. This shows the relevance to, and challenge for, peace education in developing educational responses that consider such events as part of whole societal dynamics, providing ground for radicalization. Therefore, two research questions need to be answered: how can we understand the dynamics of radicalization, manifesting in the NHF, in order to avoid onto-epistemic violence, and how does peace education approach those dynamics accordingly and thereby complement an approach of "prevention"?

---

[2] In the following, "prevention of radicalization and direct violence'" will be shortened as "prevention" for better readability.

[3] *Patriotic Europeans Against the Islamicisation of the Occident* (PEGIDA), founded in 2014 in Dresden, is a nationalist and racist protest movement against immigration.

[4] The *Querdenken* ("lateral thinking") movement protests against COVID-19 policies in Germany, consisting of a variety of participating people, with an increasing influence of right-wing and conspiracy theory actors.

[5] The data is openly available: https://neues-hambacher-fest.de/wp-content/uploads/2021/06/Anschreiben_von_Buergern_an_Frau_Ulrike_Dittrich_Managerin_des_Hambacher_Schlosses.pdf [Last access: 29.08.2022].

Writing in the context of Peace and Conflict Studies, this contribution is suggesting the concept of *"polarizing conflicts[6] over democracy,"* which allows for the analysis of relational processes of polarization, radicalization, and violence in specific situations and contexts, such as the NHF. It also allows the usage of peace (education) research's frameworks for the application and development of possible steps for transformation. The characterization of conflicts as "polarizing" is used here in the sense of a dynamic process, in which diverse contested topics align between seemingly two opposing groups (Iyengar et al., 2019). According to peace researcher Christoph Weller, only in these—for him unlikely—cases, conflicts lead to disintegration. They are an exception in pluralized societies (Weller, 2013, p. 50).

While this might be true when comparing quantity, this contribution deals with exactly these polarizing conflicts. In contrast to Weller, it follows the thesis that polarization and radicalization are a response to pluralization and (post-) modernity, not their exception. The so-called Leipzig study on authoritarianism, for example, describes a return of repressed authoritarian attitudes in response to dynamics of liberalization during the last three decades (Decker & Brähler, 2020, pp. 21–22). Therefore, the connecting issue at the surface of polarizing conflicts, which align diverse topics such as migration, health, and memory culture, is understandings of democracy. This shows the huge relevance to understanding underlying conflict dimensions, including societal structures and cultures that are complicit in polarization and correspondingly provide a nutritional ground for radicalization and violence, as has been illustrated.

This contribution applies peace education's core terms, such as different conflict dimensions, divergent forms of violence, and understandings of "peace" and corresponding approaches of peace education on the case study of the NHF, understood as a polarizing conflict over democracy. It uses an elicitive/transrational theoretical framework that allows for a relational lens. The argumentation mainly builds on preliminary examples drawn from a pilot conflict analysis of the case of the NHF.[7] As field research is still in progress, this article can be understood as a starting point to clarify peace education's concepts and locate the phenomenon within the larger discourse of peace studies. The work-in-progress data can be understood as illustrating further research possibilities.

---

[6] According to peace researcher Christoph Weller, "conflict is not understood as escalating dispute or even applying violence to handle discrepancies, opposition or contradictoriness, but only the expressed difference of positions, constituted by contrary interests, but also opposing values or normative attitudes" (Weller, 2013, p. 48, translated by the author).

[7] The conflict analysis mainly builds on media coverage, actors' online self-representation and observations at the NHF. Additionally, narrative interviews with regional actors opposing the NHF and observations of a workshop with them inform the analysis. The educational reflections built on the author's practical experiences in holding educational spaces for multiplicators in higher and further education, both in and outside university.

2 A Relational Perspective of Peace Education on Radicalization

This chapter introduces peace education by providing a typology of approaches and locating prevention of radicalization within. It gives insight into current debates on the need for onto-epistemological self-reflection regarding these approaches. Consequently, it opens a relational perspective of elicitive/transrational peace education that, following a typology by John Paul Lederach, will guide the analysis of the case study.

Peace education is a diverse field of practice and research, differentiated in regard to the specific forms of violence relevant for each context (Salomon, 2002). Generally speaking, it aims toward (a) raising awareness regarding different forms of violence, (b) exploring and developing various understandings of and approaches toward "peace," and (c) unfolding potentials for conflict transformation. Knowledge, skills, and competencies, as well as the capacity to act upon them are considered to go hand in hand didactically. Transformation of conflicts is largely understood as a continuous process and a potential for mutual learning (Groppe & Hussak, 2021, p. 6).

Norbert Frieters-Reermann uses Johan Galtung's well-known trichotomy of violence to classify peace education approaches into (1) *violence prevention* as tools for restraining direct violence (e.g., peer-mediation training), (2) *critical peace education*, which exposes structural violence (e.g., debates on armament), and (3) *education for a culture of peace*, which deconstructs cultural or symbolic violence (e.g., anti-bias training) (2019, p. 153). Within this given scope, prevention of radicalization overlaps especially with peace education as violence prevention working mainly on interpersonal micro-level. Though it is historically oldest and most widespread in practice, peace education theory warns against high expectations in fostering solely personal responsibility and informed decisions without looking at violence-reproducing structures and cultural discourses that limit the individuals' power and lead to frustration and resignation (Frieters-Reermann, 2009, pp. 52–59).

In line with this, there is a debate on widening definitions of radicalization and corresponding prevention approaches beyond individual direct violence toward a societal level (Deitelhoff & Junk, 2018).[8] For example, the *Peace Research Institute Frankfurt* (PRIF) introduces the concept of "societal radicalization" (Herschinger et al., 2018, p. 1, translated by the author). It describes the process of an increasing and intensifying quality of anti-democratic attitudes and the acceptance to act (not only but also violently) upon them within the whole society. It is based on reciprocal influence of individual radicalization and societal dynamics, e.g. the renunciation of prevalent norms such as the equality of human beings. Accordingly, the

---

[8] Prevention of radicalization and violence receive increasing attention in funding of political education. Actors in the field, dependent on this funding, are pressured to portray peace education as a branch of "prevention." This influences project design that counteracts theoretical and practical developments, which suggest a distance from an individuum- and security-centered peace education.

re-interpretation of democracy at the NHF would indicate a process of societal radicalization (Abay Gaspar et al., 2018).

A disadvantage of such a wide concept is that it puts everybody under general suspicion due to the strong normative and stigmatizing meaning of radicalization that is associated with direct violence. In the worst case, it guides a security-focused educational agenda for the broad public that effectively hampers pluralistic dialogue and freedom of unfolding within trust and creativity. This is the main argument for, precisely, keeping prevention of radicalisation narrow and, consciously, only including such measures, which, at their core, aim to reduce the likeliness of political violence (Greuel, 2018).

Peace education can provide a third and connecting perspective herein because it offers a terminology that stresses the transformative potential of radicalization's underlying conflicts. Those conflicts pervade the whole society, as they have democracy as their central issue. This does not necessarily mean that everybody is in danger of radicalizing toward political violence. But, it suggests a relational understanding of being affected and reciprocally effecting dynamics of polarization.

> [Polarization] fosters radicalization, because in politically polarized situations „a broad civil society group [faces] extremist, populist and fundamentalist milieus" (Zick & Böckler, 2015, p. 6) and due to this encounter openness towards repressive, anti-pluralistic and discriminatory preferences and attitudes can grow. (Herschinger et al., 2018, p. 1)

Consequently, educational actors and approaches also cannot claim a non/all-partisan outside perspective. Decolonial and feminist theory criticize that peace education actually privileges western individualistic, rational and national worldviews (Cremin et al., 2018). This expresses itself, for example, in a traditional prevention agenda: it protects the nation's state democracy against the deviant "evil," for instance by spreading rational understanding of its institutions and principles while prioritizing individual freedom rights over equality rights. This covers state violence within democratic institutions, such as the border control practices at the Mediterranean Sea or racist discrimination in German bureaucracy.

A growing branch following this perspective is the *Innsbruck School of Transrational Peace Philosophy*, founded by Wolfgang Dietrich, who understands peaces as plural, considering their differing underlying "cosmologies" (onto-epistemic assumptions) (2012). Dietrich strongly builds on John Paul Lederach's practice-oriented *Elicitive Conflict Transformation* (Lederach, 1995). Their merged typology identifies four conflict dimensions that follow cardinal themes of relational security, structural justice, cultural truths, and (trans)personal harmony. Those dimensions' dynamic equilibrium is called *transrational*, meaning that dominating western universalities of security, justice, and truth are complemented by the notion of harmony, to which relationality in the sense of *transpersonality* is central.

> According to transpersonal psychology, human beings are not limited to what or who they seem to be in their bodies, their egos, and their personalities. Transpersonal psychology seeks to unite the traditional personal properties of the human being with exterior aspects that lie beyond the boundaries of the person. (Dietrich, 2013, p. 57)

This perspective profoundly changes Peace and Conflict Studies' and peace education's perspective because it (1) understands the peace worker as part of the conflict and asks for awareness of their explicit subjective interventions, (2) focuses on relations, (3) considers bodily, emotional, psychological, and spiritual aspects as relevant, and (4) rejects universal (prescriptive) goals for an elicitive process- and actor-orientation (Dietrich, 2013).

By now, the elicitive and transrational perspectives are only beginning to be discussed within peace education, and they have not been applied to prevention of radicalization. This article aims to take a step in this direction by analyzing the case study of the NHF and discussing corresponding educational responses from an elicitive—and therefore explicitly relational—perspective. Therefore, the above introduced typology of peace education approaches by Frieters-Reermann will be extended to include John Paul Lederach, who distinguishes four dimensions of conflict transformation (cp. Fig. 1).

Lederach breaks down the direct physical aspects of violence into a relational and a personal dimension: while the *relational dimension* concerns the direct contact, e.g. changes in communication patterns, stereotypes, or trust, his *personal dimension* entails the individual's bodily, emotional, and spiritual changes in the

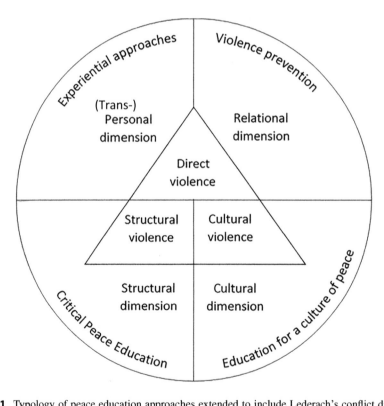

Fig. 1 Typology of peace education approaches extended to include Lederach's conflict dimensions and experiential approaches (own graph)

concerning conflict (Lederach, 1997, p. 82f.). To highlight the correspondence of internal and external processes, the "transpersonal" by Dietrich is added. These aspects of conflict transformation have recently received increasing attention in peace education (Cremin et al., 2018; Koppensteiner, 2020). Thus, a typology of peace education approaches can be extended toward what is summarized here as (*4) experiential approaches* to peace education. This will guide the following analysis of the NHF case study.

3 Analysis of the NHF Case Study

Using Lederach's typology for the following analysis of polarizing conflicts over democracy allows for reflection on different onto-epistemological perspectives of peace education's heterogenous repertoire. Empirical findings from the case study of the NHF can help to identify entry points for, but also complicity of, peace education within those conflicts. Specifically, as to the overall topic of this collection, the contribution aims to build a bridge to those aspects which can complement prevention approaches.

3.1 Relational Dimension

The relational conflict dimension affects communication between, and reciprocal perception of, the conflict parties. For example, participants and organizers of the NHF strategically perform with a moderate and non-confrontational appearance. This becomes visible when the main organizer Max Otte[9] welcomes participants by playing the guitar or labeling their protest as "going for a (patriotic) walk" (Afanasjew, 2019). On the other hand, speakers express strong distrust or make accusations and insults against politicians, opposing political groups, media, and minority groups. The "most radical" escalation of direct violence might be a barrel full of manure that was drained in front of the right-wing participants by left-wing activists (Kreitling, 2018). Beyond the annual confrontation at the castle, this relationship is also largely visible online as each group refers to or analyzes the other's texts and activities.[10]

Peace education approaches to *violence prevention* in such situations offer, for example, argumentation trainings that do not only work on content but also train to keep up relational connections.[11] Building on an individual and subject-oriented tradition that is rooted in the post-Second World War period, these approaches see

---

[9] Max Otte is an economist and political activist. He has been the chairman of the AFD-affiliated Desiderius Erasmus Foundation and was elected as leader of the Werteunion in 2021, which is associated with the conservative wing of CDU/CSU.

[10] Otherwise, the relationship between actors remains widely without direct contact, because the NHF participants travel from all over Germany, while the opposing activists live in the region.

[11] Zum Beispiel: https://www.kurvewustrow.org/argumentationstrainings

teaching of personal competencies and ethical attitudes as a key to enable people to act non-violently (e.g., K. F. Roth, 1981). These perspectives are most widespread in form of peer-mediator trainings in schools or non-violent communication groups.

There are some similarities to approaches to prevent radicalization. Due to their focus on direct violence, they allow to reach distant target groups, for example, through street work, by starting from the perspectives that clients bring in. This approach has recently been adapted by Friedenskreis Halle e.V., which cooperates with youth support organizations in the counseling center *tumult*. An important contrast remains: *tumult* is potential- rather than prevention-oriented and aims to foster community and engagement.[12] For example, those participants of the NHF and their many silent supporters that do not (yet) have a closed worldview could more likely be reached with a participatory approach, because they strongly reject the label of "radicals."

However, if structural violence is ignored, these approaches can also become complicit in reproducing inequality and exclusion if, e.g. homogenizing narratives are uncritically accepted in an open participatory room. Reversely, the demonization of any violence does not recognize differences between authoritarian and pluralistic content of underlying ideology. As exemplified in the above given case study, the drained barrel of manure by left-wing activists can also be understood as civil resistance against structural violence, standing up against the (severe) consequences for minority groups that underly the democratic structures propagated at the NHF.

Expectations of the individual choice and the potential empowerment through education appear unrealistic when confronted with structures of violence that entangled within schools, state institutions and their history of militarism, colonialism, and authoritarianism (Frieters-Reermann, 2009, pp. 52–59). Such approaches can, for example, support autocratic regimes, as they do not reflect the blurring ambivalences between structural violence and counterviolence (Gur-Ze'ev, 2010, p. 172). The described shortcomings have been extensively discussed within peace education research and have led to the development of *critical peace education*, which is introduced in the following passage.

3.2 Structural Dimension

As observed in the field research, a widely followed debate among regional actors opposing the NHF is in how far the propagated understandings of democracy have an anti-democratic potential for structural violence and how to create awareness thereof. Moreover, political science perspectives ask whether right-wing populist understandings endanger democracy and, if yes, how to democratically address them. This question is connected to decisions on whether the NHF should be allowed to take place at the Hambach Castle or be banned by the administrative foundation of the castle or political actors.

---

[12] https://tumult-halle.de/

In conflicts over the NHF, it is possible to observe re-interpretations of core pillars of democracy, such as civil liberty rights and pluralism. This is done by a construction of the German *"Volk"* as an ethnically homogenous entity that denies full democratic participation to marginalized groups, such as BIPoC, women, LGBTQI, or people who receive financial support by the state (Sturm, 2019). Thereby, speakers question the legitimacy of the existing political order and reject shared norms (e.g., equality, solidarity, and diversity), even partly suggesting the use of anti-democratic means (e.g., direct violence) to reach their goals.

Charlotte Dany portrays those structural elements as a dilemma situation: allowing violent ideas to be promoted can lead to a normalization, while restricting the possibilities for expression can strengthen the right-wing narrative of limited freedom of opinion and speech. She suggests a more nuanced response by clearly naming and criticizing those elements of the dominating understanding of democracy at the NHF that can lead to erosion of democratic cores (Dany, 2021).

Critical peace education provides a helpful lens here because it focuses on the facilitation of critical competences to identify different forms of violence and analyze one's own position and potential political actions. In times of the bipolar world order, this branch criticized (re-)militarization, while today, the global capitalistic system became central as root of violence (Bernhard, 2017). Moreover, critical trainings on right-wing structures, symbols, and ideology are part of peace education's repertoire, for example in cooperation with the project "School without racism—school with courage."[13]

In summer 2021, regional activists, politicians, and scientists that engage in the context of the NHF organized a diverse workshop series, including many critical lectures and discussion rounds.[14] Even the NHF itself understands itself as aiming toward education for peace.[15] Herein, the question of criteria for "critical peace education" arises. It becomes striking that it is deliberately not neutral:

> Rather than status quo reproduction, critical approaches in peace education and peace research aim to empower learners as transformative change agents (Freire, 1970) who critically analyze power dynamics and intersectionalities among race, class, gender, ability/disability, sexual orientation, language, religion, geography, and other forms of stratification. (Bajaj & Brantmeier, 2011, p. 221)

In contrast, the NHF shows ignorance to power structures and their historic reality (of coloniality, industrialization and patriarchy). Moreover, it does not foster participatory and plural critique from participants. Critical peace education refrains from manipulation and dogmatism and allows emancipatory learning.

Consequently, within an overly structural oriented peace education that focuses on peace as justice, polarization and, consequently, radicalization can unintentionally be strengthened. It aims to visualize conflict lines that follow modern-binary

---

[13] www.couragierte-schule.de

[14] https://hambacherfest1832.blog/2021/04/30/2021hambach1832/

[15] In 2019, the NHF had the subtitle, "Congress for security and peace in Europe" (translated by the author).

power hierarchies, such as race, class, and gender. This can have a huge potential for transformation, as power-critical approaches within peace education show (Groppe & Hussak, 2021, p. 7). At the same time, it can cement groups and their positions and strengthen affective and issue polarization.

This does not mean that polarization needs to be avoided in any case. Even those polarizing conflicts that challenge social cohesion can have transformative potential. Public discourse that often demonizes such conflicts because they "divide society" is based in a bias of peace as "national harmony," which stigmatizes perspectives of peace as justice. Polarizing conflicts can politicize and thereby strengthen democracy.

At the same time, minority rights require guaranteed protection, as it is the most vulnerable groups that suffer most directly under political violence. This needs to be brought into balance, considering how much polarization a society can withstand. Therefore, the capability to identify and resist authoritarian ideology among the wider population is an important fact that will be discussed in the following section.

3.3 Cultural Dimension

Visible aspects of a cultural dimension of conflicts in the context of NHF are the references to German democratic history, making an analogy with participants and their contexts at the Hambach Festival of 1832. According to the historian Michael Sturm, such politics of history are used strategically by right-wing actors in order to construct categories such as *"Volk,"* "nation," and "culture" as essentialist and homogenous by legitimizing them with seemingly historic arguments (Sturm, 2019, p. 21).

The underlying *völkisch*-nationalist, authoritarian, and essentialist ideology can be understood as a German continuity (Salzborn, 2017; Hufer, 2018, p. 32). This is both expressed at the NHF in postcolonial racist polemics against Islam and refugees, as well as in implicit antisemitic narratives about conspiracies of media and elites. The national-socialist crimes against humanity are not mentioned or reflected in NHF's interpretation of German history. Neither are continuities of imperialism, colonialism and global inequalities, wars, and migration. The re-interpretations fall on fertile ground, e.g. of collective repression of the perpetration of crimes against humanity during the Holocaust (Salzborn, 2017) and the continuing coloniality within dominating knowledge (Brunner, 2020).

Empirical studies on a national level back up the observation that it is not an exceptional minority who is attracted, e.g. by anti-democratic, authoritarian narratives that reproduce group-focus enmity. For Germany, they show that a large majority supports democracy as a concept, as well as its current reality, though numbers are decreasing (Faus & Storks, 2019, pp. 5–6), especially following the Covid-19-pandemic (more in common e.V., 2022). At the same time, populist ideas of a "homogenous people" are widespread not only within an "extreme milieu," but the so-called center (Zick et al., 2019). Authoritarian, nationalist, and homogenizing ideology affects western societies as a whole, manifesting in an increase of open expression of anti-modern and anti-democratic resentment, e.g. in conspiracy theories and antisemitism (Decker & Brähler, 2020). Therefore, these cultural tendencies do not only concern the right margins or societally deprived, but everybody, as it is interwoven in our systems of knowledge, education, and science.

In the case study, this becomes visible as not only participants, but also regional communal and civil society actors engage in re-interpreting symbols and history to strengthen a collective (national) identity: a pluralist, open, and cosmopolitan narrative is positioned against the patriotic and conservative one. This can be observed, for example, by the local municipality proclaiming to become "Democracy-town" or the organization of festivals promoting an (opposing) narrative of German democratic history.

For sure, there are huge differences between how actors position themselves in regard to this ever-present bias, ranging from denial over ignorance to continuous work of raising self-reflective awareness. This is a challenge and a potential for peace education. Werner Wintersteiner's approach of an "education for a culture of peace" raises awareness on collective discourses that legitimate violence. While anti-bias trainings, ideology critique and memorial education have a relatively long tradition (Schimpf-Herken, 2008), it is only recently that decolonial, post-migrant, and Indigenous perspectives on education have gained attention. They understand the Self as entangled in cultural and epistemic violence—both as person or institutionalized discipline (Groppe & Hussak, 2021, p. 7). Therefore, a second-order reflexivity that focuses on onto-epistemic roots, biases, and alternatives is suggested (Kester & Cremin, 2017):

> First, rebuffing excessively patriarchal discourses of rationality, peace education honors feminized perspectives and the role of affect and relationships, particularly in its attention to care ethics. Second, rejecting technocratic modernist values, peace education highlights diverse concepts of peace that privilege nature and ecological well-being. Third, shifting away from the Enlightenment view of religion as superstition, peace education recognizes different faith-based philosophies and traditions globally." (Bevington et al., 2020, p. 160)

These international and transdisciplinary discourses, in effect, can be connected to the practice in the German field of peace education. For example, the project #vrschwrng combines knowledge on conspiracy theory with a peer-to-peer approach, that takes the experience, identity conflicts, and challenges of ambiguity for young people as a starting point (Berghof Foundation, 2020). Here, it becomes visible that the cultural dimension, through the increasingly seen potential of self-reflection, can (be) complement(ed by) the (trans-)personal dimension of conflict transformation.

3.4 (Trans-)Personal Dimension

The high relevance that Lederach attributes to the (trans-)personal dimension of conflict transformation mirrors the mentioned turn to recognize *emotional, embodied* (timely and locally embedded), and *spiritual* aspects: Polarizing conflicts are "equally driven by psychosocial elements—long-standing animosities rooted in a perceived threat to identity" (Lederach, 1997, p. 17, 82). In the case study of the NHF, meanings of cultural symbols and history, e.g. the Hambach Festival of 1832, are connected to identity questions of both parties.

Emotional aspects are expressed when speakers and participants of the NHF express and evoke emotions, e.g. using music, joint singing, and long applause during speeches. Next to this enthusiasm, the speeches openly express anger, distrust, and experiences of powerlessness. Opposing activists, on the one hand, react to this emotionality by a strong focus on rational facts that aim to devalue emotional arguments and appear as the (superior) rational actor. Though, on the other hand, frustration and insecurity appear in irony or sarcasm, when NHF participants are being made fun of in a discrediting way. This notion also shows up in narratives connected to the barrel of manure, rather than what might be expected as serious rage.

In individual conversations, especially fear and (projections of) guilt shine through; repeatedly transgenerational transmitted narratives of complicity and/or victim's horrors during times of National Socialism are referred to. The data is still limited in number and depths for a profound analysis. What can be said is, however, that emotions are often not made explicit or reflected on and covered by a performed objectivity.

This corresponds to approaches of peace education: emotions are widely included in peace education practice, but only somewhat reflected in the light of corresponding research (Starke & Groppe, 2019). In distinction, experiential approaches work *with* instead of *against* or *around* those emotions using, e.g. body-based methods (e.g., theater, awareness, martial arts).

Embodied aspects of the conflict can be observed in their relation to the Hambach Castle as a physical place, which is described by the actors as bridging temporal "locations" throughout history. For example, by re-enacting the "march" up the hill to the castle, participants of the NHF experience their bodies in relation to demonstrators in 1832. An opposing activist expressed her impulse to hide or flee as demonstrators walked by her house.

David Abram, who explores the sensuous perception of time and space in oral cultures, diagnoses a bias in modern understandings of history as linear, stable, and place-indifferent. In contrast, communities with a mainly oral tradition of narrating stories (not history) understand "time" as inseparable from "place," both cyclical and circular (Abram, 1996, p. 181ff.). Actors' relationships to the Hambach Castle within history are mainly conceptualized as independent from their own (bodies') position in time and space. The conflicts evolve around different interpretations of a seemingly objective meta-narrative. Reflection of this onto-epistemological bias allows for the perception of memories of the Hambach Festival of 1832 as re-created in rituals and relationships of human and even inanimate bodies such as the castle and twists the meaning of "true interpretation" toward a subjective experience. Drawing awareness toward the actors' bodies allows for the experience of multiple (hi)stories of the Hambach Festival as dynamic and context-specific.

This can be a resource for peace education approaches, mainly learning from Indigenous perspectives on education, in which relationship to the land is a central pillar (Four Arrows, 2010). It leads the gaze toward transgenerational questions: how does Germany's democratic history, with all its cracks and collective traumata, including the still largely unprocessed heritage of the Shoah, shape memory, bodies and, thereby, conflicts over identity? Whose stories of emancipating struggle for democracy do we narrate, and whose are suppressed, e.g. due to patriarchal or colonial continuities? While the Vormärz period (eve of the 1848 German revolution) is widely referred to by actors, I believe that it is, rather, the not-explicitly, possibly unconscious, aspects that make those conflicts that complex. How can we learn within and about these blind spots and jointly develop transformative steps?

Spiritual aspects within conflicts over the NHF are hardly explicitly visible. Actors understand themselves as secular. Religion (both of in- and outgroup) is located at the cultural rather than (trans-)personal dimension (e.g., Muslim culture as incompatible with "German values"). Secularism for all conflict parties appears as a neutral ground, from which the others' opinion is rejected as irrational—religious—ideology. Thereby, ambiguity is hardly acceptable. In the case study, this expresses itself, for example, in debates on the danger vs. potential of left-wing meta-narratives regarding German democracy history. Plurality, though theoretically accepted on the cultural dimension of conflict, challenges the actors personally, as they need to let go of a universal historic truth. They experience vulnerability.

How should those aspects be approached practically? Norbert Koppensteiner describes the "Self" as consisting of a personal and a collective (unconscious) aspect. To approximate the latter conflict-significant, though cognitively hidden, "transpersonality,"[16] he expands learning spaces through experiential modes of knowing: sensing (somatic, embodied), feeling (empathic, affective), thinking (intellectual, cognitive), intuitive (esthetic, holistic), and witnessing (transpersonal, spiritual) (Koppensteiner, 2020, p. 96ff.). Such an experiential approach can be methodologically put into practices following Gabrielle Roths "5Rythms" (1998). It contains free movement within a group that follows cyclically changing music, which allows for bodily, emotional, and spiritual awareness of the dancers' experience of conflict. The method encourages bodily expression of new ways of movement that can be meaningful for transformative steps outside the safe learning environment.

Such approaches can also have the potential to bring groups together whose verbal and cognitive dialogue is blocked due to polarized vocabulary and communicative patterns, as well as unacceptable political positions in either direction. The basic dimensions of body, psyche, and emotionality can open a room for connectivity on another level. Of course, this also requires the facilitator's sensibility to hold a save room, e.g. not opening competitive discussion rounds, but rather subjective sharing circles. It will therefore not resolve those political issues as well, but potentially create a relationship of trust, through which further content-related processes can occur.

---

[16] Dietrich and Koppensteiner build their theoretical perspective on transpersonal psychology (cp., e.g., Grof, 2017).

Finally, context-specific reflection is key: Lederach's strong focus on the (trans-) personal conflict dimension has its roots in intractable conflict situations with severe and continuous experiences of armed violence. In such a context, further polarization that is strengthened, e.g. through critical peace education, might physically endanger participants and facilitators. This is not the case for conflicts over the NHF. In line with this, Jennifer Murphy reminds peace educators to reflect upon power structures within and trough transrational peace education (2018). Consequently, the differentiation of conflict dimensions suggests a balancing process that is discussed in the following Table 1.

3.5 Transformative Steps for Peace Education

The analysis of the case study within the frame of Lederach's conflict dimensions shows that an onto-epistemic reflection on peace education's diverse approaches, perspectives, and their corresponding entanglements within the conflicts is helpful to gain orientation within conflicts over the NHF. This chapter derives some possible transformative steps for peace education research and practice to respond to polarizing conflicts over democracy.

None of the above introduced approaches can be understood as "objective" or "non-/all-partisan," nor do any of them represent a universal normative position. On the one hand, this variety of peace education's understandings and strategies of, and for, peace(s) can be criticized for conceptual confusion, ambivalent ethical

Table 1 Summary of the conflict dimension analysis (own graph)

Conflict dimension	Relational	Structural	Cultural	(Trans-) Personal
Case study examples	Performance of non-violence; insulting political opponents	Rejection of minority rights	Nationalist interpretation of the Hambach festival	Enthusiasm, anger, powerlessness
	Resistance, e.g., with a drained manure barrel	Crisis of representation	Communal "democracy week"	Rationalization; suppressed anger, fear & guilt
Peace education approach	Violence prevention	Critical peace education	Education for a culture of peace	Experiential peace education
	e.g., peer mediation	e.g., global citizenship education	e.g., anti-bias education	e.g., Indigenous education
PE's relationship to prevention	Similar focus on peace-as-security	Contrasting evaluation of polarization	Potential of PE to complement	Reciprocal complementing
PE in polarizing conflicts	Dominating focus reproduces structural violence	Dominating focus reproduces polarization	Growing field, including unheard voices as potential	New field with potential to balance & need for reflection

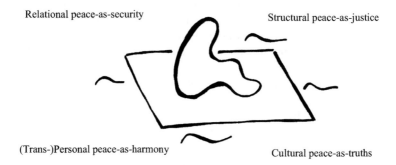

Fig. 2 Person balancing on a wooden raft, representing Dietrich's (2018) themes in a conflict that build on and correspond to Lederach's (1997) conflict dimensions (own graph)

considerations and, at worst, contradictory strategies (Frieters-Reermann, 2009, p. 61ff.; Gur-Ze'ev, 2010). On the other hand, this can also be seen as a potential for context-specific, process-oriented, and participatory practice that restrains from prescribing normative aims, such as "demarcation" from certain beliefs or behaviors (Kester & Cremin, 2017; Groppe & Hussak, 2021).

This depends on the level of awareness, for example, of the multiple relationships within the conflict, including the peace education actor's position within. Exploring peace education's relationships within polarizing conflicts over democracy is one step in this direction. Applied to the case study, conceptual differences and their complementary potential were shown.

On the one hand, the analysis reaffirms a rather well-described bias of peace education: its prevalence emphasizes the relational conflict dimension. A sole focus on conflict management skills has been discussed and criticized in literature, because it covers structural and cultural violence (Bernhard, 2017). This becomes striking when right-wing actors of the NHF refer to "non-violence" and *peace-as-security*[17] to legitimize an authoritarian and homogenizing ideology.

On the other hand, the analysis allows for the identification of another strong focus on the structural dimensions of conflict by critical approaches. They intentionally take position which strengthens polarizing dynamics. This can have a politicizing and thereby transformative effect, highlighting *peace-as-justice*. At the same time, understanding the dynamics of growing societal radicalization relationally, a dominating critical educational approach can also weaken social cohesion (*peace-as-harmony*) and undermine plurality of positions (*peace-as-truths*). This becomes visible within the hostility against "corrupt" political education, as well as the critique of migrant self-organizations regarding exclusion of PoC within peace education.

Recognizing four interrelated conflict dimensions, Lederach's framework does not end in a dualistic dilemma situation. It can be rather imagined within the metaphor of a wooden raft (cp. Fig. 2) that can be driven holding a dynamic balance. In

---

[17] The "peace families" with their main themes by Wolfgang Dietrich, as introduced above, can be aligned with Lederach's conflict dimensions (Dietrich, 2018, p. 27).

this picture, any action interacting with dynamics on one dimension will affect the others as well. Therefore, if transformation—whatever it might subjectively look like—is aimed at (which is an assumption of elicitive conflict transformation and this chapter), educators might want to let go of those prevailing approaches while unfold those identified as marginalized. Their perspective will (and should) possibly change in the course of action. Further evaluation and orientation follows in a continuous process.

Therefore, the analysis in this given moment, and from the author's presented perspective on peace education, suggests strengthening learning spaces that work on the discursive roots that reproduce cultural and epistemic violence. De- and postcolonial approaches[18] already receive some attention in the field of peace education. For example, Michalinos Zembylas asks for historization of peace concepts, practicing empathy and solidarity as well as listening to experiences of colonial continuities by people who are affected (2018). Within the given case study in Germany, such a perspective asks to build on the expertise of groups that are targeted and excluded by the NHF's ideology, within the development of programs. While there have been some attempts within educational events, there is not yet a systematic inclusion of, e.g. migrant voices.

Secondly, addressing the (trans-)personal dimension of conflict has shown the potential to connect the cultural perspective with subjective experience within democracy, repressed memory, emotions, and identity. Moreover, experiential learning about history as always relational between past and present or local and global places can help in the acceptance of the uncertainty of plural truths. Such approaches gain first attention within peace education research, e.g. they are visible within a special issue of the Journal of Peace education on transrational perspectives (Tjersland & Ditzel Facci, 2019). By now, the rationalization of emotions, ignorance regarding positionality and context and the dominance of modern secularity do leave transformative potential untouched, and they even reproduce conflict dynamics that can be observed in the case study.

Taking up the metaphor of a wood raft, the question arises as to which tools to use in order to balance between the different peace education approaches. For Lederach, the transformative steps within a conflict "elicit" form the specific context within a participatory and self-reflective process. Instead of prescribing a desired "end-state," the course of action unfolds with actors involved (Lederach, 1995). The general idea was transferred into a practical framework of *Elicitive Conflict Mapping* by Wolfgang Dietrich in relation to the *Transrational Peace Philosophy* that was mentioned beforehand (2018). Deepening the conflict analysis within such a participatory, relational and self-reflective framework within the context of the NHF can be a next step. Thereby, understanding of polarizing conflicts can gain empirical depth.

---

[18] For example, the online timeline method, *Connecting the dots*, in which participants are asked to identify the historic context of citations that carry colonial meanings, thereby experiencing the continuity of those discourses. https://www.connecting-the-dots.org/

Moreover, dialogue with the international field of peace education (including special attention to perspectives of BIPoC[19]) and neighboring disciplines of political education can enrich theory for a reflected educational response to described conflicts. In particular, perspectives from structurally, culturally, and epistemically excluded groups need to be consciously included by self-reflection, thus abolishing barriers to academic and educational settings. To understand their needs, listening and a change of perspective is needed.

4 Conclusion

The article explored, from an elicitive/transrational perspective, how approaches of peace education can complement the prevention of radicalization. It suggested the concept of *polarizing conflicts over democracy* in order to analyze underlying dynamics from a transformative and relational perspective. Lederach's differentiation of four conflict dimensions allowed for the identification of entry points for peace education, as well as their onto-epistemological entanglement within conflicts and corresponding violence-reproducing effects. This allows for conscious decisions about which kind of educational actions are helpful in the specific relational context.

For the conflicts surrounding the NHF, and potentially other polarizing conflicts over democracy in Germany, the analysis gives a first orientation: critical peace education can complement prevention approaches, providing a space to identify, criticize, and abolish structural violence—which might mean to radically challenge the nationalist status quo. Conversely, peace education can learn from prevention approaches (e.g., based on street work) as to how trustful relationships can balance and avoid animosity despite polarizing positions. These can be strengthened by including transrational/elicitive approaches, which are new to both fields. Moreover, awareness of cultural violence and pluralistic and creative remembering, e.g. of the German history of democracy, appears to be a potential approach.

These suggestions mark only a starting point for understanding the potentials for peace and challenges in regard to different forms of violence inherent in peace education within polarizing conflicts over democracy. To address and deepen them, a participatory approach, including multiple perspectives, seems to be suitable. This can be cyclically interwoven with theory development, following the challenges and potentials identified "on the ground." One could say that peace education is not only challenging homogenizing, authoritarian, and nationalist interpretation of concepts such as democracy and peace in its content, but even in its disciplinary transformation. All in all, a relational understanding of polarizing conflicts over democracy shows peace education and prevention's entanglement within the societal dynamics. Its reflection allows for conscious, transformative steps that balance the marginalized and prevailing topics. Within this perspective, peace education's diverse

---

[19] BIPoC stands for "Black, Indigenous (and) People of Color" and is a self-identification of people who experience racism because they are not perceived as *white* and *western*.

approaches can be seen as a potential for plural understandings of peace(s). Participatory and context-specific processes can open relational learning spaces in order to "unfold" conflict competences deeply rooted in (trans-)personal experience.

Acknowledgments I would, in particular, like to thank all regional partners who are engaging in, and learning about, polarizing conflicts over democracy at the Hambach Castle, as well as the team of Peace Academy Rhineland-Palatinate for their valuable feedback and support.

References

Abay Gaspar, H., Daase, C., Deitelhoff, N., Junk, J., & Sold, M. (2018). Was ist Radikalisierung? - Präzisierungen eines umstrittenen Begriffs. PRIF Report 5/2018. Frankfurt am Main: Leibniz-Institut Hessische Stiftung Friedens- und Konfliktforschung (HSFK).
Abram, D. (1996). *The spell of the sensuous: Perception and language in a more-than-human world*. Vintage Books.
Afanasjew, N. (2019). Die sanfte Rechte. Der Freitag, Retrieved June 17, 2020, from https://www.freitag.de/autoren/der-freitag/die-sanfte-rechte
Arrows, F. (2010). Indigenous spirituality as a source for peaceful relations. In E. J. Brantmeier, J. Lin, & J. P. Miller (Eds.), *Spirituality, religion, and peace education*. IAP-Information Age Publ.
Bajaj, M., & Brantmeier, E. J. (2011). The politics, praxis, and possibilities of critical peace education. *Journal of Peace Education, 8*, 221–224.
Berghof Foundation. (2020). *#vrschwrng - Ein interaktives Toolkit gegen Verschwörungstheorien*. Berghof Foundation.
Bernhard, A. (2017). *Pädagogik des Widerstands: Impulse für eine politisch-pädagogische Friedensarbeit. Pädagogik und Gesellschaftskritik*. Beltz Juventa.
Bevington, T., Nomisha, K., & Cremin, H. (2020). Peace education and citizenship education: Shared critiques. In A. Peterson, G. Stahl, & H. Soong (Eds.), *The Palgrave handbook of citizenship and education* (pp. 155–168). Springer International Publishing. https://doi.org/10.1007/978-3-319-67828-3_51
Brunner, C. (2020). *Epistemische Gewalt. Wissen und Herrschaft in der kolonialen Moderne*. transcript Verlag.
Cremin, H., Echavarría, J., & Kester, K. (2018). Transrational peacebuilding education to reduce epistemic violence. *Peace Review, 30*, 295–302.
Dany, C. (2021). Bürgerliche Antidemokraten. Max Otte und das "Neue Hambacher Fest.". *Blätter für deutsche und internationale Politik, 8*, 97–104.
Decker, O., & Brähler, E. (2020). *Autoritäre Dynamiken: Alte Ressentiments - neue Radikalität : Leipziger Autoritarismus Studie 2020*. Psychosozial-Verlag.
Deitelhoff, N., & Junk, J. (2018, April 10). Warum wir einen weiten Begriff von Radikalisierung brauchen. *PRIF BLOG*. https://blog.prif.org/2018/04/10/warum-wir-einen-weiten-begriff-von-radikalisierung-brauchen/
Dietrich, W. (2012). *Interpretations of peace in history and culture. Many Peaces*. Palgrave Macmillan.
Dietrich, W. (2013). *Elicitive conflict transformation. Many Peaces*. Palgrave Macmillan.
Dietrich, W. (2018). *Elicitive conflict mapping. Many Peaces*. Palgrave Macmillan.
Faus, R., & Storks, S. (2019). *Das pragmatische Einwanderungsland was die Deutschen über Migration denken*. Friedrich-Ebert-Stiftung.
Frieters-Reermann, N. (2009). *Frieden lernen: Friedens- und Konfliktpädagogik aus systemisch-konstruktivistischer Perspektive*. Wiku-Wissenschaftverlag Dr. Stein.

Frieters-Reermann, N. (2019). Frieden durch Friedensbildung – Grenzen und Chancen erhofften Transformationspotenzials. In G. Lang-Wojtasik (Ed.), *Bildung für eine Welt in Transformation: Global Citizenship Education als Chance für die Weltgesellschaft*. Verlag Barbara Budrich.

Greuel, F. (2018, April 16). Das (zu) weite Feld der Prävention oder: Wo Prävention beginnen und enden sollte. *PRIF BLOG*. https://blog.prif.org/2018/04/16/das-zu-weite-feld-der-praevention/

Grof, S. (2017). *Revision der Psychologie: das Erbe eines halben Jahrhunderts Bewusstseinsforschung*. Nachtschatten-Verlag.

Groppe, A., & Hussak, M. (2021). Friedenspädagogik in Transformation. Potentiale eines vielfältigen Feldes. Wissenschaft & Frieden, 2021(4)6–9.

Gur-Ze'ev, I. (2010). Philosophy of peace education in a Postmetaphysical era. In G. Salomon & E. Cairns (Eds.), *Handbook on peace education* (pp. 315–336). Taylor & Francis.

Herschinger, E., Bozay, K., Decker, O., von Drachenfels, M., Joppke, C., & Sinha, K. (2018). *Radikalisierung der Gesellschaft? - Forschungsperspektiven und Handlungsoptionen*. PRIF report 8/2018. Frankfurt am Main: Leibniz-Institut Hessische Stiftung Friedens- und Konfliktforschung (HSFK).

Hufer, K.-P. (2018). *Neue Rechte, altes Denken: Ideologie, Kernbegriffe und Vordenker*. Beltz Juventa.

Iyengar, S., Lelkes, Y., Levendusky, M., Malhotra, N., & Westwood, S. J. (2019). The Origins And Consequences Of Affective Polarization in the United States. *Annual Review of Political Science, 22*(1), 129–146. https://doi.org/10.1146/annurev-polisci-051117-073034

Kester, K., & Cremin, H. (2017). Peace education and peace education research: Toward a concept of poststructural violence and second-order reflexivity. *Educational Philosophy & Theory, 49*, 1415–1427. https://doi.org/10.1080/00131857.2017.1313715

Koppensteiner, N. (2020). *Transrational peace research and Elicitive facilitation: The self as (re) source*. Springer International Publishing.

Kreitling, H. (2018, May 5). „Neues Hambacher Fest": Wo die schweigende Mehrheit „Bravo" in die Menge brüllt. *DIE WELT*. https://www.welt.de/politik/deutschland/article176099912/Neues-Hambacher-Fest-Wo-die-schweigende-Mehrheit-Bravo-in-die-Menge-bruellt.html

Lederach, J. P. (1995). *Preparing for peace: Conflict transformation across cultures*. Syracuse University Press.

Lederach, J. P. (1997). *Building peace: Sustainable reconciliation in divided societies*. United States Inst. of Peace Press.

More in Common e.V. (2022). *Was macht die Pandemie mit dem gesellschaftlichen Zusammenhalt? Navigieren Im Ungewissen: Impulse Zur Zukunft Der Gesellschaft*. More in Common e.V. https://www.moreincommon.de/navigierenimungewissen/

Murphy, J. M. (2018). Elephant watering (W)hole: Transrational learning spaces. In J. E. Alvarez, D. Ingruber, & N. Koppensteiner (Eds.), *Transrational resonances: Echoes to the many Peaces* (pp. 263–286). Springer International Publishing. https://doi.org/10.1007/978-3-319-70616-0_13

Roth, K. F. (1981). *Erziehung zur Völkerverständigung und zum Friedensdenken* (2. überarb. und erw. Aufl. St.). EOS-Verl.

Roth, G. (1998). *Maps to ecstasy: The healing power of movement* (2nd ed.). New World Library.

Salomon, G. (2002). The nature of peace education: Not all programs are created equal. In G. Salomon & N. Baruch (Eds.), *Peace education: The concepts, principles and practices around the world* (pp. 3–15). Lawrence Erlbaum.

Salzborn, S. (2017). *Angriff der Antidemokraten: die völkische Rebellion der Neuen Rechten* (1. Auflage). Beltz Juventa.

Schimpf-Herken, I. (2008). Erinnerung braucht Zukunft, Zukunft braucht Erinnerung. In R. Grasse, B. Gruber, & G. Gugel (Eds.), *Friedenspädagogik: Grundlagen, Praxisansätze, Perspektiven* (pp. 155–184). Rowohlt-Taschenbuch-Verl.

Starke, C., & Groppe, A. (2019). Frieden fühlen?! Wie Emotionen in der Friedensbildung global-politische Bedeutung haben. *Außerschulische Bildung. Zeitschrift der politischen Jugend- und Erwachsenenbildung, 2*, 40–45.

Sturm, M. (2019). Geschichtspolitik als Kulturkampf – der Gebrauch von „Geschichte" im aktuellen Rechtspopulismus. In R. Wunnicke, & M. Parak (Eds.) Vereinnahmung von Demokratiegeschichte durch Rechtspopulismus (pp. 19–45). Gegen Vergessen - Für Demokratie e.V, Gedenkstätte Deutscher Widerstand.

Tjersland, H., & Ditzel Facci, P. (2019). Introduction: Unfolding transrational potential. *Journal of Peace Education, 16*(3), 247–251.

Weller, C. (2013). Konflikte in der pluralisierten Gesellschafft. Oder: Integration durch Konfliktbearbeitung. In M. Reder, H. Pfeifer, M.-D. Cojocaru, & A. Assmann (Eds.), *Was hält Gesellschaften zusammen? der gefährdete Umgang mit Pluralität, Globale Solidarität - Schritte zu einer neuen Weltkultur, 23*. Kohlhammer.

Zembylas, M. (2018). Con–/divergences between postcolonial and critical peace education: Towards pedagogies of decolonization in peace education. *Journal of Peace Education, 15*, 1–23. https://doi.org/10.1080/17400201.2017.1412299

Zick, A., Küpper, B., & Berghan, W. (2019). *Verlorene Mitte - feindselige Zustände: rechtsextreme Einstellungen in Deutschland 2018/19*. Edited by Friedrich-Ebert-Stiftung. Mitte-Studie. Dietz.

Part III
Selected Case Studies of Radicalization

Representation of Kurdish Female Combatants in Western Cinema

A Frame Analysis of Fiction Films on Female Combatants

Nilgün Yelpaze

1 Introduction

In January 2021, Hollywood sources reported that the former US Secretary of State Hillary Clinton and her daughter were planning to develop their own TV series on Kurdish female self-defense units YPJ (Yekîneyên *Parastina Jin—Women's Defense Units*) of North-East Syria ("Hillary and Chelsea Clinton are set to produce a TV show," 2021). This is not the first time the Kurdish women involved in armed conflict gained attention from the Western media. Since the declaration of an autonomous Kurdish region in Northern Syria and the ISIL (so-called *Islamic State of Iraq and the Levant*) attack on Kurdish cities, many Western filmmakers and journalists have traveled to the region to give publicity to the various actors involved, among which women have played a significant role. Especially after a Kurdish city at the Syrian Turkish border, Kobane, was attacked by ISIL, different media across the globe excessively covered (Shahvisi, 2018; Toivanen & Baser, 2016).

There is a significant body of literature on the representation of Kurdish female combatants in media (Dean, 2019; Fernàndez Aragonès, 2020; Şimşek & Jongerden, 2021; Toivanen & Baser, 2016). Using this as a starting point, in this chapter, I focus on fiction film to discuss further in which ways images of female combatants function. In fiction films, most of the characters, costumes and locations are reproduced and staged in a way to offer the filmmaker's own take on the issue. In this sense, it presents further possibilities for analyzing the representation of women engaging in political violence compared to documentary films or newspaper coverage.

In this chapter, I am going to analyze two films, namely *Girls of the Sun* (2018) and *Sisters in Arms* (2019). The outline of the chapter follows as such: first of all, I

N. Yelpaze (✉)
University of Marburg, Marburg, Germany
e-mail: yelpaze@staff.uni-marburg.de

© The Author(s), under exclusive license to Springer Nature Switzerland AG 2023
D. Beck, J. Renner-Mugono (eds.), *Radicalization and Variations of Violence*, Contributions to International Relations,
https://doi.org/10.1007/978-3-031-27011-6_8

will briefly discuss basic arguments from the literature on women and political violence. Second, I will briefly introduce the historical context of Kurdish women in relation to their engagement with the political violence. Third, I will shed light on the body of the literature analyzing Kurdish female combatants' media coverage. For this chapter, instead of conducting a comprehensive film analysis, I borrow the "media frame analysis" from the existing literature, which I discuss in the Methodology section. In the last section, I will conduct the analysis and discuss the results.

2 Women and Political Violence

In this section, I am going to briefly review the basic discussions within the literature on women's participation in political violence, as well as on their depiction in the media. Even though women have always participated in violent conflicts and war, their representation in the media has still been biased. Moreover, Henshaw (2016) suggests that the mainstream scholarship on women in armed rebel groups is biased as well. According to Henshaw's literature review, the key assumptions in the literature on women in armed rebel groups are: (1) Women do not participate in the majority of armed rebel groups; (2) Participation by women in active combat or leadership roles is infrequent or nonexistent; (3) Women are more likely to be present where forced recruitment or coercive recruitment tactics are used (2016, p. 42).

Henshaw's cross-national data on women's involvement in seventy-two insurgencies active since 1990 challenges these assumptions and shows that women are much more active in armed groups, they exist in the leadership roles and their participation is mostly voluntary (2016, p. 51). Several studies illustrate how women constitute a larger amount of the rebel groups than expected. For example, in organizations such as FMLN (El-Salvador), EPFL (Eritrea), or PKK (Turkey), women constitute at least one third of the members (Thomas & Wood, 2018). Even though the gendered division of labor within the military groups exist, wherein most of the time female combatants were made responsible for reproductive tasks as well as care work and working in the kitchen or hospitals (Manekin & Wood, 2020), recent cases showed that women are also taking important positions in the military duties as well as decision-making processes in several groups (Henshaw, 2016).

As a matter of fact, women's involvement in political violence is much older and much more common than the above-mentioned cases (Gentry & Sjoberg, 2011). Yet, the portrayals on women's violence have been very contested, since the women engaging in violence were in contradiction with the assumptions about the stereotypes of women. The main assumption was that women are generally more peaceful than men, that war was not in their "nature" (Alison, 2009). Scholars such as Cooper argued that women engage in terrorism for different reasons than men, mostly "obsessive and pathological" reasons and vilified the women engaging in political violence and claimed that they are deviant and, therefore, not worthy of analysis (1979 cited in Gentry & Sjoberg, 2011, pp. 72–73). The belief that women's nature is non-violent was also shared by some feminists, such as Virginia Woolf. Scholars such as Alison (2004, 2009), Sjoberg and Gentry challenged these portrayals of women as "pacifists," "fragile," or "unnatural, gender defiant, sexually deviant, psychologically unstable, or easily manipulated" (Sjoberg et al., 2011, p. 7).

Looking at the war and political violence with a gender lens does not mean only to analyze women's participation in violence, but also to consider power relations and hierarchies within states, groups, or individuals from a gender perspective (Gentry & Sjoberg, 2011; Alison, 2009). Much recent feminist theory additionally conceptualizes intersectional approaches, along with the geo-politics of women's experiences in relation to war (Begikhani et al., 2018, p. 9). The political ideology of a group also plays a significant role in both the recruitment strategies of the armed group and in women's decisions to participate (Thomas & Wood, 2017). Groups with leftist ideologies rooted in Marxist ideology tend to employ more female combatants, and anti-state or "anti-colonial movements proved a greater ideological and practical space for female combatants" (Alison, 2004). The political activities of women in colonized world significantly differ from the ones in the imperialist countries, as Alison cites from Coulter (2009, p. 104). Moreover, women in these contexts had to perform a "double-militancy organizing in and against the movement to overcome gender norms" (Cockburn cited in Alison, 2009, p. 109).

Despite their simplified media coverage, studies show a variety of ideological and political reasons for women to participate in armed groups. Viterna suggests that there are "multiple, conjunctural causes of mobilization" that lead women to participate in high-risk militant activities, that are an interaction of individual biography, networks and situational context in the case of El-Salvador (2006, p. 40). For example, Alison's research on the Sri Lankan combat group Liberation Tigers of Tamil Eelam (LTTE) conducted in 2002 and 2004 via semi-depth interviews with combatants and ex-combatants shows that women and girls had a variety of motivations for participation, including "nationalist commitment; the death of a loved one and/or other experiences or perceptions of suffering and oppression at the hands of the state (including experiences of displacement); educational disruption and restrictions; poverty; sexual violence against women; and ideas of women's emancipation" (Alison, 2004, p. 453).

So far, motivations, roles, and political agendas of female combatants have not taken much space in media frames, as it is in the case of male combatants. At present, two images operate in the media during ethno-nationalist conflicts: first, "the woman refugee gazing out hopelessly or witnessing the death of her child" and second, "a woman with a rifle over her shoulder and a baby on her back" (Drexler, 2018, p. 398). The images of female combatants are utilized for different purposes during and after the conflict, both by the media and the actors involved in the conflict.

In this chapter, I am interested in discussing the Kurdish female combatants' cinematic representations. Therefore, in this section I briefly introduced the basic discussions within the literature of women and political violence with few examples from the similar cases to Kurdish one. However, I do not intend to give an extensive account on the history of women in Kurdish armed movements and position them in the political violence literature. Instead, after briefly reviewing this history, I will focus on the literature on the Western media coverage of Kurdish female combats.

3 Kurdish Women as Combatants: Not a Novel Phenomenon

3.1 History of Kurdish Women's (Armed) Struggle(s)

In this section, I will provide a brief overview of Kurdish conflict and Kurdish women's organization within the (armed) struggle(s). After World War 1, the Kurdish population remained divided into the territory of four nation states: Turkey, Iran, Iraq, and Syria. In all these four nation states, Kurds have faced various violations and discrimination, which led to different forms of insurgency movements in every state, including guerilla warfare (Gunes, 2013).

Therefore, despite the media-coverage outbreak on Kurdish female combatants in the West in 2015–16, it was not the first time Kurdish women had been involved in armed conflict (Dirik, 2014). Begikhani et al. review the history of women's organization in different parts of Kurdistan and argue that the existing war conditions forced Kurdish women to focus on basic rights and delayed the emergence of independent women's right organizations, and continuing violence created long-lasting consequences in Kurdish women's lived realities (2018, p. 10). In conclusion, Kurdish women have always been actively involved in the conflict in different ways.

Since the scope of this chapter is too limited to give an extensive overview of the history of Kurdish women's political violence, I will try to sum up shortly the most striking examples from each part. It is important to keep the history of the Kurdish female combatants in mind, as it informs the representations in the films analyzed in this chapter. It is interesting to see how, in some moments, this history is overlooked, and how certain patterns in representing female combatants are repeated.

In Iraq, after the Saddam regime's atrocities against Kurdish population, the establishment of the Kurdistan Region of Iraq provided broader opportunities for women to organize. Their organization focused on topics such as fighting against "honor killings" and legislative reforms. However, in Iraqi Kurdistan, due to "the patriarchal structures within the political organizations, women were for many years not allowed to participate in combat, but were actively involved in underground activities, nursing and in providing logistic support" (Begikhani et al., 2018, p. 11). In Iran, women's involvement as combatants in "The Society of Revolutionary Toilers of Iranian Kurdistan" opened the way for women to be part of the national imagery of Iranian Kurds (Begikhani et al., 2018, p. 11).

In Turkey, the 1980s marked the emergence of the insurgency movement PKK (Partiya Karkeran Kurdistan, or the Kurdistan Workers' Party) and their demand for independence (Gunes, 2013). From the end of 1990s and the beginning of 2000s on, the autonomous women's organization within the PKK gained strength. Meanwhile, pro-Kurdish political parties started to actively organize among Kurds and participate in the elections, and women played significant roles in politics (Ustundag, 2019). The shift in the PKK's ideology from national independence toward "democratic confederalism," a form of autonomy based on feminist, municipalist, and environmentalist values (Jongerden, 2013), emphasized a new perspective on "women as active agents in history-making processes" (Çağlayan, 2012 cited in Şimşek & Jongerden, 2021 p. 13). Many women from different backgrounds joined independent women's forces within the PKK after this shift.

In 2012, during the Syrian Civil War, Kurdish forces declared autonomy in the North-East of Syria. In the territory controlled by the Kurdish forces, a communal local governance model was introduced, inspired by the above-mentioned ideological approach of the PKK (Dean, 2019). In this system, Kurdish women who had been organizing in the Kurdish populated regions of Syria since the mid-2000s under the name of first Yekitiya Star, and then Kongra Star, started to enjoy equal representation in the communes and became in charge of educational, juridical, or health-related governance tasks (Dirik, 2018, p. 229; Knapp et al., 2016). These developments allowed Kurdish women in Syria to establish their autonomous armed forces when ISIL started to attack the Kurdish cities. This marked the beginning of global media attention on Kurdish women as well, which will be discussed in the next session.

Since the two movies analyzed here are based on the specific context of the region of Shingal (Sinjar, Şingal), located in Iraq, I will lastly provide context on the Yazidi women. Yazidi people, a Kurmanji speaking indigenous community with their own ethnic religion, live in this region. On the third of August, ISIL took control of the Yazidi region after the KRI's Peshmerga forces withdrew (Hama, 2019). During the ISIL attacks against the Yazidis in Sinjar in 2014, thousands of men were murdered, and thousands of women and children were murdered, persecuted, kidnapped, tortured, enslaved, and raped. Sexual violence was used as a specific tool by ISIL against the Yazidi population (Castellano San José, 2020). Thousands had to flee their land and live in camps during the genocide. In response, Yazidi women established their own units similar to the YPJ in Syria and joined the armed forces.[1] However, Sinjari Yazidi women's narratives and subjectivities have been heavily silenced since then, with few exceptions. Buffon and Allison (2016) argue that the hyper-visibility of Yazidi women in Western media as sex slaves "produced a pornographic affect" (p. 182). Yazidi women were repeatedly mentioned together with the sexualized violence, rape, and genocide, despite their resistance, activism, and despite the ways they coped with ISIL's brutality (Minwalla et al., 2020; Sarac, 2020).

3.2 Western Media Depiction of Kurdish Female Combats

As discussed above, the backgrounds, motives, and goals of Kurdish woman combatants are manifold. Kurdish women played multiple roles in war and armed conflict, and "the experiences of Kurdish women in different parts of Kurdistan are

---

[1] For example, see: Al-Dhiban and Coles (2016), Khalel and Vickery (2015).

characterized by activism, resistance and pain" (Begikhani et al., 2018 p. 25). Yet, their media depiction remained insufficient in representing the complexity of it. In this part, I will review the studies on the Western media frames of Kurdish female combatants from approximately 2014 on, namely after the emergence of "women's self-defense units" in Northern Syria. The image of "secular, liberated women with a gun" against "Islamic terrorism" has circulated in newspapers, mainstream lifestyle magazines or clothing brands and inspired numerous Western film productions, both fiction and documentary. This popular image of a young woman with long, braided hair, with a gun and a colorful scarf with flowers on it, has been romanticized, exoticized, and idealized in various ways, so that even the fashion brand H&M produced a jumpsuit "inspired" by the YPJ combatants (Wyke, 2014).

Independent of the time and context, the operation of these images turns the body of Kurdish women into a battleground of war. Previously, Turkish newspapers framed Kurdish female combatants as "dishonorable terrorists." During the 1990s, print media in Turkey published the naked bodies of female combatants, captured dead by the military, in a pejorative frame. Alkan (2018) mentions the case of the state conducting forced medical tests on the bodies of female combatants in order to prove they are involved in "immoral sexuality" within the combatant groups, which was also presented by the Turkish media extensively. During the city curfews of 2015–16, soldiers of the Turkish army circulated photographs of tortured, mutilated, naked bodies of combatant women. This visual representation of Kurdish female combatants' bodies as "depraved terrorists" constituted a form of "gendered racism" in the context of the war between the Turkish state and Kurdish insurgency movement (Alkan, 2018).

The Western media depiction of Kurdish female combats after the Syrian civil war is quite far from the Turkish one. In the following parts, I will review the existing studies on these depictions. So far, the literature examines mostly newspapers and websites from the USA, UK, France, and Italy and utilize framing theories in media studies. It is important to give a brief review of these studies here, because there are certain similarities between the media and film representations of Kurdish female combatants which serve as reference points for my film analysis later in the chapter.

One of the connecting points of this media coverage of Kurdish women is the "Western fascination." As Kurdish researcher and activist Dirik (2014) emphasizes: "…these mainstream caricaturizations erroneously present Kurdish women fighters as a novel phenomenon," despite the generations of Kurdish women resisting. This fascination is derived from the mystifying Otherness of the Kurdish women that does not fit into the previous expectations of the Western gaze: weak or in need of protection (Shahvisi, 2018). They are presented as a new exotic species from a neo-Orientalist and sensational point of view (Begikhani et al., 2018), as "brown" women who are suddenly appearing with "heavy weapons," an activity usually associated with men, as "their last chance" in order to save themselves from "brown men" and who have been perceived as "underdeveloped, uneducated, passive" victims so far (Alkan, 2018; Dean, 2019). Indeed, as it is mentioned earlier, it is neither new nor scarce that women participate in the armed groups, but the images of women from the global south and/or east are regularly met with a similar fascination from Western media (Drexler, 2018, p. 398).

Shahvisi (2018) argues that the objectification of female combatants leads to a one-dimensional depiction of them, which is only interested in their being "women" soldiers as a surprising fact, and nothing else. In addition, analyzed media seems to point out the "light skin color" and "light eye colors" of Kurdish people quite often. Most of the pictures of these women, which appeared in lifestyle magazines such as Vogue or Marie-Claire or in different international media channels, such as the BBC, depict them in fashion photography-like settings, directly gazing at the camera while holding guns. For example, one picture of Rehana, also named as "angel of death," became viral after her claimed success in "killing more than 100 ISIL members" (Dirik, 2014). In this picture, we see a young blonde woman with a big gun and a big smile.

Mundane "feminine" details of hair-pins, Hello-Kitty socks, colorful bracelets repeatedly appear in media coverage in order to emphasize the femininity of these combatants (Toivanen & Baser, 2016). The Kurdish female combatants are depicted while brushing their hair, plucking their eyebrows or putting on lipstick. These media representations depicting Kurdish female bodies within the Western beauty standards present a sexualized and exoticized version of them. Next to the sexualized body of Kurdish female combatant, usually the emasculated body of the jihadist is juxtaposed in order to deepen the dichotomy between the heroic girls versus the jihadists. These images rely on the rumor that jihadists believe they go to hell if they are killed by a woman (Toivanen & Baser, 2016, p. 308). The two films analyzed in this chapter repeat this notion often as well. The peak in the circulation of Kurdish female combatant's image—as well as how they are portrayed—needs to be considered against the backdrop of a global anti-Daesh sentiment (Shahvisi, 2018).

Depoliticization is another frame commonly used. Western media narrates the Kurdish female combatants as the "opponents of ISIL" and do not include the history of Kurdish women's civil and military organization in different contexts, lands, and time frames (Dirik, 2014; Dean, 2019; Shahvisi, 2018). While some of the coverage focuses on the ideological motives of the women, such as liberty or equality, "the overall depiction is not entirely comprehensive" (Dean, 2019). In addition, Dean (2019) and Shahvisi (2018) point to the lack of media coverage on Kurdish women involved in different tasks, such as jurisdiction, education, or health, and they also point to the greater emphasis on the combatants. In addition, the self-developed ideological framework by the Kurdish women's organizations, called Jineoloji (science of woman), is not mentioned in the media coverage.[2]

Last but not least, the personal motivations of the female combatants due to concrete experiences, especially their individual history of sexual violence during the war or the loss of family members, are frequently framed in the media. This "victim frame" (Toivanen & Baser, 2016) grounds their participation almost solely in personal trauma or revenge as a motive, omitting political concerns. It goes hand in hand with the depoliticization, where the other motives of female fighters are

---

[2] For example, see: Begikhani et al. (2018), Göksel (2019), Dean (2019), Ustundag (2019).

deliberately ignored, and their taking up arms is "glorified" or "justified" via their being victims of "formidable traumatic events" (Orhan, 2019; Sabogal & Richter, 2019).

As discussed earlier, there are still certain biases on the study of gendered forms of political violence. These media frames on Kurdish female combatants repeat the existing shortcomings instead of offering a detailed picture of the motives and actions of women engaging in violence. Women's violence is granted for justification and sympathy via these frames when certain frames, such as "victimization" or "objectivization," are at work, while it is declared to be "irrational," "savage," or "evil" in some other cases. I argue an analysis of the films will reveal visual representations of female combatants in these films are in line with those biases.

4 Methodology & Case Selection

4.1 Methodological Framework

Feminist film criticism has a long history of analyzing the male gaze toward women and representation of women's sexuality in cinema (Mulvey, 2013; Sassatelli, 2011). The role of a woman in a film is crucial because their physical appearance and relation to other female and/or male characters reveal a lot about the standpoint of the filmmaker (Smith, 1972). In the following analysis, even though both directors of the films to be analyzed are female, there are certain hierarchies and contradictions between the position of the directors and the position of the subjects of the film. Since mainstream cinema is instrumental in reproducing social gender norms via mostly female sexuality, analyzing representation of female combatants with a postcolonial feminist perspective reveals interesting trends (Mulvey, 2013; Thornham, 1999).

In addition, Gaines analyzes the racial aspect of the "male gaze." According to Gaines, the male gaze symbolizes the "white perspective" at the same time. Afterwards, the authors, such as bell hooks (1992), deepened these analyses and came up with the theory of "oppositional gaze." Postcolonial Film Theory builds itself upon the early feminist film theories and brings new approaches to film analysis via questioning the role of the European/Western/white gaze as the center, and "the colonized" as the significant other. Similar to the power relations reproduced between the men and women via male gaze, certain hierarchies and power dynamics are constructed in film via geo-political distinctions.[3]

Against this backdrop, this chapter takes its inspiration for analyzing female combatants in fiction films from studies on female combatants in the media. One particular study is important in conducting the analysis: Fernandez Aragonès' study of media frame analysis in documentary film on Kurdish female combats. She writes: "frames structure the social world with meaning and the images are powerful in showing presences and absences in hegemonic discourse" (2020, p. 8).

---

[3] For example, see: Ponzanesi and Waller (Eds.), (2012), Said (1978), Shohat and Stam (1994).

Toivanen and Baser (2016) developed four main frames for Kurdish female combatants used in British and French media: (1) struggle for equality/emancipation/liberation where they are depicted as the warriors for liberation; (2) personal/emotional motivations, also named as victim frame where the motivations of participation are reduced to personal victimization; (3) physical appearance in terms of performance of mundane feminine activities; and (4) exceptionalism understood as the specific characteristics attributed to female combatants as extraordinary fighters due to their "female" situation, and they are depicted as tougher than men.

Similar to Fernandez Aragonès' analysis, I will utilize these media frames in analyzing the selected cases. This paper thus analyzes cinematic representations of Kurdish female combatants in fiction films made by Western directors. I am interested in investigating whether the existing media frames are applicable to the film. Since each frame implies what is left out of the frame at the same time by drawing a line between the information that is included and not included in the frame, I try to understand what kind of image of Kurdish female combatant is constructed via these films, and what is left out of the picture.

One of the reasons why it is possible to observe these media frames in the mentioned films is that the filmmakers of the films that are going to be discussed in this paper also accessed the topic initially via Western media resources. In one interview, the director of the *Girls of the Sun,* Eva Husson, says:

> …I came across news articles about Kurdish women who had escaped ISIL. Not only that, they had become fighters and it triggered something in me as a woman. I [thought] "Wow, for once, we are not just the victims. We have the social context and the collective support to stand up and not get victimized and refuse that position. I thought if I was so moved by a few lines in a newspaper, it'd be very powerful on the big screen for two hours. (Saito, 2019).

Additionally, both the media and film materials are produced for Western audiences, therefore, they rely on similar frames that are consumable for the Western audiences.

4.2 Case Selection

For this research, two films were selected with the criteria that they are high-budget film productions, they potentially enjoyed a large audience and that they were accepted to several film festivals through Europe and globally. The films are: *Girls of the Sun* (2018), directed by French filmmaker Eva Hussons), which was screened in the well-known European film festival Cannes, and *Sisters in Arms*, directed by French filmmaker Caroline Fourest and released in 2019.

Both films are directed by women and include at least one female character representing the Western gaze in the storyline, in the form of a French journalist in *Girls of the Sun,* and in the form of the European and American female combatants of the internationalist brigade in *Sisters in Arms.* Both films focus on the Yazidi genocide and are partly filmed in the Kurdistan Region in Iraq.

One of the reasons why many documentary films were made in the autonomous Kurdish territory in Syria, and fiction films with large crews were made in Kurdish territory in Iraq, is due to the political ambiguity and the embargo in the self-declared autonomous region of North-East Syria. The borders were mostly closed to the region, and due to the lack of international recognition, it offered a legal safety issue for the larger film crews. Thus, the region attracted mostly small crew and small budget documentary projects. On the other hand, with its legal status and emerging film industry, the Kurdistan Region of Iraq attracted more commercial projects.

In *Sisters in Arms*, the film's narrative evolves around Zara who lives in a Yazidi village that is attacked by ISIL. Her father and the other male inhabitants of the village are murdered, while Zara, her brother, and her mother are kidnapped. Zara is sold as a so-called "sex-slave" to an ISIL member. She manages to escape and meets the international women battalion based in Northern Iraq. The bulk of the film focuses on what happens once she becomes a fighter. In a similar manner, in *Girls of the Sun*, the main character Bahar and her family are attacked by ISIL. Her husband is killed alongside with the other male family members, and her son is kidnapped. She escapes ISIL captivity and joins female combatants to rescue her son. Meanwhile, she meets French journalist Mathilde, and they become friends. In the films, Zara is speaking English, and Bahar is speaking French most of the time, and the narratives are not linear, but unfold through long flashbacks. In *Sisters in Arms*, the story is told in a linear fashion, yet the voice over of Zara in the beginning suggests that it is a past story. Interrupting the chronological sequence of events with flashbacks is used in *Sisters in Arms* explicitly and vividly for the rape scenes.

For each media frame, I have watched the films from the beginning to the end through the online platforms where the copies of the films are available and took notes. Afterwards, I combined the textual and visual analysis of the sequences in which female combatants appeared (mostly, but no limited to, main characters) and combined it with the contextual analysis provided by the literature. In the following part, I will discuss the findings of the analysis.

5 Discussion: Women's Violence as an Exception and an Emotional Reaction

5.1 Struggle for Emancipation: Depoliticization

In this section, I am going to discuss the struggle for emancipation frame of Toivanen and Baser's study. This media frame depicts combatants as "they are striving for equality, emancipation and national liberation" (2016, p. 301). In the two films I am analyzing here, I observed this frame existing in a form of depoliticization where history of Kurdish female combatants is deliberately taken out, and they are presented in the film narrative as opponents of ISIL. Via depicting these female combatants emerging as an inevitable result of the ISIL atrocities, these films take these women, as well as the region itself, out of its context and history.

Alkan (2018, p. 33) argues that, at least since the publication of Orientalism, it is impossible to ignore the relationship between power and representation. Fighting ISIL creates an ontological and epistemological distinction between the West and East, where the former is represented with women's rights, and the latter with the lack of it (Şimşek & Jongerden, 2021). In these films, apolitical, secular Kurdish women embedded in happy family lives are depicted as being personally victimized by a wide variety of atrocities, and then temporarily joining the combatant forces as an inevitable result. However, even though this might be the case in some situations, the female combatant forces have a historical continuity in the Kurdish case with special ideological focuses, such as national liberation (or autonomy) and equal rights for men and women in the society or ecological transformation (Çiçek, 2015; Göksel, 2019).

The film music serves as a good example to the silencing operated by the depoliticization frame. Singing became an important part of the female combatants' life as it is an important aspect of Kurdish women's lives traditionally (Mirzeler, 2000). Gathering around the fire, singing and performing traditional collective Kurdish dances were classical images of the combatants that are in circulation.[4] These moments are used in the narratives of both films. However, instead of existing Kurdish songs that are connotated with certain Kurdish histories, the films chose to compose new songs from scratch. Even though copyrights for film music is complicated and might be the reason for composing new songs, leaving out an essential part of Kurdish female combatants' daily life that is produced by their own voice and over-writing different songs by Western composers on these scenes has a symbolic meaning, which is in line with stripping the film out of the historical/political context of the existing Kurdish female combatant organizations.

In addition, in both films, female combats wear colorful scarfs with flower patterns, as used by the YPJ and PKK members. This scarf serves as a strong visual tool to create an abstract heroic Kurdish female fighter, both in these films and in the media. Yet, in both films, political connotations of Kurdish female combatants are deliberately left out. The audience is not granted the information of the names of the groups that are shown in the movie, nor their ideological standpoints. The scarf is carrying the responsibility of telling who these women are, rather than the narrative of the films themselves.

In addition, in *Sisters in Arms,* the conflict between the government of the Northern Iraq Autonomous Region and the North-East Syria autonomous zone, as well as the PKK, is blurred, and particular images and discourses created by one are attributed to another. For example, the Peshmerga units and PKK-affiliated female combatants are depicted as working together, even though this was never the case. The particular representation of various Kurdish actors in the region in these films, and political meaning of these representations, needs to be investigated further.[5] In

---

[4] For example, see: Bakur, inside the PKK. Documentary. 2015 (dir: Çayan Demirel, Ertuğrul Mavioğlu) http://www.sidewaysfilm.com/bakur-inside-the-pkk/

[5] During the Yazidi genocide in Sinjar, after the KDP defense units Peshmerga left the zone, the Yazidis remained defenseless. The USA had started airstrikes against ISIS while PKK guerillas

conclusion, in the lack of the historical and ideological connotations of existing Kurdish women's armed groups, the struggle for emancipation media frame existing in the Western media does not exist in these films. Instead, a depoliticization frame operates through the images of women, where their political goals are limited to their personal motives and victimizations, which I will analyze next.

5.2   Personal-Emotional Motivation Frame (Victim Frame)

The second media frame common in the Western media depictions of Kurdish female combatants is the personal-emotional motivation frame, or victim frame. This frame refers to female combatants' participation in armed activities because of their personal (or family) victimization during the conflict. As the literature also suggests, women are expected to be "soft" in their nature and are not capable of making political decisions. Therefore, they can only engage in political violence due to the emotional reasons. It is possible to observe this media frame existing in both films.

The main characters have a specific goal (revenge or rescuing family members) when entering combat. Zara, the main character of *Sisters in Arms,* is kidnapped and sold in the so-called slave market by ISIL (women are captured by force and subjected to different forms of sexualized violence) where a foreign (white) man takes her home. Accompanied by screaming noises, the film uses the image of blood dropping into water as the symbol of her being raped. The representation of sexualized violence, and rape in particular, has been discussed in cinema studies for a long time. Certain feminist critiques of the American film genre "rape-revenge films" argue that the women are expected to be transformed from "victims" into "avengers" after rape (Read, 2000). The audience roots for the victim character and justifies her actions of revenge through sympathy (Henry, 2014). The film *Sisters in Arms* builds its narrative on this structure and builds the justification for women participating in the violence on the revenge.

The male gaze tends to reproduce the sexualized violence as a male phantasy by position of the camera, or by deciding what to show to what extent during the representation of it (for example, see: Smelik, 2007). For feminist film theorists, in order to overcome the male gaze, the existence of a female director may not be enough, since the existence of a camera and the relationship between "what is shown" and "who is showing" create the power dynamic inherently (Smith, 1972). This power dynamic is affected constantly by the gender, race, ethnicity, class, or political point of view of the director. At the end of the film, Zara kills the ISIL

---

managed to open a humanitarian corridor. In both films, the depiction of the organizations that are fighting in the zone is not accurate. The patches on the military uniforms and the flags are designed for the film, while in Girls of the Sun they remained clearly the Yazidi self-defense units YBŞ and YJŞ (*Sinjar Resistance Units and Sinjar Women's Units*), in the Sisters in Arms there is a totally imaginary military organization created by the director mixing all different structures including the Peshmerga units and PKK, who are actually in conflict.

member who raped her, which is interspersed with detailed flashbacks from the rape scene that we did not see earlier. Both the first symbolic scene and the second flashback scene do not differ from the mainstream cinema's depiction of rape, but rather reproduce feelings of horror and pity from the male gaze and victimize the character within the narrative. Those images carry the risk of re-traumatizing the victims and under-estimating the scope of the atrocities as it is in each case of representation of (sexualized) violence.

In *Girls of the Sun*, the rape is not directly shown, yet a screaming noise is heard in this film, too. Later we learn that Bahar's unit is a female combatant unit of the survivors. Zara and Bahar are strong and able to make independent decisions in order to escape and join the armed groups. Yet, their decision is justified "under the radar of moral acceptability without comment" (Shahvisi, 2018). Zara joins the combatants and says in her letter to her brother, otherwise I will lose my mind. Zara's main motives are the trauma of the sexual violence and finding her little brother. Both are resolved within the narrative, and we do not know whether Zara will stay as a combatant or not. Bahar, who was motivated by finding her son, finds him at the end of the film. Both films are resolved with the reunion and rescuing of the little boys from ISIL captivity, which gives the responsibility of the care work of healing the new generations from ISIL atrocities to the women, or mothers. These scenes strongly construct the characters as victims of sexual violence and family break-ups and call for a sentiment that glorifies their positions as combatants in order to right these wrongs.

In addition, motherhood is presented as a personal motive for joining the combat. At several points in the *Girls of the Sun*, the scenes where Bahar is involved with her child directly follow with the scenes where we see the emotions of the French journalist (Mathilde) engaging with her own child. The juxtaposition of motherhood scenes establishes direct continuation between Bahar's and Mathilde's motherhood and an understanding between the two. As Bahar is a mother and wants to rescue her son, and the European female character Mathilde is also a mother and thinks a lot about her relationship to her daughter, we as an audience are also invited to understand Bahar for what she is doing. Yet, was it only the wartime sexual violence and loss of family members that creates a moment for women to participate in military activities? In the case of Kurdish women, and especially including the Yazidi women,[6] history of sexual violence[7] was definitely a reason for participating in the armed movement, yet, I argue establishing a narrative structure on the victim frame due to the sexual violence for women is a highly gendered perspective, stirs a false justification for the participation in the armed movements by deliberately ignoring the other reasons, and re-victimizes women. Moreover, written and visual resources are available at an incredible level in various languages, produced by Kurdish women themselves, explaining their own standpoints, which are much more diverse than the Western media frames. Among them are critique of state-violence, gender

---

[6] Different bodies of UN recognized ISIS crimes against Yazidis as genocide ("ISIL crimes against Yazidis constitute genocide" 2021).

[7] For example, see: Aubert (2021), Pabst (2018), Oppenheimer (2020).

equality in all realms of life, including political representation, right of education in mother tongue, freedom of culture and religion, freedom of expression and release of political prisoners, stopping forced marriage of children, and stopping polygyny, to count some (Herausgeberinnen kollektiv, 2012; Herausgeberinnen kollektiv, 2021; Jineoloji Akademisi, 2015).

5.3   Physical Appearance: Sexualization of the Female Combatants

Toivanen and Başer's study suggests that the third media frame, the physical appearance frame, is visualized in various forms, such as focusing on female combatants' pink socks, hair styles, make-ups, nicknaming them as "lioness" or "tigers." In this section, I am going to analyze the physical appearance frame with a special focus on sexualization of the combatants. In both of the films, the choice of actresses, costumes, and camera angles provide an exotic overview of the female combatants. The physical appearance frame in these films is very much in line with the findings of the existing literature. However, I define sexualization as only different than exoticization in this specific frame. Specifically, to Middle Eastern, and especially Kurdish, women, the Western gaze attaches a sexual oppression to these women, who need to be educated and saved. In this section, I intend to analyze what kind of sexuality is given to the characters.

I am going to focus on one scene, which is the kiss performed between the Kurdish female combatant and the Kurdish male commander, and defend that female combatants are rescued by the Western gaze via being allowed to have their sexuality back In *Sister in Arms*, after the victory against ISIL, the combatants and the local people organize a celebration in the liberated village. During this celebration, where everyone is dancing, the male commander asks the female combatant for a kiss. After her refusal, he says: "what is our difference than the ones we fought against (ISIL), if we cannot kiss?" I believe this scene is highly symbolic in terms of showing the operation of these representations in a crystalized way. Kurdish women inside of the PKK have developed a position of sexual relationships, and it fueled a discussion among the scholars of the Kurdish women's movement. For example, Al-Ali and Kaeser, in their article "Beyond Feminism? Jineolojî and the Kurdish Women's Freedom Movement," wrote that "sexuality as a practice is viewed and treated as a form of violence and repression as opposed to pleasure and mutual desire. This attitude…is problematic, as it essentializes men as rapists" (Al-Ali & Kaeser, 2020, p. 22). They continue that, for their respondents, sexuality is a side effect of capitalism which should be avoided, as it is seen as a threat to the struggle. They conclude: "This idea clearly emerges out of the militarized culture of the Kurdish Freedom Movement as a whole, in which the bodies of guerrillas are strictly policed and required to refrain from sexual and romantic relationships" (Al-Ali & Kaeser, 2020, p. 25).

In return, the Kurdish Women's Movement has published an open letter where they suggest, according to the previous article,

...the refrainment of women and men guerrillas in the Kurdistan Freedom Movement from sexual relations shows that despite all their claims, Kurdish women remain oppressed and repressed. While in the West, asexuality is accepted as a queer identity, while respected feminists like Adrienne Rich spoke of "compulsory heterosexuality," while Black feminists like Audre Lorde broke ground when speaking of eroticisms outside of sexuality, why is it that the Kurdistan Women's Movement's political choice to opt for asexuality under patriarchal conditions, and their struggle to conceptualize the philosophical meaning of love in relation to notions of freedom, nature, life, and humanity, are seen as forms of suppression? (Jadaliyya Reports, 2021).

The Kurdish Women's Movement has developed a certain analysis of "patriarchal relations" between men and women, arguing that, under the patriarchal circumstances, the relationships lead to exploitation of women, and freedom is not possible to achieve, therefore, the social structures leading to certain gender roles should be replaced (Jineoloji Akademisi, 2015; Ustundag, 2019). Yet, their approach, developed by the Kurdish female combatants affiliated with PKK, does not exclude the possibility of "sexual relationships" totally. In a similar manner to taking away the voice of the Kurdish female combatants via changing the songs, the film *Sisters in Arms* takes Kurdish women's ideological standpoint away and gives them their sexuality "back." The "innocent kiss" in the end of the film provides Middle Eastern underdeveloped women to finally be able to "keep their sexuality," as at the moment that they have fought against ISIL, they are granted the right of enjoying what European women are able to enjoy. The political stand and discussions developed by the Kurdish women themselves that are discussed above are put aside by this scene. The strong, independent female combatant characters created in this film are returned back to the male gaze by this plot, namely resolving the tension with romance.

Judith Butler discusses that sexual freedom has been recently declared as an "ultimate sign of development and modernity," as opposed to the new religious minorities of Europe (2008). In this new trend, the sexual freedoms that are seen as inherently European values are put into a contradiction with the threat of religion or migration. The global anti-ISIL sentiment that Shahvisi (2018) mentions can be thought of together with this line of arguments: as long as Kurdish female combatants are secularly organized against the backward values, they are invited to the secular modern timeline of Europe. I argue that this scene is embedded in such a dichotomy, and at the cost of silencing Kurdish female combatants' own political standpoint, the narrative of the film "liberates" them from their sexual oppression.

Regarding the *Girls of the Sun*, the fascination toward the female combatants is produced by the French journalist Mathilde, with whom the audience is expected to associate themselves, while the combatants are "the other." She points her objective toward the women and makes pictures of them through the film. The moments where combatants are captured into her objective are mostly when they are with their guns, shooting, strong, and determined, and sometimes during the daily life activities. In the end, she calls the main combatant character Bahar as a queen from the past with her colorful scarf on her head. The characters are chosen based on their acceptability by the Western audiences (a former lawyer, speaking foreign language, survivor of violence), and we can definitely observe the exoticization frame. Bahar's sexuality, on the other hand, is limited to the family. During the flashbacks and her dreams, the film depicts her as having a normative, nuclear family life with her husband. Overall, the sexualization of the female combatants is very subtle in *Girls of the Sun*.

5.4 Exceptionalism: Mystic Death Machines

In this part, I am going to discuss the findings that are categorized under the exceptionalism frame, namely extraordinary characteristics attributed to the female combatants due to their gender. Exceptionalism in these films is operated via two aspects: one of them is "female combatants as irrational though death machines," and the second one is the motherly instincts that was already discussed in the second frame.

It is very symbolic that in the first moment we are introduced to the female combatants' unit and watch them from a voyeuristic point of view as they perform their rituals, we get to know about them via three male characters speaking to each other: a Kurdish commander, an American commander, and a European journalist. These three men talk about the female soldiers in an objectifying language, and the audience sees them through the gaze of these men. These rituals are not explained to the audience by the subjects themselves, so the whole military ceremony and practice take place in an observatory documentary mode, where we are invited to alienate from the subjects and just observe. This mystifies the female combatants from the beginning on. In *Sisters in Arms*, the female combatants are shown as extraordinary, exotic "death machines" who are like ninjas (where they make a raid into the headquarters of ISIL they literally move as ninjas and transfer the burqas into a ninja-like costume as a classical action-movie move). In this scene, as well as in other scenes where female combatants are using guns, they rake with the gun swiftly, often accompanied by screams.

When Bahar is using guns, she screams and shoots targets more than several times in a row, while there is no extra focus or emotion in the scenes of men with guns. The motherhood comes back into play in the decision-making processes of female combatants: in one scene in *Sisters in Arms,* another (non-Kurdish) female combatant resists against the group decision and acts individually in order to follow the sound of a crying child, which ends up being a trap and putting the whole team in danger. Overall, the female combatant unions are pictured as wild, irrational, and Amazon-like fighters who cannot be tamed and who do whatever their "female or motherly instincts" tell them to do. Parallel to the findings of Toivanen and Baser (2016) in this frame representing female combatants as "tougher than men" warriors based on their gendered characteristics, these films operate in a way that the female combatants make braver decisions, fight harder, even revolt against their male comrades and attack harder. And, all this happens because they are women, they are mothers, they have suffered more. For example, Bahar decides to organize an attack on the headquarters of ISIL, where she thinks her son is held as a captive. In order to achieve this goal, she challenges the male leader of the Kurdish combatant units in the region. Even though the other team members do not think it is a good idea, Bahar insists on holding the attack due to her motherly instincts. In *Sisters in Arms*, the Kurdish combatants succeed in capturing the ISIL leader (the one who held Zara as a captive earlier) as a war prisoner who could be a source of further information. The group decides to keep him alive as a prisoner, yet Zara attacks and stabs him during a nervous breakdown. Zara's character acts intuitively and irrationally in this moment against the group decision to keep the prisoner alive. The rape-revenge movie plot is concluded in this scene, and the audience is expected to show understanding for Zara. Character is depicted as she is hysterical in these moments, and rape scenes are shown in order to strengthen the dramatic effect.

This representation is very much in line with the media frames analyzed earlier. Tamang (2017, p. 244) shows that, in the case of ex-combatants in Nepal, media played a key role in "constructing and perpetuating motherhood ideologies as central tools in reinforcing gendered identities... that puts women back into the box of domesticity." It is valid for these films as well. In these films, female combatants are seen as irrational, over-emotional characters who are putting their emotions before the group decisions and, of most of the things they are doing, they do it for their children.

6   Conclusion

In this chapter, I expanded media frame analysis with the four frames developed by Toivanen and Başer on Western media representations of Kurdish female combatants to fiction films produced by the Western directors. The four frames I analyzed follow as such: depoliticization, the personal/emotional motivation (victim frame), sexualization, and exceptionalism. I found out that the representation of the female combatants in these films is similar to the frequently used media frames. Kurdish female combatants are presented as novel, exotic characters without a historical framework, victimized, granted the right to fight at only one frozen moment and context, and sexualized via being allowed into "secular European values" due to their anti-Islamist positions. As Şimşek and Jongerden argue, through the portrayal of women fighters, "the idea of the Middle East is reproduced as a geography of fear, backwardness and violence" (2021, p. 18).

I propose that cinema can provide us further insights in conflict research, especially in the subjects of feminist research and "women and conflict," where the studies and data are limited compared to the conventional fields of conflict research. So far, the majority of media coverage on female militancy reproduces the existing biases and does not offer a deeper insight to women's political violence. The increase in circulation of the images of female militancy does not automatically offer an increase in the diversity of their stories. The orientalist gaze, global anti-ISIL sentiment (rooted in Islamophobia), and the stereotypes about the women's relation to violence work together in the construction of these representations.

In the case of the Kurdish conflict, visual materials, including films produced by the actors of the conflict, are not scarce. The most well-known example is Halil Dağ, who himself was a combatant and a filmmaker at the same time (Smets & Akkaya,

2016). Renowned movie Beritan, produced collectively by Halil Dağ and other combatants in 2006, focuses on the life of the Kurdish female combatant Beritan, where all the characters are played by combatants themselves (Smets & Akkaya, 2016). Further study of such films might unlock new data on the Kurdish female combatants from their own perspective and contribute to the field of women and political violence from non-Western perspectives.

References

Al-Ali, N., & Kaeser, I. (2020). Beyond feminism? Jineolojî and the Kurdish Women's freedom movement. *Politics and Gender, 2020*, 1–32. https://doi.org/10.1017/S1743923X20000501

Al-Dhiban, U. & Coles, I. (2016, May 13). On patrol with the Sinjar resistance units. *Reuters*. Retrieved from https://widerimage.reuters.com/story/on-patrol-with-the-sinjar-resistance-units

Alison, M. (2004). Women as agents of political violence: Gendering security. *Security Dialogue, 35*(4), 447–463. https://doi.org/10.1177/0967010604049522

Alison, M. (2009). *Women and political violence: Female combatants in Ethno-National Conflict* (pp. 1–275). Routledge. https://doi.org/10.4324/9780203013458

Alkan, H. (2018). The sexual politics of war: Reading the Kurdish conflict through images of women. *Les Cahiers Du CEDREF, 22*, 68–92. https://doi.org/10.4000/cedref.1111

Aubert, B. (2021, July 27). ISIS' use of sexual violence as a strategy of terrorism in Iraq. *E-International Relations*. Retrieved from https://www.e-ir.info/2021/07/27/isis-use-of-sexual-violence-as-a-strategy-of-terrorism-in-iraq/

Begikhani, N., Hamelink, W., & Weiss, N. (2018). Theorising women and war in Kurdistan: A feminist and critical perspective. *Kurdish Studies, 6*(1), 5–30. https://doi.org/10.33182/ks.v6i1.432

Buffon, V., & Allison, C. (2016). The gendering of victimhood: Western media and the Sinjar genocide. *Kurdish Studies, 4*(2), 176–196. https://doi.org/10.33182/ks.v4i2.427Castellano

Çağlayan, H. (2012). From Kawa the blacksmith to Ishtar the goddess: Gender constructions in ideological-political discourses of the Kurdish movement in post-1980 Turkey. *European Journal of Turkish Studies* 14.

Castellano San José, P. (2020). The rapes committed against the Yazidi women: A genocide? *Comillas Journal of International Relations, 18*, 50–71. https://doi.org/10.14422/cir.i18.y2020.003

Çiçek, M. (2015, January 13). Did the women of the YPJ simply fall from the sky? Kurdish question. *Deftera res a meral Çiçek*. http://defterares.blogspot.com/2015/01/did-women-of-ypj-simply-fall-from-sky.html

Dean, V. (2019). Kurdish female fighters: The Western depiction of YPJ combatants in Rojava. *Glocalism: Journal of Culture, Politics and Innovation, 1*, 5. https://glocalismjournal.org/wp-content/uploads/2019/05/Dean_gjcpi_2019_1.pdf

Dirik, D. (2014, October 29). Western fascination with 'badass' Kurdish women. *Al Jazeera*. https://www.aljazeera.com/opinions/2014/10/29/western-fascination-with-badass-kurdish-women

Dirik, D. (2018). The revolution of smiling women: Stateless democracy and power in Rojava. In O. U. Rutazibwa, & R. Shilliam (Eds.), *Routledge handbook of postcolonial politics* (1st edition [Online], pp. 222–238). Routledge. https://doi.org/10.4324/9781315671192.

Drexler, E. F. (2018). Victim-warriors and iconic heroines: Photographs of female combatants in Aceh, Indonesia. *Critical Asian Studies, 50*(3), 395–421. https://doi.org/10.1080/14672715.2018.1487311

Fernàndez Aragonès, A. (2020). Women, body and war: Kurdish female fighters through commander Arian and Girls' war. *Media, War and Conflict, 15*(3), 298–314. https://doi.org/10.1177/1750635220948554

Gentry, C. E., & Sjoberg, L. (2011). The gendering of Women's terrorism. In C. E. Gentry & L. Sjoberg (Eds.), *Women, Gender, and Terrorism* (pp. 57–80). University of Georgia Press.

Göksel, N. (2019). Gendering resistance: Multiple faces of the Kurdish Women's struggle. *Sociological Forum, 34*(S1), 1112–1131. https://doi.org/10.1111/socf.12539

Gunes, C. (2013). Accommodating Kurdish National Demands in Turkey. In E. Nimni, A. Osipov, & D. J. Smith (Eds.), *The challenge of non-territorial autonomy: Theory and practice* (pp. 71–84). Peter Lang.

Hama, H. H. (2019). Framing the fall of Sinjar: Kurdish media's coverage of the Yazidi genocide. *Middle Eastern Studies, 55*(5), 798–812. https://doi.org/10.1080/00263206.2019.1580192

Henry, C. (2014). *Revisionist rape-revenge: Redefining a film genre*. Palgrave Macmillan.

Henshaw, A. L. (2016). Where women rebel: Patterns of women's participation in armed rebel groups 1990–2008. *International Feminist Journal of Politics, 18*(1), 39–60. https://doi.org/10.1080/14616742.2015.1007729

Hillary and Chelsea Clinton are set to produce a TV show about 'defiant' all-female Kurdish militia unit that helped to defeat ISIS in Syria, after buying the rights to new book about the women. (2021, January 25). *Daily Mail*. https://www.dailymail.co.uk/femail/article-9185967/Hillary-Chelsea-Clinton-make-TV-female-militia-unit-fought-ISIS.html

Hooks, B. (1992). *Black looks: Race and representation*. Routledge.

ISIL crimes against Yazidis constitute genocide, UN investigation team finds. (2021, May 10). *UN News*. Retrieved from https://news.un.org/en/story/2021/05/1091662

Jadaliyya Reports. (2021, May 24). Open letter to the public about the article "Beyond Feminism? Jineolojî and the Kurdish Women's Freedom Movement" [Open letter]. *Jineoloji Committee Europe*. Retrieved from https://penandthepad.com/cite-open-letter-8551629.html

Jineoloji Akademisi. (2015). *Jineoloji'ye Giriş.[Introduction to Jineoloji]*. Aram Yayınları.

Jongerden, J. (2013). Confederalism and autonomy in Turkey: The kurdistan workers' party and the reinvention of democracy. In C. Gunes & W. Zeydanliouglu (Eds.), *The Kurdish question in Turkey: New perspectives on violence, representation, and reconciliation* (pp. 186–204). Routledge. https://doi.org/10.4324/9780203796450

Khalel, S., & Vickery, M. (2015, February 23). Yazidis battle ISIL: Disaster 'made us stronger'. *Al Jazeera*. https://www.aljazeera.com/news/2015/2/23/yazidis-battle-isil-disaster-made-us-stronger

Knapp, M., Flach, A., & Ayboga, E. (2016). *Revolution in Rojava: Democratic autonomy and women's liberation in Syrian Kurdistan*. Pluto Press.

Manekin, D., & Wood, R. M. (2020). Framing the narrative: Female fighters, external audience attitudes, and transnational support for armed rebellions. *Journal of Conflict Resolution, 64*(9), 1638–1665. https://doi.org/10.1177/0022002720912823

Minwalla, S., Foster, J. E., & McGrail, S. (2020). Genocide, rape, and careless disregard: Media ethics and the problematic reporting on Yazidi survivors of ISIS captivity. *Feminist Media Studies, 00*(00), 1–17. https://doi.org/10.1080/14680777.2020.1731699

Mirzeler, M. K. (2000). The formation of male identity and the roots of violence against women: The case of Kurdish songs, stories and storytellers. *Journal of Muslim Minority Affairs, 20*(2), 261–269. https://doi.org/10.1080/713680369

Mulvey, L. (2013). Visual pleasure and narrative cinema. In C. Penley (Ed.), *Feminism and film theory* (pp. 57–68). Routledge. https://doi.org/10.4324/9780203699362

Oppenheimer, S. (2020, October 9). The world celebrated Kurdish women's fight against ISIS. Now it's silent as they're raped and tortured. *HAARETZ*. Retrieved from https://www.haaretz.com/middle-east-news/syria/2020-10-09/ty-article-magazine/.premium/the-world-celebrated-kurdish-womens-fight-against-isis-why-is-it-silent-now/0000017f-e7dd-df2c-a1ff-ffdda3150000

Orhan, M. (2019). The intersectional dynamics of political violence and gender in the Kurdish conflict. *Studies in Ethnicity and Nationalism, 19*(3), 269–288. https://doi.org/10.1111/sena.12308

Pabst, S. (2018, December 10). Nadia Murad: One woman's fight against 'Islamic State'. *DW*. Retrieved from https://www.dw.com/en/nadia-murad-one-womans-fight-against-islamic-state/a-36172104

Ponzanesi, S., & Waller, M. (Eds.). (2012). *Postcolonial film studies*. New York.

Read, J. (2000). *The new avengers: Feminism, femininity and the rape-revenge cycle*. Manchester University Press.

Sabogal, L. C. B., & Richter, S. (2019). Las Farianas: Reintegration of former female farc fighters as a driver for peace in Colombia. *Cuadernos de Economia (Colombia), 38*(78), 753–784. https://doi.org/10.15446/cuad.econ.v38n78.73540

Said, E. W. (1978). *Orientalism*. Penguin.

Saito, S. (2019, April 13). Interview: Eva Husson on fighting for a female perspective of War in "Girls of the Sun". *The Moveable Fest*. https://moveablefest.com/eva-husson-girls-of-the-sun/

Sarac, B. N. (2020). UK newspapers' portrayal of yazidi women's experiences of violence under ISIS. *Journal of Strategic Security, 13*(1), 59–81. https://doi.org/10.5038/1944-0472.13.1.1753

Sassatelli, R. (2011). Interview with Laura Mulvey: Gender, gaze and Technology in Film Culture. *Theory, Culture & Society, 28*(5), 123–143. https://doi.org/10.1177/0263276411398278

Shahvisi, A. (2018). Beyond orientalism: Exploring the distinctive feminism of democratic Confederalism in Rojava. *Geopolitics, 26*(4), 998–1022. https://doi.org/10.1080/14650045.2018.1554564

Shohat, E., & Stam, R. (1994). *Unthinking eurocentrism*. Routledge.

Şimşek, B., & Jongerden, J. (2021). Gender revolution in Rojava: The voices beyond tabloid geopolitics. *Geopolitics, 26*(4), 1023–1045. https://doi.org/10.1080/14650045.2018.1531283

Sjoberg, L., Cooke, G. D., & Neal, S. R. (2011). Introduction. In C. E. Gentry & L. Sjoberg (Eds.), *Women, Gender, and Terrorism* (pp. 1–25). University of Georgia Press.

Smelik, A. (2007). Feminist film theory. In P. Cook (Ed.), *The cinema book* (pp. 491–504). British Film Institute Publishing. https://doi.org/10.5040/9781838710484.0065

Smets, K., & Akkaya, A. H. (2016). Media and violent conflict: Halil Dağ, Kurdish insurgency, and the hybridity of vernacular cinema of conflict. *Media, War and Conflict, 9*(1), 76–92. https://doi.org/10.1177/1750635215611611

Smith, S. (1972). The image of women in film: Some suggestions for future research. In S. Thornham (Ed.), *Feminist film theory: A reader* (pp. 14–19). Edinburgh University Press.

Tamang, S. (2017). Motherhood containers: Cantonments and the media framing of female ex-combatants in Nepal's transition. In M. Hutt & P. Onta (Eds.), *Political change and public culture in Post-1990 Nepal* (pp. 223–250). Cambridge University Press. https://doi.org/10.1017/9781316771389.011

Thomas, J. L., & Wood, R. M. (2017). Women on the frontline: Rebel group ideology and women's participations in violent rebellion. *Journal of Peace Research, 54*(1), 31–46. http://www.jstor.org/stable/44511194

Thomas, J. L., & Wood, R. M. (2018). The social origins of female combatants. *Conflict Management and Peace Science, 35*(3), 215–232. https://doi.org/10.1177/0738894217695524

Thornham, S. (1999). Women's Cinema as Counter-Cinema. In *Feminist film theory a reader*. https://www.academia.edu/20269802/Sue_Thornham_Feminist_Film_Theory_A_Reader_Book_Fi

Toivanen, M., & Baser, B. (2016). Gender in the representations of an armed conflict: Female Kurdish combatants in French and British media. *Middle East Journal of Culture and Communication, 9*(3), 294–314. https://doi.org/10.1163/18739865-00903007

Ustundag, N. (2019). Mother, politician, and guerilla: The emergence of a new political imagination in Kurdistan through Women's bodies and speech. *Differences, 30*(2), 115–145. https://doi.org/10.1215/10407391-7736077

Viterna, J. S. (2006). Pulled, pushed, and persuaded: Explaining women's mobilization into the Salvadoran guerrilla army. *American Journal of Sociology, 112*(1), 1–45. https://doi.org/10.1086/502690

Wyke, T. (2014, October 6). H&M apologises after being accused of modelling £15 khaki outfit on uniform worn by Kurdish female fighters battling ISIS. *Daily Mail Online*. https://www.dailymail.co.uk/news/article-2782418/H-M-apologises-Peshmerga-chic-jumpsuit-Clothing-chain-embarrassed-accused-modelling-15-khaki-outfit-uniform-worn-Kurdish-female-fighters-battling-ISIS.html

Manifestations of Violence in the Causality of a Radicalization Episode

A Case Study on the Margins of La Paz-Bolivia

María Fernanda Córdova Suxo

1 Introduction

For the past 15 years, Bolivia has registered an average of 70 episodes of social conflicts per month (UNDP-PAPEP, 2013; UNIR, 2021). This average increased twice during previous years, which positions Bolivia with one of the highest conflict indices in Latin America. These conflicts have the characteristic of being led by social groups and individuals who protest against tangible issues that directly affect their living conditions and point up to deficiencies in public institutions (UNDP-PAPEP, 2013).

The main reforms of the country in the last years, such as the Bolivian Constitutional Reform (2009), took place within the framework of this conflict dynamic, which would not have occurred without the pressure generated by the radicalization of conflicts. Radicalization prompted democratization and the recognition of fundamental rights, to name a few examples: access to water after the Water War in 2000, the redistribution of natural resources as a result of the Gas War in 2003, or the establishment of a constituent assembly in 2006, including hitherto marginalized populations. This observation suggests that the country's development—understood as the expansion of fundamental rights, the redistribution of wealth, and the exercise of democracy—has been achieved through high levels of conflict led by organized civil society (Inksater, 2005; UNDP – PAPEP, 2013). In general, the social conquests resulting from conflict dynamics, due to their reformative character, tend to minimize the degree of violence. The manifestation of this violence and its different expressions are produced and located in the causality of the conflict process. Therefore, the "democratic" character attributed to conflict dynamics tends to cover up forms of violence rather than denounce them.

M. F. C. Suxo (✉)
University of Kassel, Kassel, Germany

This article argues for the perspective that an episode of radicalization finds important reasons to be established in the process—in its causality—rather than in the episode as such. Causality, however, is not assumed from its empirical perspective, which would concentrate and list the events that precede the episode of radicalization, but from its structural dimension, making it possible to describe the systems and mechanisms that sustain the occurrence of the events in the way they are triggered. To this end, the meta-theory of Critical Realism (CR) (Bhaskar, 1978, 1998; Sayer, 2000, 2004; Martins, 2006) is incorporated in order to apply a stratified perspective of reality and, likewise, to open the way to an analysis that questions the ontology of the episode of radicalization. In the first part of the article, this meta-theoretical approach of CR is described, together with its philosophical and theoretical foundations for the present research.

In order to contextualize and approach the case study, the second and third parts describe the theoretical foundations, followed by the case study setting—methodology and background—of the radicalization episode. The specific case of Macrodistrict VI - Mallasa is analyzed, a community on the fringes of the city limits of La Paz, Bolivia, which evidences a permanent state of conflict. As in most of the Bolivian territory, this community experienced an episode of radicalization between October and November 2019 as a result of a government crisis triggered by questionable presidential elections.

In the following, the causality of the radicalization episode is configured on the basis of the foundations on the stratified ontology. Bhaskar (1978) proposes the stratified ontology for causality analysis, distinguishing three ontological domains: the empirical, the actual, and the real. Based on these three dimensions, the relationships, structures, and mechanisms underlying the episode in question are described. The empirical domain narrates the incidents of violence evidenced by the episode of radicalization that occurred between October and November in the Mallasa territory. The actual domain reveals unobservable events of the episode; from the recognition of the forms of structural and symbolic violence, it describes the substantial relationships and necessary conditions that sustain the events of the empirical domain. The real domain highlights the forms of epistemic violence in structures of radicalization. This dimension leads us to a process of reconceptualization and dimensioning of the radicalization as such by questioning the structures that sustain events with a high degree of violence.

The concluding remarks develop reflections on the findings and the application of the stratified ontology to the analysis of radicalization processes and conflicts in general. Based on the case analyzed, the concept of radicalization is confirmed and broadened as a way of contesting the order, but also as an episode conditioned by previous social and historical experiences, where unresolved demands and grievances converge.

2 Critical Realism

In order to identify forms and expressions of violence in the causality of an episode of radicalism, the present case study is guided by the meta-theory of Critical Realism (Bhaskar, 1978, 1998; Sayer, 2000, 2004; Martins, 2006). Critical realism proposes a philosophical system that distinguishes the empirical world—observable—from the real world—unobservable—configured in structures, mechanisms, laws, and properties that underlie and generate certain empirical events. In this way the stratified ontology establishes: "a reality independent of our concepts and knowledge (and) this reality and the way it behaves are in important respects not accessible to immediate observation" (Danermark et al., 2002, p. 20). This distinction will formulate the "stratified ontology" (Bhaskar, 1978), which posits two dimensions underlying an empirical domain: the actual and the real. The actual and the real domain are constituted by structures and mechanisms, not always visible but describable through theory, whose "real" dimension does not lie in the materiality of their properties, but in the causal powers they contain.

While critical realism upholds the existence of an objective reality, it differs from classical realism with respect to the way in which causality is perceived, problematizing not only its observability, but also its entire constitution. CR formulates that the social world is both socially constructed and real, sustaining the important dependence of concept and language on social phenomena (Sayer, 1992).

Critical realism research "aims at developing causal explanations that map the components of a social phenomenon across stratified reality, spelling out what the relevant objects, structures, mechanisms and conditions are to that phenomenon" (Hoddy, 2019, p. 113). A critical realist case study will then be concerned with seeking theoretically supported explanations of social phenomena, in this case, the episode of radicalization. The approach entails the assumption that there is a dimension (truth) underlying the empirical episode, which is describable and analyzable by researching the social causes and effects of the object of study (Danermark et al., 2002). Therefore, this case study, in addition to analyzing and characterizing the configurations of a given space and episode of radicalization, mainly documents the structures that sustain the phenomenon, that shape the context in the way it will manifest itself.

3 Theoretical Framework

Based on these principles of critical realism, the assumed concepts and theoretical frameworks are supportive, as they acquire the property of being reconceptualized in a retroductive phase (see methodology). Thus, the concepts of radicalization, violence, and conflict are explained in a heuristic extent (Kelle quoted by, Hoddy, 2019); methodologically, the combination of observation and theoretical production integrated by retroduction will be enabled.

Radicalization, in the context of this article, is configured on the basis of the scale of Glasl (2004), which proposes a stratification and characterization of the escalation of social conflicts. According to this model, radicalization is manifested when the conflict escalates to the level that "the transformation of the image of the counterpart takes place (...) a sudden perception of the true, and very different, nature of the other" (Glasl, 2004, p. 236). The positions of the parties are no longer considered in terms of inferiority or superiority, but in the taking of sides, in an antagonistic binarism (good, bad), accompanied by the increase of both direct and symbolic violence (Glasl, 2004, p. 236). The visualization of different expressions of violence allows, through critical realism, to analyze the events under the dimensions of the stratified ontology. That is, not only the forms of manifested violence are identified, but also their causality is configured through the analysis of the empirical, actual, and real dimensions.

In addition to Glasl's characterization, in the historical context of Bolivia, and more specifically, of the Andean highlands, radicalization is associated with the conflict dynamics. According to Jordán Prudencio (2016) and Rojas (2015), the processes of radicalization are described as the adoption of extreme measures, implying violent episodes with fatalities. This form of radicalization has not led to armed conflict, but has the characteristic of operating as a spring (Jordán Prudencio, 2016). The analogy with the spring is intended to describe the action of straining, as the tension of the conflict and its recurrence accumulates until it reaches the point of release and rebounds in a concentrated period of clashes, high rates of violence, and the toll of injuries and deaths.

Radicalization in this context sustains an important symbolic background, aligned to the culture of protest in Bolivia. A symbol of radical protest is associated with the encirclement of cities. The siege can be traced back to the historical cleavage that refers to the uprising of Tupac Katari in 1781, long before the constitution of the Republic. The characteristic of Katari's rebellion was the siege of the city of La Paz. The social configuration imposed by the Spanish colony positioned the "Indian villages" on the margins of the city; the margins of La Paz are hills and mountains that, because of their great height, create the impression of a bowl whose base, to this day, constitutes the urban center. The encirclement blocked this urban center, preventing any kind of transit. This rebellion demanded the vindication of the indigenous Aymara people in pursuit of independence from the Spanish colony (see Thomson, 2002; Del Valle de Siles, 2019). The legendary "siege of Katari" has since then been a symbol of radicalization and struggle repeatedly employed to this day. The blockade of roads and the siege of cities is reproduced as a radical measure of pressure; it is a resource historically used by the marginalized indigenous class (Hylton & Thomson, 2007; Rivera Cusicanqui, 2010).

The symbolic elements of radicalization are incurred in a dimension of long memory (Rivera Cusicanqui, 2010) by expressing through an act the vindication of a struggle of several centuries. Although the demands of protest differ from those of colonial independence, the act denounces in its practice the marginalization, the symbolic position of cornering the nucleus from where oppression is exercised, and thus confronting the established centralized regime. Therefore, the meaning gained by the act of radicalization, through its historical and political contextualization, makes it necessary to problematize both the visible forms of violence that are registered in an episode and those that are configured as forms of epistemic, symbolic, and structural violence.

The concept of epistemic violence is understood as an indirect form of violence which reinforces pretensions of absolute truth by contributing to the legitimization of existing structural processes (Korf, 2006; Brunner, 2020). Epistemic violence is anchored in the power of definition and of legitimization, so that it produces hegemonic discourses. These hegemonic discourses define limits whose formats and objectives are justified with violence (Korf, 2006; Brunner, 2020.). This form of violence is expressed in "(...) the 'rationalization' and naturalization of *geographical imaginaries* [italics used by the author] that makes possible the legitimization of political aspirations over territorial spaces and the use of natural resources" (own translation of Korf, 2006, p. 632). This concept helps to identify forms of structural violence, housed in processes of validation of knowledge, which are configured in the normative body—the legislature, development plans, supreme decrees, among others—and, from its application, seek to define and impose concepts and practices of development, welfare, but also justice, its limits, and scope.

In the same structural dimension, the lens of symbolic violence (Bourdieu, 1977) is also applied, understanding it as a form of non-physical violence that manifests itself in the difference of power between social groups and as an unconscious agreement on both sides. It manifests itself in the imposition of the norms of the group with greater social power on those of the subordinate group. Symbolic violence can manifest itself in the marginalization and instrumentalization of the narrative that legitimizes each of the polarized parties in the process of escalation of the conflict and its culmination in radicalization.

In addition to this manifestation of violence that addresses hierarchies in human social interactions, it is also important to contextualize structural violence as the interaction with institutions; this refers to social circumstances, often aspects of social structures or institutions that prevent individuals from meeting basic needs, i.e. a healthy existence (Galtung, 1990).

In addition to the forms of direct violence, evidenced in empirical dimensions, the exercise of epistemic, symbolic, and structural violence can be identified in the causality of the episode of radicalization described below. Being able to dimension their forms of expression in a concrete case allows us to conceptualize the structures and causes underlying radicalization.

4   Case Study Setting

The case study is part of an independent research project, conducted between 2014 and 2021 (Cordova Suxo, 2021), with the objective of analyzing the dynamics of conflict in Bolivia and its correlation with the country's development. In this period of time, the conflict index maintained a regularity of 70 conflicts per month (UNDP-PAPEP, 2013; UNIR, 2021), positioning the country with one of the highest indexes of social conflict in Latin America. The year 2019 bore witness to an episode of radicalization triggered by a political and social crisis, which revealed distrust in public institutions and polarization, despite a major structural reform of the State in 2006. The initial empirical dimension of the case study has exhausted the explanatory capacity of the causality of the episode of radicalism, so it was deemed pertinent to incorporate an approach that allows us to problematize the structures of power dynamics underlying the crisis. Thus, Critical Realism is introduced in order to develop causal explanations that account for the structures, mechanisms and conditions of the phenomenon.

In what follows, I concentrate on describing the causality of radicalization episode, which started with the presidential elections on October 20, 2019 and ended on November 11 of the same year. This episode took place in a territory conflict Macrodistrict VI, Mallasa, where a boundary struggle was already taking place. The methodological design consisted of data collection based on ethnographic techniques. Specifically, with respect to the radicalization episode, semi-structured interviews were conducted with local residents and former authorities. An exhaustive review of press releases, journalistic interviews, and reports of the facts registered in the radicalization event in the mentioned period of time was carried out. For the analysis of this information, the case study is configured in the stratified ontology, which was analyzed by means of retroduction[1] (Danermark et al., 2002) in conjunction with coding techniques of content analysis (Mayring & Fenzl, 2014).

4.1 Background Information

In 2019, the Bolivian political situation deepened the polarization of the population due to the presidential electoral process conducted in October of the same year. The then-president Evo Morales was once again (for the fourth time in a row) running for election as a candidate. This run was an unconstitutional action; also, a referendum denied the possibility of changing the constitution to modify the reelection possibilities. Notwithstanding, in the midst of the distrust, Morales ran for election under the approval of Bolivia's Constitutional Court. The procedures and results leading Morales to win unleashed the fraud narrative, later contrasted by a coup d'état (See Bernard-Menguz, 2020; Weisbrot, 2020; Kurmanaev & Trigo, 2020). A series of geographically isolated events, but articulated by a massive diffusion of photos, audios, videos, memes, were inciting confrontation: the "defense of democracy" against the "wild mob"; "marginalized groups" against the "white elite," "the old right" (Kurmanaev & Trigo, 2020). The polarization of the cities reproduced

---

[1] By retroduction, methodologically proposed by Danermark et al. (2002), we understand the reconstruction of the primary conditions for a particular phenomenon. Retroduction transcends the empirical events' observation and conceptualizes conditions (2002). The reconstruction was carried out through an inferential analysis; this type of analysis allows theorizing the characteristics of the mechanisms and structures found in the properties that constitute causality of the radicalization episode. In other words, we reconstruct the system of social positions, norms, laws, and the acquired social and cultural dispositions (*habitus*) that structured a particular action (2002, p. 98), building a transfactual argumentation based on the theory of violence and its manifestations.

Katari's image of a siege by pointing out the threat of wild mobs coming down from the mountains to take over the cities.

Many inhabitants of capital cities such as La Paz and Cochabamba were quartered in the nuclei of their neighborhood associations, meeting places such as neighborhood schools, or private homes, gathering wooden sticks, rubble, old tires, and all kinds of debris. These tools built protective walls and blocked the streets and avenues connected with the country's interior since the mob's arrival was announced. On the margins of the capital cities, the social organizations, peasants, miners, indigenous peoples were also articulated. The discourse of threat and fear of the "return of the neoliberal right" emanated from these nuclei, which in most cases were aligned with the ruling political party, the Movement al Socialismo (MAS) also headed by Morales. Although the dissidence and division of the movements with respect to this alignment was evident, the narrative of fear prevailed.[2]

Macrodistrict VI, Mallasa (Mallasa from here on), as a microcosm of the general situation, reflected and reproduced the polarization that existed throughout the country. Mallasa is a territory south of the city of La Paz; despite being part of the urban area, it remains on the margins of the city due to its highly rural characteristics. For more than 80 years, this territory has had conflicts with neighboring municipalities over internal limits.

Factors such as hyper-regulation (Horn, 2021), clientelism (Revilla, 2011), and a deep problem of a society fragmented by classes and colonial experiences (Inksater, 2005; Cordova Suxo, 2021) had led to the polarization of the local community. In a context rife with tension, these factors had already pre-established, matured, and fostered the radicalization of its population.

4.2 Radicalization Episode: The Empiric Domain

On November 10, 2019, Evo Morales presented his resignation as president after 20 days of protests and clashes that generated social unrest due to the polarization between those who joined the civic strike against the alleged electoral fraud and those who denounced the establishment of a coup d'état. Morales' act of resignation generated a new wave of violence:

> That same night, groups of protesters attacked several police stations, destroyed public transport buses, and looted and burned the houses of people with a public profile. Due to rumors circulating that groups of citizens were preparing to move to different neighborhoods to loot the houses and businesses in the area, the population organized vigils to protect their neighborhoods (Own translation, Méndez et al., 2021, p. 92).

Among these circumstances, the sub-mayor's office and a police station in Mallasa were attacked, looted, and burned. Press reports describe "a mob of about 50

---
[2] This information is part of personal experience and can also be contrasted with the factual reconstruction reports of Méndez et al. (2021) and with the report "Relato de un pueblo" of the Permanent Assembly of Human Rights in Bolivia (APDHB, 2021).

people, identified as MAS supporters" (Méndez et al., 2021). This event consummated several threats made by unions and local organizations related to the dominant political party regarding the seizure of institutions by force, along with the discourse of recovering buildings that belong to them (El Diario, 2014). The materialization of this violent episode —of the burning of the sub-mayor's office and the police property— was the result of a short-term individual and collective maturation; following Khosrokhavar (2014), the radicalization actions evidenced in this short-term is entailed and a result of a long process of maturation, in which the assimilation of affectivities and the social environment converge (p. 38).

The historical reference to the Katari siege mentioned at the beginning of this article refers to the symbolic role of radicalization through the blockade as an element of protest that prevails over time. To date, the configuration of the siege is a coercive measure to raise attention to the demands claimed, but also a symbol of struggle for self-determination, which is still in the process of concretizing for indigenous peoples. The feeling in individuals who radicalize "of being the victim of a profound injustice, with the certainty that the intentions of reform are not enough" (Khosrokhavar, 2014, p. 52.) is materialized through the symbolic value of the siege. The frequent use of this instrument of rebellion and the causes that lead to its use reproduce the long struggle to overcome a marginal situation. This practice intends to reflect the insufficiency of the system, the injustice to which its protagonists are exposed and the need to radicalize their actions in order to be heard.

4.3   Revealing Unobservable Events: The Actual Domain

The actual domain is "where events happen whether we experience them or not" (Danermark et al., 2002, p. 20); the domain encloses the conditions of the establishment of the substantial relations (Danermark et al., 2002, p. 46) expressed in the empirical event of radicalization. It was mentioned above that the hyper-regulation of the territory (Horn, 2021), a growing clientelism (Revilla, 2011), and social fragmentation by classes and colonial experiences (Inksater, 2005; Cordova Suxo, 2021) are elements that precondition the polarized and conflicting scenario. The analysis and retroduction of these factors allowed us to identify striking forms of violence that shape the actual domain: marginality as structural violence and the instrumentalized narrative that deepen polarizations. These elements configure the conditions of substantial relations of the causality of the episode of radicalization and are discussed below.

4.3.1   Marginality

Marginality, as an expression of structural violence, is considered a necessary property of causality. Structural violence is understood as intrinsic to the social, political, and economic systems that govern societies, states, and the world (Galtung, 1990). The social establishment that positions the city's margins in a precarious situation results from implementing plans of modernity inspired by ideal capitalist models that proclaim the "freedom of choice" of where to live, what to own, and how to move around (Angotti, 2013). In such a configuration, the rural is then positioned as marginal and problematic because it does not condone modern characteristics and will settle in the limits of legality in its transition to the modernity. The location and precariousness to which inhabitants are exposed result from the imposition of a city model alien to local dynamics and only accessible to a minority.

In addition to the families that have occupied Mallasa in the last century, the settled population is migrant, commonly established in this territory due to displacement and eviction processes linked to internal migration flows (Espósito Guevara, 2008, p. 296). The high population concentration is evident in the urban centers with the most significant economic activity (2008), one of them being the city of La Paz. The city's expansion generates pockets of growth with high levels of vulnerability due to its unplanned expansion, which is normally established on the margins of legality. The inequality generated by migrant settlements, contrasted by phenomena such as the expansion of private housing, deepens into social gaps (Harvey, 2005; Vidal-Koppmann, 2005).

Mallasa is not only a territory in transition, on the margins of modernity, but also in conflict. Territories in conflict have been identified as places of high vulnerability since this condition generates unworthy living conditions for their inhabitants (Espósito Guevara, 2008, p. 2). It is common to experience the neglect and postponement of managing the populations' needs since the conflict condition endows the territory with a frozen situation. Under this frozen condition, it is impossible to manage, move, or initiate any development or improvement plan; therefore, attention to the demands for basic and public services, such as the installation of sewage systems, provision of drinking water, or road construction, is also postponed. In addition to the unattended demands and the impossibility of management, there are, as mentioned earlier, sanitation processes and judicial processes for the 'illegality of the territory' that demand much time, economic resources, and stress from the target population.

In the early 2000s, the marginalization of indigenous populations was a constant feature of human development reports. The 2004 HDR report concluded the evident existence of "a limited multiculturalism, reinforced by a strong social and ethnic stratification" (UNDP, 2005, p. 110). Development data and indicators also supported this discourse linking the indigenous with poverty and the margins. This situation promised to be reversed with the articulation of indigenous and peasant social organizations in the political instrument MAS-IPSP, established in the government in 2006. Based on data from the municipal human development index, Mallasa does not show to have had any variation, and especially concerning the access to basic services has not registered a categorical improvement. In 2002, only 56% of the population had access to basic services such as drinking water, sewage, health and education, data that decreases and had an average of 33% between 2012 and 2018 (Municipal Government of La Paz (GAMLP), 2020; National Institute of Statistics Bolivia (INE), 2013, 2020). In contrast, the economic gap in the country had widened between 1994 and 2003 and had not achieved a significant reduction until 2018 (UNDP, 2018).

4.3.2 The Implications of the Narrative

The narrative emerges as a result of the inferential analysis of retroduction. In this sense, we understand narrative in the constructivist framework as a form of discourse with the capacity to generate meaning and reality. The instrumentality of the narrative has been identified as an indispensable condition that allowed the configuration of the radicalization event by fostering the consolidation of opposing identities and political roles, using the validation of symbolic violence, manifested in the power difference between social groups (Bourdieu, 1977).

A dominant narrative of empowerment emerged with the installation of the MAS-IPSP government in 2006. This administration positioned itself as the product of an organic accumulation of native and indigenous peasant organizations that establish an indigenous government, representing *all* indigenous peoples (Zuazo, 2009). Many social organizations and rural municipalities in the periphery adopted the discourse and joined the cause. The inherent diversity of the parts that made up this discourse began to unmask the essentialization of the indigenous narrative that had acted as a political instrument to achieve the idealized hegemony. This "unifying" narrative had annulled the capacity of political incidence of the actors, making invisible the diversity of their demands, which on numerous occasions contradicted the official discourse. This dismemberment of the narrative instrument led to the splitting of social organizations and of the MAS-IPSP itself (Tapia & Chávez, 2020). The weakening of the party/political instrument MAS-IPSP relied on reinforcing the figure of a single leader, accentuating populist and clientelistic characteristics. This way of exercising leadership from the government has implied costs for the quality of democracy (such as forced reelection) and evidence of the erosion of accountability and transparency (see the case of the Indigenous Fund, TIPNIS, among others).

The division of the social movements became more pronounced as their narratives became aligned with those of the government institutions or with those of their political dissidents. In order to achieve attention to local demands, the organized population established political party alliances. This affiliation directly impacts the deepening of polarization because it adopted and fed the dissemination and reproduction of opposing narratives. The reproduction of narratives fostered the creation of social imaginaries which, in the sphere of territorial conflict, drew the clear distinction between rural and non-rural habitants and spaces. In this way, stereotypes define the indigenous as rural "time-stalled" and contrasted them with the modern subject, who is located in urban spaces. The functionality of these seemingly competing narratives was reinforced over time, especially in confrontational situations in which it was necessary to validate identities and positions to legitimize the presence, access, and occupation of the territory.

Tackling a specific example: It was noted, the indistinct use of the terms "loteadores or avasalladores" (land-grabbers) to name the group of people who settle in Mallasa National Park or another area considered protected. These adjectives are intended to disqualify the community members, diverting attention from their original demand. Although there is a distinction between land-grabbers and families claiming land, being both active figures in this type of conflict, this generalization is very common. It is attributed to the fact that the passage of time has generated the diversification of actors in the conflict; to date, families have grown, and the land has been sold, thus involving new actors and dynamics in the dispute. In this dynamic situation, the validation of the narrative is straightforward, as the role of the actors is also blurred.

This exercise of identification based on the other, "in mutual and unequal opposition, through the relative attribution of inferiority and/or radical alienation towards the other/outsider of the group" (Brons, 2015, p. 87) framed a process of otherness in the territory in conflict, fueled by the political forces of passage. Social divisions were accentuated and incurred in the misuse of institutional and citizen resources by using resources of citizen participation, such as assemblies, town meetings, marches, and blockades, from positions of power and disseminating discourses of fear and distrust, making allegory to the alleged danger to which society was heading.

Institutional action in the conflict territory is conditioned to the dominant party of the institution, as well as the provision of basic services, emergency attention, citizen security, among others. Mediation and possible solutions have only been established, and with little success, to the extent that the same political party was present in the institutions involved (see, e.g., Quispe, 2016; Valdés, 2016). Therefore, the viability of any territorial management could only be achieved when related parties are represented in the institutional framework.

4.4 Structures and Mechanisms: The Real Domain

The real domain of the stratified ontology contains the structures, relations, mechanisms, and tendencies of power, in a constant flux of enduring properties (Danermark et al., 2002). The analysis and configuration of this dimension aims, then, to answer: what elements sustain the systems that perpetuate the marginalities of the boundaries and the narratives of separation? What structures allow the permanence of conflicts that underlie violence and violent episodes? What forms of violence are embodied in these structures? The contingent and necessary properties analyzed in the actual domain are sustained by the interaction of elements of validation and legitimization, such as legal instruments and concepts with imperative character: development, peace, security, and actors that enable their interaction. The real domain reveals the configuration of these elements located in structures and mechanisms. Its dynamic has not primarily revealed expressions of direct violence, but symbolic and epistemic violence.

4.4.1 Laws as a Mechanism of Symbolic Violence

In the present case, laws develop a normative body on managing the territory and the conflict, which involves decrees, criminal and legal processes, management mechanisms, sanctions, lawsuits, and forms of compensation. In the territory of Mallasa, there is an overlap of laws where both conflict parties sustain their legitimate presence (see Horn, 2021). On the one hand is the municipal government, backed by a supreme decree that delimits the park (Paz Estenssoro, S.D. No.4309,

February 06, 1956), and on the other hand, the inhabitants support their ownership and possession of land based on the laws that decree the creation of Mecapaca as a territorial unit (National Congress of the Republic of Bolivia, 1912; Honorable National Congress of Bolivia, 1947). It is also within the framework of law that the inconveniences that arise from this overlap are alleviated or intervened. In this scenario, expressions of violence are only perceptible under a detailed analysis of the impact of the norm. Two cases are described below, one regarding legal proceedings against "illegal occupants" and the second regarding the referendum as a tool for democratic participation to resolve the conflict over limits.

We understand a legal process as a "Set of legally regulated procedures for the substantiation [sic] of a criminal case or a lawsuit of another nature, and that concludes with a legal sentence" (Own translation, DPEJ.RAE, 2022). The processes have been evoked as a legitimate defense resource and are commonly used in the conflict of the present investigation. As examples, newspaper headlines that tell about their common use are cited below:

> The Sub-mayor's Office of Mallasa opened at least 36 processes for illegal occupation of municipal land (La Razón, September 28, 2014).
> The Director of Governance announced that he will file a legal claim against the trespassers who threatened criminal actions against the municipal government (El Diario, 2014).

The processes are initiated in the rule by the Municipal Government of La Paz, as the means to regain control over the disputed territory are scarce. The processes are not argued based on illegal settlements since the quality of the territory in conflict relativizes this "illegality"; instead, they sustain arguments of economic damage, direct aggressions, and settlements in risk zones.

This procedure confronts individuals with government agencies, exposing them to an enormous asymmetry of power between plaintiffs and defendants and involving a large amount of economic and human resources. The anecdotes of settlers with this experience point to endless bureaucratic processes and the physical and psychological wear and tear to which they are subjected. The following quote is about the experience of a Mallasa community member (Arsenio Quelqa), told by a former local authority:

> Arsenio Quelqa had lawsuits brought against him by the Mayor's Office of La Paz. He tells with bitterness that he has been beaten and violated. So, he (Mr. Quelqa) said, and it was the whole thought of the people who lived here, peasant-indigenous people, he said: 'I am going to leave, because they have mistreated me, they have put me in jail, they have made lawsuits against me (…) I must move further inland, to the south' referring to the lowlands (Mendoza, 2014. Own translation from Spanish).

The conduct of a legal process depends not only on the power to set it in motion legally, but also on the availability of sufficient resources. The use of this procedural resource only deepens the disproportion of forces and increases the vulnerability of an already marginalized population. In this sense, the quote reflects the vulnerability and violence to which the population is subjected, and it also reflects a consequence of this, which leads to the necessary displacement—stating that the solution lies in "move further inland"—because of the intractable conditions that comprise the laws.

Another legal element refers to the laws that regulate the political-administrative units and, therefore, the conflict. The Autonomy Framework Law (Plurinational Legislative Assembly, 2010) dictates that the last resort to resolve a dispute of territorial belonging is the referendum. This consultation mechanism would allow the inhabitants to decide on the territorial jurisdiction to which they wish to belong. The most appropriate democratic resource to conclude the dispute requires the consensus of all parties to be carried out. The lack of consensus has been repeatedly evidenced, mainly with the objection that the popular vote cannot define land ownership since it is an individual matter. The delegate for the dialogue process on the boundary conflict conducted in 2016 made a public statement denouncing that: "A vote of a neighbor cannot define the lands that we have bought and obtained through the Agrarian Reform Law" (Delegate of Dialogue Mecapaca in: Valdés, April 01, 2016).

Through this analysis, it is unveiled that the aforementioned legal means lead to symbolic violence by confronting the individual with the power of a government institution or a "democratic" tool at the expense of their fundamental rights and welfare. Furthermore, there is the binary order in which conflict management is configured. Through the application of a referendum, the population is subjected to decide in binary terms; it is not only about the administrative unit to which to belong, but also about the representation that has been attributed to each territory. As analyzed in the actual domain, the representations are defined by a narrative created from the politicization of the conflict, determined by the ruling elites. This representation defines aspects of identity and belonging framed in the two poles of urban-rural, native/indigenous-modern. Beyond the evident struggle between legality and constitutionality, a human level is being permanently affected and eroded by this kind of dynamics, leading to the accumulation of frustration.

4.4.2 The Uncritical Position on the Law

In the incursion of symbolic violence in the cases described, the role of public officials/servants plays a crucial role in perpetuating it. Even though government agencies are aware of an uncertain compensation, they remain firm in upholding the law that legitimizes their jurisprudence, even though it implies contradictions. The lack of questioning of the bureaucracy by bureaucratic officials and the justification for using the *raison d'État* to validate their acts, even if these are violent, refer us to what Hannah Arendt calls "the blind obedience of a law-abiding citizen" (1999, p. 83). The dissonance of being aware of inconclusive procedures, and yet protecting the institution and the norm that perpetuates injustice, has been justified by the argument that the supremacy of the law is the only recourse for individual protection. In other words, safeguarding compliance with an inconsistent law is safer than refuting it, especially in a politicized environment where the narrative has gained more value than factual evidence. Going beyond the law, as Arendt (1999, p. 84) suggests, becomes a task that reveals the actual scope of political action (*politisches Handeln*) (Arendt, 2003).

The conditions that have allowed these laws to be established and govern in the way they do can be traced back to the constitution of society through the state. Modern societies are characterized by having to produce and justify the regulations they issue since these are contingent and no longer subject to a religious power; therefore, the space in which they emanate and are issued is in politics (Bonacker, 2003, p. 288). Adorno (1971) addresses the fundamental dialectic of the norm between its genesis and validity: legal, political norms must be justified in the sense that they legitimize their validity. The validity reasons, which should also reflect the political identity of society, are structurally contingent because validity and its genesis are mutually referential. Nonetheless, this political identity is never static, and for this reason, norms must be justified, but they can never be entirely legitimated; this is the legitimization problem of political societies (Bonacker, 2003, p. 294). Returning to Arendt, political acting is often confused with political production. While production is carried out within a normative framework, acting—which occurs independently of a structure—encompasses more; it transcends the normative framework by questioning it. Assuming, then, that acting is dynamic and permanent, the capacity to formulate and reformulate is integrated to political action, which confers the capacity to question the establishment of things (the ontological dimension).

The strategies for the constitution of the Bolivian nation-state brought with it unresolved problems of representation and territorial legitimization. Moreover, the imposition and over-positioning of state ideals deepened the original issues and created new ones. In recent years, the legislature that applies to the Bolivian territory has made the participation of the majority of its population feasible. However, the logic of political participation is one of aggregation—it formally adds participants, but does not deal with the diversity they implicitly bring with them—preventing political action from questioning structures of origin (genesis). As a consequence, the validity of the law prevails absolute. The rupture of the colonial legacy—that shapes the nation-state in the way it is experienced today—starts from an ontological and epistemological questioning, which also breaks the logic of political participation of aggregation in order to reconceptualize it, based on current configurations and needs. Under this argument, not only is an institutional exercise of modifying the law sufficient, but also the conception of political society, insofar as the active exercise of its political action allows for its efficient modification. It appears that this questioning of the order has been carried out through radicalization.

5   Conclusion

The causality determined from critical realism made it possible to identify structures that validate the application of direct, symbolic, and structural violence through mechanisms of law and narratives of power. The marginal condition in which the Mallasa territory has developed, accentuated by conflicts and the demographic formation of the city, is allegedly maintained by government institutions and systems that define the dominant guidelines of modernity and economic and political priorities. This dynamic results in the local accumulation of frustration, impotence, and the perpetuation of violence as a basis for reproducing episodes of radicalization.

Many violent practices underpin radicalization, but it is apparently radicalization itself which is a historical and coercive resource that challenges the order and opens the space for political action, a fact that will give rise to a possible reform of the structures of the State. As the article introduces radicalization in the context of Bolivia, it refers not only to an accumulation of conflicts and violent practices that trigger the "spring bounce," in reference to the metaphor that alludes to the tension of the conflict as a spring (Jordán Prudencio, 2016), but also to a historical feature of resistance against the established order, which perpetuates exclusions and fosters polarization. In the case of the episode of radicalization in Mallasa in October and November 2019, we evidenced radicalized actors who have been systematically deactivated by polarization and segmentation, followed by an impenetrable normative system. These impotent actors resort to radicalization to achieve their activation; then, the vicious circle becomes evident, in which change is only possible under political action, but political action occurs within the framework of conflict. Mechanisms identified, such as polarized politics and government officials uncritical to the norm, are the elements to take hold of this system, thus enabling the insurgency of radicalization.

An additional consideration put questions to the validation of instruments that define the function and use of territory, which are generally based on development guidelines and dominant policies applied locally, but planned externally. As described above, one of the elements that define marginality as a condition and exercise of violence happens from encasing a model of city and development alien to local needs, which impacts on the precariousness and a permanent situation of transit and instability. The impact of external standards transcends economic development plans, as it also defines narratives of belonging and identity according to ideal characteristics of spaces. These characteristics define, distinguish, and hierarchize the "rural" from the "urban," the "city dwellers from the town dwellers" they impose binary and inadequate characteristics to those that the locality transmits and practices.

Although this fact is framed within the exercise of structural violence, the validation of knowledge that generates violence refers to epistemic violence. Through the legitimacy of discriminatory policies, e.g. "the naturalization of *geographical imaginations* (that) create legitimacy for political claims to territorial spaces and the use of natural resources" (own translation Korf, 2006, p. 632) leads to a process of validation of knowledge that sustains and configures the normative body—the legislature, development plans, supreme decrees, among others—that govern the territory in conflict from the hierarchy of power; this case refers to a violent process of rationalization and validation that defines the order that we assimilate as development, conflict, territory, among others, and that, despite discrepancies, defines the actual day to day.

Under this perspective, there is not only an institutional exercise of modifying the law sufficient, but also the conception of political society as long as the active exercise of its political action is guaranteed not from the emergency and the recourse to radicalization, but from a democratic framework that allows it. There is an imminent risk in attributing to conflict a democratic role, given that this denomination hides the levels of violence perpetrated under the name of "citizen participation." While conflict is necessary to make adjustments and permanently negotiate legitimacy, it must also be on a common basis, where fundamental rights are guaranteed.

Finally, the high degree of specificity of critical realism, required for the analysis of causality, has enabled the study of a micro example of a territory that is not necessarily representative, but addresses dynamics that are replicated on a large scale. In addition, the extension of the methodology toward retroduction allows for an understanding of the phenomena of violence and radicalization that is contextual and not imposed. This induction exercise, facilitated by the techniques of content analysis, allows for the broadening of the theoretical spectrum of the phenomena investigated, providing the necessary exhaustivity that corresponds to the analysis of each case of conflict in which social complexities are implicit.

References

Adorno, T. W. (1971). Zur Metakritik der Erkenntnistheorie. In *Gesamelte Schriften* (Vol. 5, p. 80). Suhrkamp.
Angotti, T. (2013). *The new century of the Metropolis: Urban enclaves and orientalism*. Routledge.
APDHB. (2021). *Relato de un pueblo. Asamblea Permanente de Derechos Humanos en Bolivia*.
Arendt, H. (1999). *Eichmann en Jerusalén. Un estudio sobre la banalidad del mal*. Lumen.
Arendt, H. (2003). Personal responsibility under dictatorship. In J. Kohn (Ed.), *Responsibility and judgment*. Schocken Books.
Bernard-Menguz, S. (2020, May 18). Understanding the situation in Bolivia: Between fraud and coup d'état. *Le journal International*. http://www.lejournalinternational.info/en/comprendre-la-situation-en-bolivie-entre-fraude-et-coup-detat/
Bhaskar, R. (1978). *A realist theory of science*. Harvester Press.
Bhaskar, R. (1998). *The possibility of naturalism: A philosophical critique of the contemporary human sciences*. Routledge.
Bonacker, T. (2003). Die Kontingenz politischen Handelns. In D. Auer, J. S. Wessel, & L. Rensmann (Eds.), *Arendt und Adorno* (pp. 286–310). Suhrkamp.
Bourdieu, P. (1977). Sur le pouvoir symbolique. *Annales. Histoire, Sciences Sociales, 32*(3), 405–411. https://doi.org/10.3406/ahess.1977.293828
Brons, L. (2015). Othering, an analysis. *Transcience, 6*(1), 69–90.
Brunner, C. (2020). *Epistemische Gewalt*. Transcript Verlag.
Cordova Suxo, M. F. (2021). *Vivir en el Conflicto: La relación conflicto - desarrollo, en el caso del Macrodistrito VI-Mallasa, municipio de La Paz* [Master Thesis, Universidad Mayor de San Adrés]. https://doi.org/10.13140/RG.2.2.22265.54884.
Danermark, B., Ekström, M., & Karlsson, J. C. (2002). *Explaining society: Critical realism in the social sciences*. Routledge. https://doi.org/10.4324/9781351017831
Del Valle de Siles, M. E. (2019). *Historia de la rebelión de Tupac Catari, 1781–1872*. Vicepresidencia del Estado Plurinacional.
DPEJ.RAE. (2022). *Diccionario panhispánico del español jurídico*. Retrieved September 4, 2018, from https://dpej.rae.es/lema/proceso
El Diario. (2014, October 17). Loteadores anuncian toma de predios de Subalcaldía de Mallasa. *Cedib*.Org. https://www.cedib.org/post_type_titulares/loteadores-anuncian-toma-de-predios-de-subalcaldia-de-mallasa-el-diario-17-10-2014/.

Espósito Guevara, C. A. (2008). Exclusión política, des-ciudadanización y profundización de la pobreza urbana en Bolivia. In S. del Hombre & CLACSO (Eds.), *Procesos de urbanización de la pobreza y nuevas formas de exclusión social: Los retos de las políticas sociales de las ciudades latinoamericanas del siglo XXI* (pp. 295–317). Clacso.

Galtung, J. (1990). Cultural violence. *Journal of Peace Research, 27*(3), 291–305. https://doi.org/10.1177/0022343390027003005

Glasl, F. (2004). *Konfliktmanagement. Ein Handbuch für Führungskräfte, Beraterinnen und Berater*. Haupt.

Harvey, D. (2005). *A brief history of neoliberalism*. Oxford University Press.

Hoddy, E. T. (2019). Critical realism in empirical research: Employing techniques from grounded theory methodology. *International Journal of Social Research Methodology, 22*(1), 111–124. https://doi.org/10.1080/13645579.2018.1503400

Honorable National Congress of Bolivia. (1947). Ley de 24 de octubre. Créanse la segunda y tercera sección Municipal de la Provincia Murillo del Departamento de La Paz, (1947). https://www.lexivox.org/norms/BO-L-19471024.xhtml.

Horn, P. (2021). The politics of hyperregulation in La Paz, Bolivia: Speculative peri-urban development in a context of unresolved municipal boundary conflicts. *Urban Studies*, 1–17. https://doi.org/10.1177/00420980211031806.

Hylton, F., & Thomson, S. (2007). *Revolutionary horizons. Past and present in Bolivian politics*. Verso.

Inksater, K. (2005). *Análisis de conflicto en Bolivia. Equilibrio en medio de caos*. International Consulting Services.

Jordán Prudencio, N. (2016). *El resorte de la conflictividad en Bolivia: dinámicas, riesgos y transformaciones, 2000–2008*. Vicepresidencia del Estado Plurinacional de Bolivia, Centro de Investigaciones Sociales (CIS).

Khosrokhavar, F. (2014). *Radicalisation*. CEP Europäische Verlagsanstalt.

Korf, B. (2006). Hydraulischer Imperialismus, Geographie und epistemische Gewalt in Sri Lanka. In E. Kulke, H. Monheim, & P. Wittmann (Eds.), *GrenzWerte. Tagungsbericht Und Abhandlungen, 55. Deutscher Geographentag Trier 2005* (pp. 627–633). Deutsche Gesellschaft für Geographie.

Kurmanaev, A., & Trigo, M. S. (2020, November 9). *In Bolivia, a bitter election is being revisited*. The New York Times.

La Razón. (2014, September 28). En Mallasa hay 36 procesos por ocupación de terrenos ediles. Cedib.Org. https://www.cedib.org/noticias/en-mallasa-hay-36-procesos-por-ocupacion-de-terrenos-ediles-la-razon-28-09-2014/

Martins, N. (2006). Capabilities as causal powers. *Cambridge Journal of Economics, 30*, 671–685. https://doi.org/10.1093/cje/bel012

Mayring, P., & Fenzl, T. (2014). Qualitative Inhaltsanalyse. In N. Bauer & J. Blasius (Eds.), *Handbuch Methoden der empirischen Sozialforschung* (pp. 543–556). Springer VS. https://doi.org/10.1007/978-3-531-18939-0_38

Méndez, J., Burger, J., Correa, M., Weichert, M., & Tappatá, P. (2021). Informe sobre los hechos de violencia y vulneración de los derechos humanos ocurridos entre el 1 de septiembre y el 31 de diciembre de 2019. GIEI – Grupo Interdisciplinario de Expertos Interdependientes. https://embassyofbolivia.nl/ootsegla/2021/08/2021-GIEI-Bolivia-informe-final.pdf

Mendoza, R. (2014). Interview. In Cordova Suxo, M. F. (2021). *Vivir en el Conflicto: La relación conflicto - desarrollo, en el caso del Macrodistrito VI-Mallasa, municipio de La Paz* [Master Thesis, Universidad Mayor de San Adrés]. https://doi.org/10.13140/RG.2.2.22265.54884.

Municipal Government of La Paz (GAMLP). (2020). *Objetivos de Desarrollo Sostenible*. Retrieved January 13, 2021, from http://sitservicios.lapaz.bo/sit/ods/objetivos.html.

National Congress of the Republic of Bolivia. (1912). Law: Provincia «Murillo». -Se da esta nueva denominación a la provincia del Cercado del departamento de La Paz, Pub. L. No. GOB-38 (1912). https://www.derechoteca.com/gacetabolivia/ley-17-10-1912-3-del-17-octubre-1912/.

National Institute of Statistics Bolivia (INE). (2013). CENSO 2012 de Población y Vivienda. *Base de datos*, Retrieved July 21, 2021, from https://nube.ine.gob.bo/index.php/s/YjT4QxyKqeYsYFf/download.

Paz Estenssoro, V. Presidente Constitucional de la República de Bolivia (1956). Supreme Decree No. 4309 06th of February. 'Parque Nacional de Mallasa. Se lo declara de utilidad y necesidad pública así como las aguas del Choqueyapu y otros. Gaceta Oficial de Bolivia.

Plurinational Legislative Assembly. (2010). "Framework Law on Autonomies and Decentralization 'Andrés Ibañez'", No. 031. Gaceta Oficial de Bolivia, 19 de Julio de 2010.

Quispe, J. (2016, April 8). Mecapaca señaliza Mallasilla y La Paz rompe diálogo por límites. La Razón. https://www.la-razon.com/sociedad/2016/04/08/mecapaca-senaliza-mallasilla-y-la-paz-rompe-dialogo-por-limites/.

Revilla, C. (2011). Understanding the mobilizations of Octubre 2003, dynamic pressures and shifting leadership practices in El alto. In N. Fabricant & B. Gustafson (Eds.), *Remapping Bolivia: Resources, territory and indigeneity in a Plurinational state* (1st ed., pp. 121–145). SAR Press.

Rivera Cusicanqui, S. (2010). *Oprimidos pero no vencidos. Luchas de campesinado Aymara y qhechwa 1900–1980*. Hisbol.

Rojas, R. C. (2015). *Conflictividad en Bolivia (2000–2014) ¿Cómo revertir la normalización de la presión social?* Friedrich Ebert Stiftung-Bolivia (FES).

Sayer, A. (1992). *Method in social science: A realist approach* (2nd ed.). Routledge.

Sayer, A. (2000). *Realism and social science*. Sage.

Sayer, A. (2004). Why critical realism? In S. Fleetwood & S. Ackroyd (Eds.), *Critical realist applications in organisation and management studies* (pp. 6–20).

Tapia, L., & Chávez, M. (2020). *Producción y reproducción de desigualdades Organización social y poder político*. CEDLA.

Thomson, S. (2002). *We alone will rule: Native Andean politics in the age of insurgency*. University of Wisconsin Press.

UNDP. (2005). Informe de Desarrollo Humano Bolivia 2002. https://www.undp.org/es/bolivia/publications/informe-de-desarrollo-humano-2002

UNDP. (2018). Informe de Desarrollo Humano Bolivia 2018. https://annualreport.undp.org/2018/es/

UNDP-PAPEP. (2013). *Understanding Social Conflict in Latin America*. https://www.undp.org/sites/g/files/zskgke326/files/migration/latinamerica/Understanding-Social-Conflict-in-Latin-America-2013-ENG_0.pdf

UNIR. (2021). *Infografías Enero - Junio 2021* [Infographic]. Fundación UNIR Bolivia. Retrieved February 01, 2022, from https://analisisdeconflictos.unirbolivia.org/wp-content/uploads/sites/4/2022/01/Infoconflictos-diciembre-2021.pdf

Valdés, K. (2016, April 1). Mecapaca rechaza referéndum por límites. La Razón. https://www.la-razon.com/sociedad/2016/04/01/mecapaca-rechaza-referendum-por-limites/.

Vidal-Koppmann, S. (2005). La ciudad privada: nuevos actores, nuevos escenarios ¿nuevas políticas urbanas? Revista Electrónica de Geografía y Ciencias Sociales, IX. http://www.ub.edu/geocrit/sn/sn-194-15.htm.

Weisbrot, M. (2020, September 18). Silence reigns on the US-backed coup against Evo Morales in Bolivia. The Guardian. https://www.theguardian.com/commentisfree/2020/sep/18/silence-us-backed-coup-evo-morales-bolivia-american-states.

Zuazo, M. (2009). *¿Cómo nació el MAS-IPSP? La ruralización de la política en Bolivia*. Friedrich Ebert Stiftung-Bolivia (FES).

Radical Politics in Post-Conflict Settings

Stratis Andreas Efthymiou

1   Introduction

Much is said about anti-EU, racist, anti-immigration discourses when discussing radical right European parties. This chapter will explore how radical far-right ideological agendas can emerge in contemporary post-conflict settings. It does so through the case of the leading radical right party in Cyprus, ELAM, an abbreviation in Greek for National Popular Front (in Greek: Εθνικό Λαϊκό Μέτωπο/ΕΛΑΜ, *Ethniko Laiko Metopo*/ELAM). ELAM is the first and largest radical far-right party in Cyprus after the island's war and division in 1974, making Cyprus a good case study examining radical ideology in a post-conflict setting. The Cyprus Problem is a prolonged conflict between Cyprus and Turkey and stands as the last unresolved issue between Greece and Turkey following the Ottoman Empire's collapse. The politico-military and para-military actions of radical far-right movements in the 1970s led to the war and subsequent division of the island into two monoethnic areas. Therefore, the emergence of ELAM carries historical, political, and social weight in a community that has suffered the consequences of radical politics for the last 47 years. ELAM's presence is an integral discursive mechanism of the conflict's changing politics and Europeanization of Cypriot society and state. It is the counter-discourse to a European Union state with open borders.

Conflict is something very dynamic that keeps changing. We tend to think of conflict as something static, and indeed, the conflict between Cyprus and Turkey and, similarly, the conflict between North and South Korea, both seem like they have been frozen in time. However, significant changes to the conflict politics have occurred since the accession of Cyprus to the EU (Efthymiou, 2019; Vassiliou,

S. A. Efthymiou (✉)
London Policing College, London, UK
e-mail: Stratis.Efthymiou@LondonPolicing.co.uk

2004). The opening of the internal borders (Demetriou, 2007) mainly related to the security felt by the general population on both sides of the divide. It was precisely the changing post-conflict context that opened the space for the formation of radical far-right organisations.

ELAM began as a small party with trivial political power. In 2016, it entered the Cyprus House of Representatives with two members of parliament (out of the 56). ELAM's continuing support growth translated into four seats in the parliament in the 2021 election. ELAM garnered 6.8% of the vote, narrowly replacing the Movement of Social Democrats (Edek) as the fourth biggest political force in the island's Greek Cypriot party system for the first time in 45 years (Smith, 2021). Looking at the Cypriots who supported ELAM in the elections (Data.gov.cy, 2017), one can easily observe the distinctive variation of political orientations and previous political affiliations. Similarly, Zanotti and Rama (2020) observed that the supporters of Vox in Spain did not necessarily hold xenophobic, pro-race supremacy or anti-EU beliefs. Arguably, ELAM drew much of its support by challenging the long-standing dominance of mainstream parties and, at a time, as the analysis will later show, the general Cypriot public felt deeply disappointed for quite some time by the political leadership in terms of making progress on the Cyprus Problem. Indeed, the ability of the party's leadership to strategically take advantage of anti-establishment popular resentment (see Sigmalive, 2013) has scaffolded its steep growth, resulting in ELAM's voters more than doubling in five years (2011–2016), from one parliamentary election to the other (Parliamentary Elections: Official Results, 2011, 2016).

The recent history of fascism and authoritarian regimes still vividly resonated in Southern European states and rendered little discursive space for the rise of far-right parties observed elsewhere. However, the legacy of authoritarianism and the absence of post-industrial welfare states perhaps limited the electoral wish for the far-right (Ellinas, 2010, p. 38; Kitschelt, 1995, pp. 52–54). As Ellinas (2014, p. 543) explains, post-authoritarian far-right groupings were absorbed by the mainstream right or relegated to the fringes of the political system with minimal voter support. The understanding that it is the extraordinary conditions Southern European countries such as Greece, Spain, and Portugal faced in the past years that led to the breakthrough of their respective far-right parties could be the extent of post-conflict settings. Thus, while Greece experienced an outbreak of its sovereign debt crisis, it received an international bailout with associated austerity measures, which pushed the country into one of the deepest post-war recessions. Similarly, Cyprus faced extraordinary conditions as a post-conflict divided society after opening its internal borders and accession to the EU that allowed the discursive space and perhaps created a discursive configuration in which the need for a far-right party was deemed by society as necessary.

This chapter proceeds in the following steps. I first discuss the methods used to collect the data on which the analysis draws. What follows is a discussion of how radical politics implicates the Cyprus Problem. I then move forward to illustrate the sociopolitical backdrop against which the ELAM successfully seized the opportunity to emerge, in a political landscape where radical politics where in a fast hibernation since the division of the island in 1974. As I will show ELAM emerged after the crossing of citizens across the internal divide was made possible for the first time after 37 years. The analysis shows how ELAM, although perceived as the fraternal party of the Greek Golden Dawn at its inception, distanced from its Greek counterpart and adapted its agenda to the post-conflict setting. I conclude the chapter by providing transferable lessons from the case study.

2   Methods: Investigating Radical Politics in Post-conflict Settings

The perceived fighting spirit in the national struggle was undermined after the opening of the borders and after 50 years of unsuccessful international peace negotiations. As in the case of post-war Sri Lanka (Ramasamy, 2021), such undermining is a potential driving factor in propelling radicalisation in the post-war scenario. According to Bustikova and Kitschelt (2009), legacies of past mobilisation under communist rule affect the potential for radical right-wing politics across the post-communist region. They claimed that in countries with a gift of deep post-conflict nationalism mobilised and supported by the state and the larger society, an environment of general societal dissatisfaction with the political efforts for a peace settlement creates a most fertile breeding ground for the radical right.

I draw on elite interviews that I conducted in Cyprus with radical right politicians in 2011, as well as on the content analysis of their party materials and of newspaper coverage of ELAM from 2011 to 2021. I conducted extended elite interviews in Cyprus with the acting representative of ELAM. In my analysis, I also indirectly draw from elite interviews conducted with other radical right political organisations and situate the analysis within Cyprus' broader radical right political space. The article focuses on ELAM, as it is the radical right organisation that has become the most successful, yet other organisations are currently active, too. The Nationalist Democratic Party (EDHK) is of special attention, as its President, Loucas Stavrou, founded ELAM together with Christos Christou, current president of ELAM, and then left the party to create EDHK. DRASIS-KES is also of special attention as, while it's the oldest youth radical right political organisation created in 1973 before even the division of the island, a lot of ELAM's leading members were leading members of DRASIS-KES before ELAM was created. Furthermore, interviews also took place with the president or a representative of NEDHSY, the youth section of the DHSY right-wing political party, which is the party in government, and METWPO, the independent radical right political youth group which has become very active in the UK student population, as the UK is the second most popular destination for Cypriots to study after Greece.

In terms of the content analysis of newspaper coverage, I compiled all articles from all five daily newspapers in the Greek language and one in English, from first January 2011 to 30th July 2021, that contained a reference to the keywords in Greek and English: ELAM (in Greek: Εθνικό Λαϊκό Μέτωπο/ΕΛΑΜ). The newspapers by readership numbers in declining order are Phileleftheros (in Greek: Ο

Φιλελεύθερος, 26,000 copies daily), Alitheia (In Greek: Η Αλήθεια, meaning 'The Truth', 11,000 copies), Simerini (in Greek: Η Σημερινή, 9000 copies), Haravgi (Greek: Χαραυγή, meaning 'Dawn', 9000 copies) and Politis (in Greek: Πολίτης, 7000 copies). The next most widespread newspaper is Makhi (in Greek: Μάχη, meaning 'Battle' or 'Struggle'), with close affiliation to radical right-wing and nationalist ideas, which is a weekly one. Furthermore, the Cyprus Mail, the fifth, was included in the sample as the only English-language daily newspaper published. When choosing the daily newspapers, I was aware that a broad spectrum of political ideologies is represented in the sample. In Cyprus Newspapers, I take a political orientation concerning conflict politics (Christophorou et al., 2010; Karlekar & Marchant, 2008).

My positionality also rendered me a particular discursive space from which to analyse far-right radicalism in Cyprus. I grew up in Cyprus shortly after the war in a political family that was involved in creating the Cyprus peace movement. The movement was considered radical because, while the general society was supporting a nationalist and militarist solution to the Cyprus Problem, the social circles where I grew up thought that Turkish Cypriots were our brothers and we needed to find a peaceful solution. The Cyprus Peace movement was, at the time, the first movement to adopt a somewhat feminist agenda in Cyprus, so from a young age, I began reflecting on both nationalism and gender. Moreover, these circles defined themselves in opposition to right-wing populism and its representatives.

The following sections will illustrate the rise of ELAM as the first radical far-right political power after the war and how the party managed to grow its support by adapting to the changing post-conflict context.

3 Case Study

3.1 How Radical Politics Implicate in the Cyprus Problem

To better understand ELAM's development, it is important to place it within the Cyprus Problem shaped after the island's division in 1974. The Cyprus Problem revolves around the fact that there are two main ethnic populations on the island: the Greek and Turkish Cypriots. In 1974, the radical right Greek Cypriot political space that ELAM represents today, in conjunction with the end-time military regime of Greece, overthrew the Cypriot government, aiming to unite Cyprus and the Greek state into one, and thus creating an enlarged Greece. Turkey invaded as a response and occupied the northern part of Cyprus, making it a puppet state recognised only by Turkey and Pakistan. The violent intervention of radical political movements in the Cypriot ethnic landscape led to the country being divided by the huge internal border that stretches across it. For almost 40 years, none had crossed the border. Cyprus is heavily militarised; the global militarisation index systematically ranks Cyprus as one of the most militarised countries. In 2020, Cyprus was ranked 13th in the world and fourth in Europe most militarised country by the Global Militarisation Index (Global Militarisation Index, 2020).

Growing up in Cyprus, I experienced first-hand how nationalist and militarist ideas become naturalised through key state institutions like schools and the army. Moreover, because I grew up in a political family involved in the leadership of the peace movement, this experience provided me with discursive space for reflection on the culture of nationalism that state institutions and popular culture endowed with the generations that followed the war. At the same time, the agenda mobilised by the social circles in which I grew up incited deep criticism towards right-wing radicalisation, instigating my interest to understand it, rather than reject it. In the southern part, there was always mystery about what lay on the other side (Said, 1978), accompanied by the fear that Turkey would occupy the country. The post-conflict situation was all about intelligence and spying on each other. Because the Greek Cypriot society blamed parties with radical right agendas for causing the war and division of the island, they became marginalised, silent in political discourse, and did not form a political party after the war. In Cyprus, radical far-right politics appeared shortly after the island's independence in 1960, arguing against autonomy and supporting the unification (in Greek: Ένωσις) of Cyprus with Greece. At that time, the National Organisation of Cypriot Fighters (EOKA-B), a Greek Cypriot para-military organisation formed in 1971 aimed at unification (Efthymiou, 2019), mobilised the radical far-right ideology. The political agenda of ELAM today is mostly a continuation of the politics of that time. However, these agendas were not represented in an organised political formation in post-conflict Cyprus (Efthymiou, 2019). Instead, these factions remained marginal after the division, and they remained dispersed within already-existing right-wing parties, such as the Democratic Rally (DHSY).

Generally, the Greek Cypriot (GC) far-right has maintained a continuous stance against the Turkish Cypriot (TC) community, favouring an ethnically cleansed Cyprus that would be 'pure' Greek (Efthymiou, 2019). The history of radical politics developed in parallel between Cyprus and Greece because of the joint efforts of radical organisations in both countries. In terms of political participation, far-right parties in both Cyprus and Greece after the 1974 invasion of Cyprus by Turkey had traditionally remained on the margins of the political system, mainly because of 'the interconnection between the far-right and the Junta' (Alkiviadou, 2021a), whose actions led to the 1974 war. For this reason, in both countries and since the re-establishment of democracy in 1974, radical right organisations made poor attempts, mostly failing to leave any distinctive mark in Greek and Cypriot politics. In only a few years, radical political organisations acquired a significant say in the governance of Greece. Scholarly attention on political radicalism in Greece has primarily focused on the far-right fascist Golden Dawn party (Angouri & Wodak, 2014). Golden Dawn, which became the third-largest parliamentary party in Greece, drew significant support by promising revenge against the 'older political system' and providing 'hope for alternatives' (Ellinas, 2015). The research on Golden Dawn reflects a general increase in studies on the European radical right, neo-populist and neo-fascist parties (Carter, 2005). Golden Dawn, a party that stayed on the margins of parliamentary politics, made a breakthrough in 2010 amid the economic crisis (Ellinas, 2014). While fraternal parties stemming from the same ideological Greek and Cypriot roots gained immediate, significant popular support, the two parties, as this chapter will show, have had a different trajectory because ELAM operates in a post-conflict context.

ELAM was created instead in 2008 and had originally intended to register as Golden Dawn of Cyprus, but the authorities did not allow the name. Its symbol is a blue flag with a white cross charged in the centre with the party's emblem, represented here as an old black shield with a white sword pointing upwards. It describes its ideology as 'popular and social nationalism' (ELAM, 2022). While ELAM denies the National Socialist or Nazi label that others used to describe it, its direct affiliation to Greek Golden Dawn (which at a later point ended) makes no secret of an ideological lineage from interwar ideologies. Moreover, ELAM's ideology is reinforced by ELAM's anti-system and anti-Communist rhetoric. Such ideological elements unfold the backdrop of a post-conflict ultra-nationalist, the ideology that sees the Cyprus Problem as a manifestation of the antagonism created and sustained between Greece and Turkey following the collapse of the Ottoman Empire. As of May 2011, it has been approved as a legal political party by Cyprus authorities.

ELAM became very active from its inception around the island, and the founding leaders of ELAM were prominent members of the Greek Golden Dawn (Baider, 2017). Also, their youth section (called Youth Front) is tightly linked to the political youth Drasis-Kes, which was created in 1968 by Cypriot students studying in Athens and supporting the Union of Cyprus with Greece and Georgios Grivas, the then leader of the para-military organisation EOKA-B. ELAM and, similarly, its former Greek counterpart, Golden Dawn, draw from an existing discursive ideological stock of vigilantism and para-militarism, as they both have a long tradition in Modern Greek (Vrakopoulos & Halikiopoulou, 2019) and Cypriot history (Efthymiou, 2019). The military junta (1967–1975) is an example of political violence in Greece, expanding its influence to Cyprus. In 1967, the Greek military took power over the Cyprus National Guard. With the Republic of Cyprus essentially losing legitimacy over its army, President Archbishop Makar created the 'reserve force' with the role of protecting him from EOKA-B para-military (Efthymiou, 2019, p. 26). The military junta in Greece ordered a coup d'état on 15 July 1974 in Cyprus, and Turkey invaded in response and has since then occupied the northern third of the country. While vigilantism was directed towards political opponents, it is primarily aimed towards ethnic minorities and migrants.

Understanding the strategies employed by ELAM, as will be discussed in the sections below, would shed light on how far-right radicals can take advantage of the post-conflict context in today's sociopolitical landscape to gain popular support.

3.2 ELAM Emerging After Border Opening

In 2003, the border between the two sides opened. Most people never visited the other side or interacted with members of the TC community when they crossed to the South part of the border. However, what did happen is that those intense nationalist feelings were eased because the community could see that what lay on the other side was not so threatening, but just people (Efthymiou, 2019). Moreover, being part of the EU, specific nationalist arguments could no longer be uttered by the government. Thus, rhetoric shifted from being more patriarchal, militarist, and nationalist to being softer and more diplomatic. In this context, ELAM is a brother party of the Greek Golden Dawn. Because the Greek Golden Dawn is one of the most extremist political parties in Europe, it is generally seen as a neo-fascist party (Ellinas, 2014). Moreover, the party has been dissolved, and its leadership has been sentenced to prison. The court ruled that it is a criminal organisation, as they had also murdered Pavlos Fyssas, a young Greek anti-fascist rapper in 2013 (Kitsantonis & Magra, 2020). The Greek Golden Dawn became one of the most closely observed far-right parties in Europe and tried many times to expand to Cyprus, but holders of radical right ideology did not welcome it because they, although being nationalists and anti-communists, did not share Golden Dawn's neo-fascist agenda.

Standing in a world of ruins; the last faithful believers, a prominent slogan used by the ELAM, describes 'ruined' Cyprus and the 'believers' of the far-right ideology of ELAM (Efthymiou, 2019). The case of the Cyprus ELAM is particularly interesting because it emerged in 2008 shortly after the opening of the internal borders and the conduction of the peace referendum for reunification and the accession of Cyprus to the EU. The emergence of ELAM as a counter-discourse to the Cypriot society shows significant transformations since the opening of the borders, which have led to a re-adaption of notions of 'national struggle' and 'security'. Thus, ELAM emerges as a discursive reaction against the national struggle against Turkish 'occupation' re-adaptation. Moreover, I will illustrate that while ELAM began as a fraternal party of Golden Dawn, it gradually detached from its Greek paternal nationalist organisation, and by separating, it has been able to focus its agenda further on a radical nationalist post-conflict ideology and tone down the anti-immigration, racist, and anti-EU agendas of European radical far-right organisations. Moreover, while it has continuously grown, it holds the potential to accumulate additional political capital. In contrast to non-post-conflict societies, ELAM can draw from an existing stock of nationalist, militarist, and patriarchal ideas that characterise post-conflict societies.

ELAM's appearance in Cyprus' so-called accessible areas generated much debate and controversy in the last few years. It has emerged against the backdrop of the electoral success of radical far-right organisations in Europe that have recently raised concerns about the menace posed by fascism. Recent studies on radical far-right parties have developed one-dimensional analyses of racist agendas. Some scholars have attributed the rise of these parties to anti-EU, anti-immigration and pro-national sovereignty discourses (Hayton, 2010; Lynch & Whitaker, 2012) or the severity of the recent economic crisis (Dimitrova, 2009). In Cyprus, however, it is the changing post-conflict context that opened the space for radical far-right organisations. ELAM prioritises the border closure between the North and the South for national, social, political and economic prosperity. These groups perceive the government's role in the national struggle after the opening of crossing points on the internal divide, particularly its defence policy and continuous peace negotiations, together with the fading 'fighting spirit' in the community, as submissive and effeminate postures. Trimikliniotis and Demetriou (2011, p. 3) comment that ELAM is 'claiming that it is the only party that speaks for the "liberation of our enslaved lands". By embodying bold masculinity typical of radical far-right groups in Europe (see Hörschelmann, 2013, pp. 129–131), these groups claim to sustain the true nationalist spirit. In this context, ELAM has been created and has attracted more supporters. Thus, its emergence during a period of little public hope for the reunification of the country has allowed ELAM to capitalise on the legitimacy of the righteousness of the national struggle by projecting a solid anti-system message. By extension, they believe that a small group of men can drive the nation to liberation and continue the assertive masculine stance developed in the conflict, promoting men as defenders of the borders. In contrast to the general public and the state's disinvesting in nationalist masculinity (Onoufriou, 2010), commemorations and military parades publicly perform in a hyper-masculinized fashion during national celebrations and anniversaries uttered in a heroic-like discourse of 'active leading' (Foucault, 1983). Thus, their ideology is presented through hyper-masculinist politics and is embodied in militias' masculinity (Efthymiou, 2019).

3.3 Radical Far-Right Ideology and Post-Conflict Politics

Drawing on empirical research with the party, I will analyse the formation of ELAM by discussing how post-conflict politics interact with radical far-right ideology, and how the radical far-right ideology becomes contextualised within post-conflict settings. This chapter aims to put on the agenda that post-conflict settings provide a particular social, political, and cultural ground for forming and expanding radical far-right organisations. ELAM's 'struggle' emphasises the need to revive the post-1974 national struggle against Turkey in the form before the opening of the border and EU accession, whilst it is fused with radical far-right ideological elements. These parties' political discourse confronts any argument for a solution and peaceful co-existence of the communities as feminised, weak, and disgraceful. This position is largely shared by other GCs as well. The creation of ELAM presents the manifestation of radical far-right politics in Cyprus for the first time since 1974. ELAM's presence is an integral discursive mechanism of the conflict's changing politics and Europeanization of Cypriot society and state. It is the counter-discourse to a European Union state with open borders. The empirical research findings presented from the next section onwards would help to understand the particular way in which radical politics became adapted within post-conflict or conflict settings, and how these adaptations can be used by radical right parties to accumulate increasing political capital.

3.4 Close Borders

The opening of the borders was a discursive opening for Golden Dawn to make its appearance in Cyprus. After the opening of the borders a few members of Golden

Dawn moved from Greece to Cyprus to create ELAM (Alkiviadou, 2021b). The party assumes that the Cyprus national struggle for liberation from Turkey has lost its direction because of the opening of the borders. So, ELAM's primary goal is for the divide to close again so people cannot cross. ELAM states on their website that, as part of their political positions, they require: 'The immediate closure of the checkpoints that are the gate which maintains the occupation army and the 'pseudo-state" (ELAM, 2021b). As a representative of ELAM, (ROE: representative of ELAM) noted in an interview I conducted with him in 2011 in Nicosia, Cyprus: 'The barricades should be closed immediately! We are subsidising the conqueror financially'. ELAM shares their interpretation with the most prominent narrative in the accounts of the public that the opening of the borders and the subsequent crossings is a recognition of the 'pseudo-state' (Boedeltje et al., 2007, p. 18; Webster & Timothy, 2006, p. 176). They strongly assert the need for their immediate closure, as they expect this to restore the 'fighting spirit' (Efthymiou, 2014). Yet, ELAM further wants the borders' closure to restore a state of 'occupation', where war is rendered once again visible to the community's eyes (Efthymiou, 2019). The emergence of ELAM following the opening of the borders is a discursive response to this opening, the perception of the weakening of the 'fighting spirit' in the GC community, the undermined 'defence' and the weakening of masculinist militarist discourses of the national struggle (Efthymiou, 2019). This view is further supported by other far-right political organisations. For example, Stylianos Soteriou, the president of Drasis-Kes, states in an interview I conducted with him in 2011 in Nicosia, Cyprus:

> I believe that the borders should close; we will be holding an event next week in favour of the symbolic closing of the borders in order to promote and project some messages, we have done this three to four times in the past.

In their somewhat anachronistic yet also modified discourse of the 'national struggle', while the opening of the borders and the accession to the EU have eased the 'existential threat' in the general community, such notions of 'existential threat' are now mobilised by ELAM itself. As the representative of ELAM comments, in an interview I conducted with him in 2011 in Nicosia, Cyprus 'By opening the borders, we endangered our national sovereignty...they should be closed immediately! ... [it is] the moral duty that we have towards the dead and the ones that are not yet born'.

Whereas the financial crisis and the migration challenges faced by many EU states have been tightly linked to the rise of radical right-wing parties across Europe, my concern here is what made these political parties possible from within the post-opening of the borders in Cyprus. Characteristically, the representative of ELAM comments in the interview I conducted with him in 2011:

> We organise protests at the borders regarding the closing of the borders... we try to promote this as much as we can to make people understand all the negative aspects that brought the opening of the borders.

ELAM does not trust the destiny of the 'Greek nation' in the hands of the state of Republic of Cyprus (RoC), whose role in the national they perceive struggling and especially in armed defence today as submissive. The demand for the closure of the borders precisely and integrally relates to this non-re-adaptation of these groups' position under the new parameters. The refusal to accept the open borders allows them to continue mobilising their nationalist, militarist masculinist position against the existence of a 'should-be' un-crossable border (Efthymiou, 2019). Their stance against the borders allows them to continue mobilising the 'existential threat' and need for a 'nation-in-arms' (Rapoport, 1962), contingent on a potent army and discourses of heroism and collective virility as a defensive and offensive stance against the 'occupation' forces. The role of the government in the national struggle, that has modified its discourse to less nationalistic and more European, particularly in relation to defence policy and negotiations, and the fading 'these groups perceive fighting spirit' in the community as submissive and effeminate postures. Thus, they are protesting against change, as they favour preserving a masculinist nationalist struggle which, in Cyprus, is changing under the EU reality and opened borders. Their understanding of the armed part of the struggle extends beyond the mostly shared understanding of the public to fortify the National Guard (NG) to perform not only a defensive but also an assertive role. In this understanding, the revival of the Single Area Defence Doctrine (In Greek: Ενιαίο Αμυντικό Δόγμα Ελλάδας-Κύπρου) was expressed by them to be integral to the reiteration of the post-war position assertion. While ELAM has drawn much support from groups that feel resentment towards the political establishment by, for example, asking for state funding for political parties to stop (see Sigmalive, 2013), their supporters do not necessarily support this anachronistic junta-phile version of the national struggle.

In this understanding of the national struggle, they support the reconstruction of the imagined unified monoethnic community (Anderson, 1983) of a 'Greece of Greek Christians' that will 'not forget', predicated on the collective national struggle (In Greek: Ελλάς Ελλήνων Χριστιανών). This understanding of the need for such a community goes further than the public's criticism of the adoption of an individualist self-interested attitude because it directly links to their support of a society that produces the militarist and heroic types of masculinity, and, by extension, men that will sacrifice themselves for the community's interest, namely, the national struggle. Moreover, the masculinity of the parties discussed here, as Hörschelmann (2013, p. 138) has argued concerning Neo-fascist groups in Germany, challenges the assumption that non-hegemonic masculinities of these specific parties become subordinated forms of masculinity. These groups that personify distinct masculinity from the dominant definitions of transnational entrepreneurial masculinity (Connell, 1998), as described above, assert their hegemony over others.

Andreas Yiallouridis's appearance at the interview portrayed his political beliefs. He was a built-up muscular young man with a big moustache dressed in black. This created an interesting yet heavily charged environment at the coffee shop we were at, as the people sitting at tables around us kept staring at him. Moreover, by allowing me to enter his world, I began to understand the emotional depth of such nationalist and militarist beliefs. These feelings of deep emotional attachment to national sentiments can be interpreted through the primordial understanding of nations that often characterises nationalist thought and provides a sense of national kinship that extends beyond clear-cut kin connections (Puri, 2004, p. 44; Smith, 1986, p. 12; specifically on Cypriot nationalism see Papadakis, 2008, p. 5). In my endeavour to deepen my understanding of them, they also increasingly shared with me some of the difficulties they were facing in Cypriot society and political circles due to their extreme political beliefs. When working with extremist organisations of any sort, one has to, as Sluka (2007) points out, 'learn how to walk softly. Be sensitive to what sorts of questions may be asked and what sort of questions are taboo'. Having established rapport, taboo areas were disregarded and questions were asked that could have been previously considered appropriate. Moreover, the strong critical attitudes discussed above towards the state for the weakening of the national struggle and undermined condition of the NG are not only appearing among the groups representing a substantial shift from traditional social and military-defence values to the European and Western-like individualist attitudes and aspirations (see Efthymiou, 2019). Rather, they have also appeared—albeit articulated in inverse terms—among some of the most newly formed, ultra-nationalist political parties. Drawing from the case of Cyprus, it therefore appears that, when the state in a post-armed conflict, society moves away from the nationalist masculinist militaristic discourses it previously mobilised, and this can contribute to the masculinist militarisation of ultra-nationalist groups. The ideology that ELAM embodies, evokes, and mobilises is that the community has lost its true path to liberation. Yet this ideological position is not a discursive setback to a pre-opening of the borders type of radical right-wing ideology, as it is fused with neo-Nazi and junta-phile ideological elements.

Since ELAM clearly does not trust the state in doing the 'necessary' in the national struggle, it appears that they see it as their responsibility to become mobilised for action. ELAM is ideologically against the state, and their militant groups are constitutive of this ultra-nationalist neo-Nazi ideology. In the increasing political investigations into the para-military actions of these ultra-nationalist parties following the murder of Pavlos Fissas (in Greek: Παύλου Φύσσα) by a member of Golden Dawn, the fraternal party of ELAM, the issue of the militant groups of these parties has been intensely on the political agenda in Cyprus and Greece. In the scope of these political developments, the Cyprus Ministry of Justice has begun to investigate these groups under the charge that they organise para-military trainings in abandoned camps of the NG. On 24 September 2013, Philelepheros newspaper (see Phileleptheros, 2013) writes 'In the abandoned camp of LOK (translators note: LOK are a division of the special forces of the NG), … seems that trainings were taking place with weapons or replicas of weapons'.

In the scope of the weakening ideology of defence, these parties and groups have been formed who do not trust the destiny of the 'Greek nation' to the state, whose role in the national struggle, and especially in armed defence today, is perceived by them as submissive. Moreover, after ELAM entered the Cyprus parliament in 2016, and Golden Dawn was declared a criminal organisation by the Greek state in 2020,

ELAM, as the analysis will later show, adapted to these new realities of the post-conflict context (Panayiotou, 2020).

ELAM's grand objective is to reinstall awareness of the national struggle in the GC community as a way of combatting 'forgetting' and thus firing up the 'fighting spirit' (Efthymiou, 2019). As ELAM notes on its website, part of its main political objectives is: 'The immediate growing of fighting spirit in people and combating the climate of defeatism' (see ELAM, 2014). Moreover, in my interview with ELAM and other radical right-wing organisations, they used 'I do not forget, and I struggle' to illustrate the weakened 'fighting spirit', and how they have modified this slogan presents a central part of the struggle to which they aspire. The Greek Cypriot national slogan 'I do not forget and I struggle' (In Greek: Δεν Ξεχνω και Αγωνίζομαι) was the pivotal axis of the post-war Greek Cypriot identity. While, for the GCs, the 'other' living across the border was imagined, the 'other' side was part of the 'imagination' of what Cyprus became for the GC community following the partition. What was perceived to have been lost, existing across the border, was imagined or remembered. Therefore, memory, which in this instance takes the form of the official pronouncement of 'I do not forget' (Christou, 2006), has been a function of resistance (Hobsbawm & Ranger, 1983) in maintaining the GC nationalist imagination in the territory of Cyprus that GCs are no longer able to control and were also unable to visit. The resistance to forgetting maintained an 'imagination' that was ideologically turned into the need to 'I struggle' to 'return'; 'I do not forget, and I struggle' for the GC community. As said above, 'I do not forget' is now used by ELAM to illustrate that society has 'forgotten'. Characteristically the representative of ELAM (ROE) in an interview I conducted with him in Nicosia, Cyprus in 2011, commented 'Now it's an empty phrase and nothing more'.

ELAM has come to assert 'Never Forget'. The President of Drasis-Kes, in an interview I conducted with him in 2011 in Nicosia Cyprus, elaborated further, making clear the position of the broader Greek Cypriot radical right space, which ELAM shares, commenting that 'I don't consider [the GCs who cross the border] to be my enemies, they are victims of this situation we've forgotten, let's have a good time, it's over'.

The reference to the community as, 'let's have a good time, it's over' relates precisely to this criticism of the adoption of an individualist, self-interested attitude of the general community at the expense of the unified national struggle. However, ELAM mainly directs their disapproval of the current situation towards the government. Besides, ELAM had posted on their website a few years after the opening of the borders (see ELAM, 2012) that 'In recent years, the current political leaders follow a methodical policy leading mathematically from the 'I don't forget and I struggle' to 'delete memories and compromise'.

The disappointment of ELAM with the political direction in which the Cyprus Problem is heading, following the opening of the borders and the community's acceptance of this, has meant that they felt that the political organisation needed to be formed *to* restore their version of the post-war national struggle. This is also evident in that they are aiming to demonstrate that there are GCs who do not forget: 'Nobody Forgets Nothing is Forgotten' (In Greek: Κανενας Δεν Ξεχνα Τιποτα Δεν

Ξεχνιεται), this being a widespread slogan used in the rather newly formed ultra-right-wing area of the political scene of Cyprus. It is important to describe one of the many videos they have published, as these videos have been important in the identity and solidarity of the group. The youth division of ELAM organised an anti-occupation march through Nicosia (15 November 2010) and uploaded the video to their website with the title 'Student march for the condemnation of the pseudo 'state''. The video is introduced by titles appearing on the screen[1]:

> At the same time when some were in concerts with their 'brothers' *[translators note: meaning TCs]* and they were singing about 'a united country' as well as about Greek Turkish 'friendships'. At the same time, when some others were in coffee shops drinking their coffee, stress-free. At the same time, some others-the uncompromising ones-have come, disciplined, unrepentant and nationalist to agitate the calmness of the day (ELAM, 2011).

The video begins with ELAM youths marching in military alignments and chanting cadences loudly and uniformly. The video of the march interchanges with images and titles appearing on screen, and a military rhythmic song is playing in the background. The young men of ELAM chant:

> ELAM race, blood and honour
> > We will be back, and the earth will tremble
> > Morality? Blood!
> > Turks, Mongols, Murderers
> > The Turks of Cyprus are not our brethren
> > Listen to what the wolf said: we will return to
> > take our land one day.
> > Solomou, Isaak, the border is going to break!

The titles appearing on the screen, mentioned above, refer primarily to Cypriot society—which they condemn for its passiveness in the national struggle—and a call to join them in an assertive struggle. Their hyper-masculine, militarist performativity (Butler, 1990) asserts the masculinist heroic and militarist debilitated ideological link of the 'I struggle' of the Cypriot state and society while calling the public to join them in the struggle.

Therefore, the strong army in a post-conflict society (Enloe, 2007) is raised as a need by these parties, calling for an armed liberation of Cyprus from occupation. This need is embodied, retained and reiterated through expressions of masculinity, which have been historically central discourses of the ideology of defence and the idea of 'Greek self' assertion, previously mobilised strongly by the state. They aim to bring awareness of the fading ideals of heroism to the GC community. In this way, the necessary models are re-instilled in the national struggle, whilst they see themselves as the only ones who continue to honour national heroes substantially. As one of the most prominent slogans of ELAM states 'We honour, not forget', they clearly say that national heroes are the role models that should be followed for

---

[1] The video can be found in the ELAM's event video archives: https://elamcy.com/category/ekdiloseis/

liberating Cyprus. They organise anti-occupational marches, attend, and organise ceremonials and informative events about national heroes. As the ROE comments in an interview I conducted with him in 2011 in Nicosia, Cyprus, 'That's what we mean with 'We honour, not forget' because honour for a hero and a person is to find someone to carry on their purpose'.

The slogan aiming to motivate the community to 'honour, not forget' relates precisely to this criticism of adopting an individualist, self-interested attitude of the GC community at the expense of the unified national struggle. The masculinity of ELAM embodies and performs against the 'occupation' and the successive post-war governments of the RoC. ELAM sees negotiations to solve the so-called Cyprus problem as a feminised GC posture concerning 'occupation'. It discursively draws from the nationalist understanding encapsulated in the post-war slogan, that the only solution is a liberation' of the 'enslaved lands' (in Greek: Απελευθέρωση η μόνη λύση), to promote an assertive united stance by Cyprus and Greece against Turkey. Most symbolically, it was the only party that did not escort the RoC government in the five-member meeting for setting the plan for a potential new round of negotiations for the reunification of Cyprus in Switzerland in 2021. It appears that the state disinvestment from its post-war discourses, which sustained the masculinist nationalism and the broader social undermining of these discourses, gave space to the reiteration of masculinist militarist discourses by ultra-nationalist movements through a neo-fascist version, representing a discursive response to the perceived notion of feminisation of the national struggle (Efthymiou, 2019). Yet, while ELAM maintains a hardline position towards the Cyprus Problem, its political agenda towards other issues have been updated in such ways that distanced the party from its Greek counterpart, Golden Dawn.

As the next section will illustrate, ELAM distanced itself from its Greek counterpart, Golden Dawn, in an effort to gain further support within the post-conflict context.

3.5 Distancing from Greek Golden Dawn

ELAM initially spoke about race supremacy and harsh policies towards immigrants. However, by reading the public announcements of ELAM in the five newspapers I studied and on their website from 2011 to 2021, it becomes clear that they gradually began to tone down the typical radical right rhetoric and distance themselves from Golden Dawn's neo-fascist agenda. There are two reasons for this. Firstly, Cyprus is a small country, so radical political ideologies tend not to be accepted by the Greek Cypriot population. In the beginning, they were organising nationalist camps in the mountains, where they were training young men with military skills. In 2013, the Cyprus Ministry of Justice began to investigate these groups under the charge that they organised para-military trainings in abandoned camps of the NG. On the 24 September, 2013, Philelepheros newspaper (see Phileleptheros, 2013) wrote, 'In the abandoned camp of LOK (translators note: LOK are a division of the special forces of the NG), ... seems that trainings were taking place with weapons or replicas of weapons'.

They were also allegedly accused of assaulting some immigrants (Politis, 2010). But, these types of actions were quickly condemned by the Cyprus population, and they stopped. Secondly, it is much more challenging to raise arguments about race and immigration in a situation that is already extremely sensitive about these issues. For example, if we were to talk about racial differences in a post-conflict context, it would have meant that the differences between Turks and Greeks are natural. Moreover, how can you utter harsh immigration politics when the war internally displaces one-third of the population, and especially there are about one in four Cypriots to date still living in refugee housing (International Displacement Monitoring Centre, 2005). Thus, the racial supremacy argument would have gained a different dimension in a divided post-conflict context.

In the begging, ELAM said that it was the Cypriot wing of Golden Dawn. Slowly, it noted that it only shared its ideology, and in this was the Cypriot ideological representation of the doctrine in Cyprus. Then, it distanced more and more, saying they shared some ideological elements. ELAM found itself in a very precarious position, given that it was publicly understood to be the Golden Dawn fraternal party. At the same time, the latter's leadership was imprisoned, making headline news, and the court rule was positively commented on by Prime Ministers of key states across Europe. On that day, the British newspaper Guardian wrote, 'Neo-Nazi leaders of Greece's Golden Dawn sentenced to 13 years' (Smith, 2020). While Golden Dawn's leader, Nikolaos Michaloliakos, and MPs were sentenced to about 13 years each, over 57 defendants were convicted of murder, assault, weapons possession and either running or participating in the criminal outfit, amounting to a total of more than 500 years behind bars (Smith, 2020). In Cyprus, the most widely spread newspaper Phileleptheros Newspaper wrote that 'ELAM is flesh of the body of Golden Dawn and since Golden Dawn has been condemned by Greek justice as a criminal organization, ELAM cannot remain unharmed' (Panayiotou, 2020).

ELAM did not take sides with Golden Dawn after the court ruling. Rather, it disassociated from its former fraternal party. It was repeatedly certainly made clear by the leadership of ELAM that now claimed the two parties have no relation apart from occupying a similar ideological space in Cyprus and Greece. The president of ELAM commented that 'ELAM now moves in its course and strategy and that the decision to end the relationship with Golden Dawn is official'. ELAM was in the process of toning down the neo-fascist ideological parts of its agenda. This process reached its peak after the imprisonment of the leadership of Golden Dawn and the official cutting off from ELAM. In 2020, ELAM cut off its umbilical cord by publicly separating itself from its fraternal party, Greek Golden Dawn (AlphaNewsLive, 2020). This allowed it to take a political and ideological course on its own, which, as the next section will show, has been very much about adapting its agenda to the particularities of the post-conflict context.

3.6 Adapting the Agenda to the Post-Conflict Setting

ELAM had to be very careful about taking any radical stance towards social and political issues from its inception. The party was walking on ideological eggshells in a compassionate, towards radicalism, divided post-conflict setting. Given that it was the actions of the ideological ancestors of ELAM that led to the war and division of the island in 1974, it would be effortless to become ostracised. Yet, ELAM is increasingly gaining widespread support and political power. A part of its success is the ideological chameleon's ability [to conform camouflage], which is illustrated in becoming tuned to the contemporary post-conflict context. At large, the post-conflict Cyprus community did not favour any radical ideology. From the division of the island to the emergence of ELAM, there was no radical right or left party in Cyprus (Trimikliniotis & Demetriou, 2011).

At the same time, the public feels deeply disappointed by the parties that have ruled the country since the war and, most importantly, have led the peace negotiations (Efthymiou, 2019). ELAM managed to gain increasing popularity in this context by toning down aspects of its radical ideology, cutting away from Golden Dawn, and adopting a harder line than established parties on the Cyprus Problem, thus managing to express, in this way, the frustration of a segment of the Greek Cypriot population. With the increasing popularity in the post-conflict context, ELAM quickly adapted to usual parliamentary politics and joined in the mainstream political issues discussed in parliament and media. The media, which was highly critical of ELAM, also gradually relaxed its position towards the party.

Moreover, ELAM had to face one more significant challenge. No political party in post-conflict Cyprus held radical far-right views since the war. The political factions that voiced this kind of discourse in the 1960s and 1970s are considered responsible for the war. While in Europe, radical right-wing organisations were coming out and uttering intense agendas, ELAM had to be very careful about taking any radical stance towards social and political issues. It would have been straightforward to become ostracised. To put it in Baider's (2017) words, Christos Christou, the founder and leader of ELAM, has not opted for aggressive rhetoric like that of the leader of Golden Dawn (Michaliliakos) because, locally, that style would not take him very far. Notably, ELAM did not also adopt the imagery and symbols typical of European neo-nazi movements, like the flags with crosses. Yet, ELAM manoeuvres its ideology so that it is increasingly gaining widespread support and political power. A few years after its emergence, it became a parliamentary party and now has a small parliamentary team, which keeps growing (Reuters News Service, 2021).

Most importantly, ELAM, from an organisation that other political powers were completely sceptical about, and one which none wanted to talk to, is gradually gaining more political credibility and is taken more and more seriously by political powers and the general population. Many Cypriots do not subscribe to racist and anti-EU rhetoric, but they subscribe to nationalist ideas. Discursively speaking, ELAM tries to reverse the national struggle to its form before the border opening. It succeeded in this and focused on advocates for the same values that the GC population at large strongly supported in the few decades that followed the division of the island, such as heroism and spending much more on defence and armament, and it is finding a good amount of support in this.

ELAMs initially spoke about race supremacy, preserving the 'Greekness of island' and harsh policies towards immigrants. Notably, the party's 2011 manifesto proclaimed a strict Greek-centered public education and a zero-tolerance, anti-immigration policy on illegal immigration Ε.ΛΑ.Μ. (ELAM, 2011). Yet, today, the party's immigration policy focuses on holding a relatively hard line on immigration that concentrates mainly on 'thorough examination of applications for political asylum and immediate expulsion of those whose applications are rejected' (ELAM, 2021a). Most symbolic of their ideological adaptiveness to immigration, they initially asked for IDs when creating a food bank and only gave food to Greek Cypriots. Later on, they dropped this policy. It is much more challenging to raise arguments about race and immigration in a post-conflict situation that is already extremely sensitive about these issues. Journalists had repeatedly asked ELAM how they could ever adopt a hard stance towards immigration when so many Greek Cypriots became economic migrants after the war, and so many more were internally displaced people. Moreover, even though racial supremacy is toned down in ELAM's official discourse on immigration when compared to other European radical right parties, immigration is a post-conflict fusion becoming discursively parallelised with the Turkish occupation. In Baider's (2017) study of ELAM's immigration discourse and the dialectics of threat he argues that in its discourse, there is a vague commingling of the Cyprus problem with the immigration phenomenon. Thus, illegal immigrants are conflated with the 'occupiers', therefore the military Turkish presence in north Cyprus, in such ways that migration is seen as an 'invasion' similar to the 1974 one by Turkey. In this way, migration as invasion reverts to old fears, inscribing a well-established frightening scenario (IBID: 25). Moreover, ELAMs also tone town its masculinised rhetoric on the army. Initially, it spoke about adopting a much more militarised defence policy, involving more money spent on armament and the revival of Greece's 1990 single area defence doctrine. Today, it has adopted a more modest and realistic view of the limited defence capabilities that Cyprus currently has, arguing that the main focus should be 'strengthening the National Guard' (ELAM, 2021a). Most symbolically, in 2021, there is no section dedicated to defence on ELAM's website in the section regarding their policies.

Given the many corruption scandals made public in recent years involving the major Cypriot parties, anti-corruption political discourses are becoming popular in Cyprus politics. Most notably, President Nicos Anastasiades' administration (in power since 2013) has been badly hit by allegations of corruption linked to a controversial cash-for-passports scheme. ELAM sought the opportunity of circumstance and promoted itself as 'the only party to have never been involved in corruption'. It has helped transform the seashore city of Limassol with gargantuan apartment blocks, built with the sole purpose of luring investors (Smith, 2021). Given that it is a very newly established party, it successfully projected itself as one that has never been accused of corruption and is not part of the base political system of parties. The approach of easing typical neo-fascist rhetoric and focusing on anti-corruption is not entirely new. Both Matteo Salvini in Italy and Marine Le Pen in France attempted a similar policy shift to broaden support.

Any political organisation would have found it difficult to gain popularity and legitimacy in the political landscape of post-conflict Cyprus by mobilising a neo-fascist ideology. The holders of radical right ideology are primarily blamed for the events leading to the 1974 war and subsequent island division. ELAM has, in its thirteen years of existence, changed its doctrine from a typical neo-fascist one to an ultra-nationalist one that incorporates a hard line on the Cyprus Problem and an increasing focus on anti-corruption politics. ELAM initially spoke about race supremacy and harsh policies towards immigrants. But, today, it has dropped these aspects of its agenda and only holds a relatively hard line on immigration. Notably, ELAM has moved away from critical aspects of typical neo-fascist ideology and has officially cut away from Golden Dawn. By shifting its agenda towards focusing more on a hard line on the Cyprus Problem and anti-corruption, it adopted what can be termed an ultra-nationalist, post-conflict ideology. This ideological shift has allowed ELAM to gain increasing popular support, doubling its seats in the parliament and holding a solid potential to have a European Union Member of Parliament in the next elections. Still, it gives them a radical right-wing twist. For example, they believe that a small group of men can drive the nation to liberation, which is typical of radical far-right groups in Europe.

4 Conclusion

This article has argued that the emergence of radical far-right ideological agendas in contemporary post-conflict settings are intrinsically linked to the changing politics of the conflict created a political vacuum as the government's nationalist and militarist rhetoric was toned down. A radical right organisation was created to claim that space. Therefore, when looking at another context beyond Cyprus in terms of the emergence of radical far-right ideological agendas, particular attention needs to be directed to the radicalisation of movements during the change of conflict politics. Similarly, Ramasamy's (2021) analysis of pathways to radicalisation in the post-war context of Sri Lanka argues that policy measures considering prevention must address community grievances. In Cyprus, the community is grieving for a considerable investment it has made in the national struggle to liberate north Cyprus, which today, after almost 50 years of unsuccessful international peace negotiations and an undermined fighting spirit in the community after the opening of the borders, seems futile. The point of attention here is that anti-systemic politics in post-conflict societies could mean political violence towards the state and any political opponents of radicalism, thus hindering, on the one hand, the efforts made by the state for peace and its ability to act as an agenda in international politics to help bring peace to the country and, on the other hand, deepening political divisions within the country by mainstreaming any systemic culture where frustration towards the establishment turns into support for radical right politics. Another transferable lesson is that ELAM is continuously growing; it holds the premise to accumulate additional political capital. The potential for increasing popular support is because, in contrast to non-post-conflict societies, it can draw from an existing stock of nationalist, militarist and patriarchal ideas against the enemy characteristics of post-conflict societies. Thus, radical right organisations in post-conflict societies can distance themselves from typical radical right agendas and draw from another stock ideologically available in post-conflict settings.

The case of Cyprus is significant as a comparative case for other post-conflict contexts. Post-conflict societies are particularly vulnerable to political radicalisation, because as has been shown the grieving of what has been lost and the hope that it can be regained can be exploited by radical organisations at times when trust has been lost in mainstream parties. Moreover, divided post-conflict societies present an incredibly fertile ground for establishing radical organisations. Divided post-conflict societies have constructed 'enemy-within', which serves as a structured target for radical ideology to be projected against. Therefore, as we can learn from the case of Cyprus, particular attention needs to be directed towards the radicalisation of movements during the conflict politics change. While radical organisations can draw from an existing stock of nationalist, militarist and gender ideas against the enemy characteristics of divided post-conflict societies, they are presented with the opportunity to remove from this ideologically available stock and distance from typical radical right agendas. This particularity of divided post-conflict settings renders them especially vulnerable towards radicalisation, yet also presents a scene where radical organisations are rendered chameleon-like abilities and can grow faster and gain longevity. Cyprus offers a clear case of the vulnerability of divided post-conflict societies towards the growth and adaptiveness of radical organisations compared to other cultures because ELAM began as the representation of the Greek Golden Down in Cyprus. As of writing this chapter in late 2021, ELAM continues to grow, having outcasted mainstream political parties with a long history and holding much potential to gain further political power in the Cyprus divided post-conflict context.

References

Alkiviadou, N. (2021a, June 27). Golden Dawn and the rise of its 'sibling' Elam. *Cyprus Mail*. Retrieved July, 14, 2022, from https://cyprus-mail.com/2021/06/27/golden-dawn-and-the-rise-of-its-sibling-elam/

Alkiviadou, N. (2021b). The far-right in Greece: The elephant *and* the room. *Interdisciplinary Journal of Populism, 1*, 48–71.

AlphaNewsLive.(2020,June23).ΟΧρίστουεξηγεί:ΓιατίτοΕΛΑΜδιέκοψετιςσχέσειςμετηνΧρυσή Αυγή (ΒΙΝΤΕΟ). *AlphaNews.Live*. Retrieved August 7, 2020, from https://www.alphanews.live/politics/o-xristoy-exigei-giati-elam-diekopse-tis-sheseis-me-tin-hrysi-aygi-binteo

Anderson, B. (1983). *Imagined communities: Reflections on the origin and spread of nationalism*. Verso.

Angouri, J., & Wodak, R. (2014). 'They became big in the shadow of the crisis': The Greek success story and the rise of the far-right. *Discourse and Society, 25*(4), 540–565. https://doi.org/10.1177/0957926514536955

Baider, F. (2017). Thinking globally, acting locally: Analyzing the adaptation of mainstream supremacist concepts to a local socio-historical context (ELAM in Cyprus). *Journal of Language Aggression and Conflict, 5*(2), 178–204. https://doi.org/10.1075/jlac.5.2.02bai

Boedeltje, F., Houtum, H., & Kramsch, O. (2007). The shadows of no man's land: Crossing the border in the divided capital of Nicosia, Cyprus. *Geographica Helvetica, 62*(1), 16–21. https://doi.org/10.5194/gh-62-16-2007

Bustikova, L., & Kitschelt, H. (2009). The radical right in post-communist Europe. Comparative perspectives on legacies and party competition. *Communist and Post-Communist Studies, 42*(4), 459–483. https://doi.org/10.1016/j.postcomstud.2009.10.007

Butler, J. (1990). *Gender trouble: Feminism and the subversion of identity*. Routledge.

Carter, E. (2005). *Extreme right in Western Europe: Success or failure?* Manchester University Press.

Christophorou, C., Şahin, S., & Pavlou, S. (2010). Media narratives, politics and the cyprus problem. PRIO Report. https://www.prio.org/publications/7303.

Christou, M. (2006). A double imagination: Memory and education in Cyprus. *Journal of Modern Greek Studies, 24*(2), 285–306. https://doi.org/10.1353/mgs.2006.0019

Connell, R. W. (1998). Masculinities and globalization. *Men and Masculinities, 1*(1), 3–23. https://doi.org/10.1177/1097184X98001001001

Data.gov.cy. (2017). *Επίσημα Αποτελέσματα Βουλευτικών Εκλογών 2016 (Σταυροί Προτίμησης) [Official Results of Parliamentary Elections 2016 (Preference Crosses)]*. Retrieved May 20, 2020, from https://www.data.gov.cy/node/494?language=en

Demetriou, O. (2007). To cross or not to cross? Subjectivization and the absent state in Cyprus. *Journal of the Royal Anthropological Institute, 13*(4), 987–1006.

Dimitrova, K. (2009). The economic crisis closes in on Bulgarian Roma. *Roma Rights Quarterly, 1*, 39–43.

Efthymiou, A. S. (2014). Issues arising out the non-professionalization of the Cyprus National Guard: Positive motivations for enlistment. Government report. Ministry of Defence of Cyprus (distributed internally). Available online: (PDF) Army and society Positive motivations for enlistment (researchgate.net).

Efthymiou, A. S. (2019). Radical nationalism, militarism and masculinity after the opening of the border. In A. S. Efthymiou (Ed.), *Nationalism, militarism and masculinity in post-conflict Cyprus* (pp. 191–215). Palgrave Macmillan.

ELAM. (2011, March). A Greek: Δελτίο Τύπου - Βουλευτικές εκλογές 2011 ("Press release—Parliamentary elections 2011"). *ELAM's blog*.

ELAM. (2012). *ανθελληνικο κρατος* [Anti-Greek state]. ELAM. http://www.elamcy.com/tipos/chapters.html

ELAM. (2014). Διώξεις του καθεστώτος Αναστασιάδη. ELAM. http://www.elamcy.com/latest-articles/item/5150-diokseis-tou-kathestotos-anastasiadi.html.

ELAM. (2021a). *ΘΕΣΕΙΣ - Εθνικό Λαϊκό Μέτωπο (Ε.ΛΑ.Μ.)*. ELAM Policies. https://elamcy.com/theseis/

ELAM. (2021b). Όταν τα απαιτούσε το Ε.ΛΑ.Μ. μας έλεγαν ακραίους, ΚΛΕΙΣΤΕ και τα οδοφράγματα! - Εθνικό Λαϊκό Μέτωπο (Ε.ΛΑ.Μ.), ELAM Press Office. https://elamcy.com/otan-ta-apaitouse-to-e-la-m-mas-elegan-akraious-kleiste-kai-ta-odofragmata/

ELAM. (2022). *ΘΕΣΕΙΣ*. [online] Available at: https://elamcy.com/theseis/ (Accessed 20 October 2022).

ELAM (ELAM Blog) (in Greek). (2011, March 18). Archived from the original on 15 August 2011. Retrieved 19 August 2021.

Ellinas, A. (2010). *The media and the far right in Western Europe: Playing the nationalist card*. Cambridge University Press.

Ellinas, A. (2014). The rise of Golden Dawn: The new face of the far right in Greece. *Southern European Society and Politics, 18*(4), 543–565. https://doi.org/10.1080/13608746.2013.782838

Ellinas, A. (2015). Neo-Nazism in an established democracy: The persistence of Golden Dawn in Greece. *South European Society and Politics, 20*(1), 1–20. https://doi.org/10.1080/13608746.2014.981379

Enloe, C. (2007). *Ethnic soldiers: State security in divided societies.* Penguin Books.
Foucault, M. (1983). The subject and power. In H. Dreyfus & P. Rabinow (Eds.), *Michel Foucault: Beyond structuralism and hermeneutics* (2nd ed., pp. 208–226). University of Chicago Press.
Global Militarisation Index. (2020). *Global Militarisation Index (GMI)* [online]. Available at http://www.bicc.de/program-areas/project/project/ global-militarization-index-gmi-43/. Accessed 19 September 2020.
Hayton, R. (2010). Towards the mainstream? UKIP and the 2009 elections to the European parliament. *Politics, 30*(1), 26–35. https://doi.org/10.1111/j.1467-9256.2009.01365.x
Hobsbawm, E., & Ranger, T. (1983). *The invention of tradition.* Cambridge University Press.
Hörschelmann, K. (2013). Deviant masculinities: Representations of neo-fascist youth in eastern Germany. In K. Hörschelmann & B. van Hoven (Eds.), *Spaces of masculinities* (pp. 128–141). Routledge.
International Displacement Monitoring Centre. (2005). Cyprus: failure of political settlement prevents the displaced from repossessing their properties. Retrieved November 30, 2019, from https://web.archive.org/web/20070812185328/http:/www.internal-displacement.org/802570 8F004CE90B/%28httpCountrySummaries%29/404B5F063033BD4B802570C00056B6EA?OpenDocument&count=10000
Karlekar, K. D., & Marchant, E. (Eds.). (2008). *Freedom of the press 2007: A global survey of media Independence.* Rowman and Littlefield.
Kitsantonis, N., & Magra, I. (2020). *Golden Dawn found guilty of running criminal Organization in Greece.* New York Times. https://www.nytimes.com/2020/10/07/world/europe/golden-dawn-guilty-verdict-greece.html.
Kitschelt, H. (1995). *The radical right in Western Europe: A comparative analysis.* University of Michigan Press.
Lynch, P., & Whitaker, R. (2012). Rivalry on the right: The conservatives, the UK Independence Party (UKIP) and the EU issue. *British Politics, 8*(3), 285–312. https://doi.org/10.1057/bp.2012.29
Onoufriou, A. (2010). "Proper masculinities" and the fear of feminisation in modern Cyprus: University students talk about homosexuality and gendered subjectivities. *Gender and Education, 22*(3), 263–277. https://doi.org/10.1080/09540250903283413
Panayiotou, Y. (2020, October 18). Χρυσή Αυγή και ΕΛΑΜ. Philenews. https://philenews.com/f-me-apopsi/paremvaseis-ston-f/article/1039859/chrysi-avg-kai-elam.
Papadakis, Y. (2008). Narrative, memory and history in divided Cyprus: A comparison of school books on the history of Cyprus. *History & Memory, 20*(2), 128–148. https://doi.org/10.2979/his.2008.20.2.128
Parliamentary Elections 2011: Official Results. (2011). Retrieved June 28, 2020, from http://results.elections.moi.gov.cy/English/PARLIAMENTARY_ELECTIONS_2011/Islandwide
Parliamentary Elections 2016: Official Results. (2016). Retrieved June 28, 2020, from http://results.elections.moi.gov.cy/English/PARLIAMENTARY_ELECTIONS_2016/Islandwide
Phileleptheros. (2013). *Phileleptheros Newspaper.* Available at: http://cyprusnews.eu/newsitcykipros/1470318. Accessed on 24 September 13.
Politis. (2010, July 22). Racism went out in the Streets (Ο ρατσιμός βγήκε στους δρόμους). Politis Newspaper. Retrieved November 26, 2013, from.
Puri, J. K. (2004). *Encountering nationalism.* Blackwell.
Ramasamy, R. (2021). Youth radicalization and violent extremism: A study of pathways in the post-war context of Sri Lanka. *Journal of Youth Studies.* https://doi.org/10.1080/13676261.2021.2010684
Rapoport, D. C. (1962). A comparative theory of military and political types. In S. Huntington (Ed.), *Changing patterns of military politics* (pp. 71–100). Free Press.
Reuters News Service. (2021, May 30). Nationalist Elam gain big in parliament vote. *Cyprus Mail.* Retrieved July 14, 2022, from https://cyprus-mail.com/2021/05/30/nationalist-elam-gain-big-in-parliament-vote/
Said, E. (1978). *Orientalism: Western representations of the orient.* Pantheon.

Sigmalive. (2013, October 18). ΕΛΑΜ: Ζητεί κούρεμα στις κομματικές χορηγίες [ELAM: Demands a haircut for party sponsorships]. Sigmalive. Retrieved April 29, 2020, from https://www.sigmalive.com/news/local/71025/elam-zitei-kourema-stis-kommatikes-xorigies.

Sluka, J. A. (2007). Silent but still deadly: Guns and the peace process in Northern Ireland. In C. Springwood (Ed.), *Open fire: Understanding global gun culture* (pp. 56–73). Berg.

Smith, A. D. (1986). *The ethnic origins of nations*. Blackwell.

Smith, H. (2020, October 14). Neo-Nazi leaders of Greece's Golden Dawn sentenced to 13 years. *The Guarduan*. Retrieved August 25, 2021, from https://www.theguardian.com/world/2020/oct/14/greece-golden-dawn-neo-nazi-prison-sentences

Smith, H. (2021, May 30). Cyprus election: Far-right party linked to Greek neo-Nazis doubles vote share. *The Guarduan*. Retrieved August 25, 2021, from https://www.theguardian.com/world/2021/may/30/far-right-cyprus-election-parliament

Trimikliniotis, N., & Demetriou, C. (2011). *Accept Pluralism. Tolerance and cultural diversity discourses in Cyprus*. European University Institute, Florence, Robert Schiman Centre for Advanced Studies. Retrieved from http://cadmus.eui.eu/bitstream/handle/1814/19789/ACCEPT_2011_01_WP1_background_report_Cyprus.pdf?sequence=1

Vassiliou, G. (2004). EU entry: Catalyst for a Cyprus solution. *Global Dialogue, 5*(3/4), 1–8.

Vrakopoulos, C., & Halikiopoulou, D. (2019). Vigilantism in Greece: The case of the Golden Dawn. In T. Bjørgo & M. Mareš (Eds.), *Vigilantism against migrants and minorities* (pp. 183–198). Routledge.

Webster, C., & Timothy, D. J. (2006). Travelling to the "other side": The 'occupied' zone and 'Greek Cypriot' views of crossing the green line. *Tourism Geographies, 8*(2), 162–181. https://doi.org/10.1080/14616680600585513

Zanotti, L. & Rama, J. (2020, March 2). Spain and the populist radical right: Will Vox become a permanent feature of the Spanish party system? *LSE blog*. Retrieved April 30, 2020, from https://blogs.lse.ac.uk/europpblog/2020/03/02/spain-and-the-populist-radical-right-will-vox-become-a-permanent-feature-of-the-spanish-party-system/

Uncovering the Complexities of Radicalization and Violence: A Summary

Daniel Beck

Current political developments increasingly show the necessity of a deeper and more nuanced understanding of the term "radicalization", its dynamics and various forms, as well as the need for insight into the various forms of associated violence on a global level.

This edited volume therefore focused on spheres of consensus, disagreement and doubts or unclarity in peace and conflict research in regard to the causes and dynamics behind "radicalization", specifically connected to violence. In its three parts, our edited volume highlighted the areas of theocratization of radicalization and its interaction with violence, as well as the area of prevention and measures against radicalization, and, finally, it put a spotlight on new and original case studies in an evidence-based way of studying the phenomena. In general, this edited volume provides no reinvention but a substantial advancement.

The nine contributions show the connection of radicalization and violence in societies around the globe with a focus on various levels of analysis. As mentioned in our introduction, a definition of the key terms is crucial, but quite hard to achieve in times when "radical" and "radicalization" have become an inflammatory aspect of the common vernacular, which contributes to difficulties in being precise about the specific scientific meaning and interpretation of the terms. The same is true for violence, where different forms are observable and manifest in the examples provided (see, e.g., Córdova Suxo, this volume). Many of the case studies show "manifestations of symbolic, structural and epistemic violence in the causality of a radicalization episode" (Córdova Suxo, this volume).

D. Beck (✉)
Institute for Social Sciences, Otto-von-Guericke University Magdeburg, Magdeburg, Sachsen-Anhalt, Germany
e-mail: Daniel.beck@ovgu.de

© The Author(s), under exclusive license to Springer Nature Switzerland AG 2023
D. Beck, J. Renner-Mugono (eds.), *Radicalization and Variations of Violence*, Contributions to International Relations,
https://doi.org/10.1007/978-3-031-27011-6_11

Models of radicalization processes and their relation to violence, as well as measures for their prevention, are largely related to the individual realm, which was argued in several contributions. As has been shown, radicalization can describe the development process from extreme belief structures to ideologies. A further understanding of radicalization refers to the process of diminishing acceptance of an existing order, which might be associated with a corresponding willingness to act, often called extremism (Kaluza, 2022).

1 Examining Factors and Causes for the Constitution of Radicalization

The contributors to this work dealt with distinct possibilities for furthering and developing research in regard to theories, theory tests and methods on violence and radicalization. One suggestion, which is not necessarily new, but has received renewed support, is in respect to the necessity of pushing beyond isolated factors for radicalization processes and, instead, examining manifold enabling factors and potential risks more collectively.

Originally, we used the term "collective violence" (Tilly, 2003) to invite scholars to our conference in 2019 because of the need to use a specific and distinct term. However, the question remains as to when exactly violence can be seen as collective (de la Roche, 2001). It seems more adequate and functional to speak of "organised political violence", as Clément does in this edited volume, and to look at the whole spectrum of types of violence and the various connections between violence and radicalization by calling these "the variations of violence". In the first contribution, Clément explores the interconnection between organized political violence and narrative emotionalization. At the same time, she questions more conventional approaches to radicalization.

Nevertheless, when dealing with the term "radicalization", it becomes more and more obvious, how different the understandings are, and how much they are shaped by different contexts. As pointed out in the introduction and reinforced by several of the contributions, "radicalization" is highly context dependent and exists as a rather unprecise term in everyday language, as it is still frequently seen as synonymous with "terrorism". Regarding terminology, there is a difference between radicalization and extremism, and one also must make a distinction "between Foreign Fighters and transnational or national terrorism" (Strunk, this volume).

In particular, the mechanisms behind radicalization are often controversial topics of discussion, as Merhej and Fahed show in the second contribution. Their chapter argues for "a lesser role of ideology in de-radicalization processes and political violence". While ideology and individual paths of radicalization (McCauley & Moskalenko, 2017) are often seen as key aspects and components of violence, the contributions in this volume showed a broader picture and questioned the role of ideology (see Merhej & Fahed, this volume). As a consequence, it has been shown that it is difficult to generalize about individual radicalization processes because they are "unique, personal and nonlinear" (Merhej & Fahed, this volume), while the role of groups still can be seen as vital and fundamental in the radicalization processes. For Merhej and Fahed, there are two new mechanisms of radicalization visible: "I did not know – I did not trust & Normality of violence" (Merhej & Fahed, this volume).

Each of our contributors addressed the problematic developments from their own regional and theoretical area of expertise, and each of the nine chapters addressed the connection between radicalization and violence. The nine chapters do so by analyzing the connection of violence and radicalization in the following relations:

Emotions and narratives (Clément)
Foreign fighters and protest (Strunk)
Radicalization and the role ideology (Merhej & Fahed)
Governmental narratives as an adequate reaction to actions of radical groups (Tichatschke)
The potential of peace education (Groppe)
The prognosis regarding an escalation of violence in specific situations (Unverdorben)
The potential of legislative actions and land conflicts for radicalization (Córdova Suxo)
The stereotypical representation of female fighters in violent actions and their motivations (Yelpaze)
The dangers and chances for radical actors and parties in post-conflict societies (Efthymiou)

2   Analysing Violence and Radicalization in Empirical Case Studies through Innovative Methods

From a methodological point of view, this edited volume can be seen as innovative, as it deals with new suggestions, and further develops existing ideas or tests established outcomes by challenging their plausibility (see, e.g., contributions by Strunk; Unverdorben; Merhej).

The chapters also showed a clear need for further innovations and developments regarding methods. In various empirical studies, the authors brought up a variety of methodological expertise in the areas of visuality as well as film and video (Yelpaze), narratives and discourse (Clément; Tichatschke), interviews (Merhej & Fahed) and the use of personal experiences (Efthymiou) and observations.

As an outcome, incorrect causalities were uncovered when it was refuted that protests are an enabling factor for foreign fighters (Strunk), and it was shown that the role of ideology in explaining radicalization is rather limited. Furthermore, a sole focus on recorded video scenes of violence does not enable a prediction about the escalation of violence when the concrete levels of context are unknown.

The examples for the role of visuality are films (Yelpaze) and video footage from demonstrations and confrontations of the Yellow Vest movement (Unverdorben). Both clearly show how visuality can provide further insights for conflict research when done in a progressive way. Most media coverage of female militancy perpetuates pre-existing conceptions and fails to provide a deeper understanding of women's political violence. Further research into movies about female fighters may reveal further information about the female Kurdish soldiers from their own point of view, and add to the field of study that deals with women and political violence from non-Western viewpoints (Yelpaze, this volume).

In her contribution, Yelpaze deals with the representation of Kurdish female combatants in the media. She shows a problematization of the representation of women in conflict because women "are presented as novel, exotic characters without a historical framework, victimized granted the right to fight at only one frozen moment and context". The analyzed films portray female combatants in a way "that they engage in political violence due to personal reasons rather than the ideological ones, that they are sentimental and take decisions sentimentally rather than rationally and that the major reason behind women's violence is their victimization during the war" (Yelpaze). Further investigation is needed regarding the representation of their motivations.

Micro-level studies of violence carry out a visual analysis of video footage of violent confrontations (Unverdorben). But, in order to follow up on these leads, one should consider data in addition to the visual analysis used here.

3 Levels of Analysis

The focus in studies of radicalization is on the individual level, but the influence of groups is still vital. In other words, context is often missing in contemporary studies, which tend to focus more on the micro level. Critics thus see an empirical deficit in addressing the causes of organized violence applications at a micro (intrapersonal), meso (interpersonal), and macro (social and group) level. These points have been addressed here, as for example, Unverdorben shows in his contribution.

And, the case study of Bolivia can, for example, be seen "as a microcosm of the general situation, reflected and reproduced the polarization that existed throughout the country" and has made it possible to investigate a small-scale, non-representative example of a territory that focuses on dynamics, which are duplicated on a much larger scale (Córdova Suxo).

Both publications include a problematization of micro-theories of violence, as interactional theories focus too much on micro-sociological situations and, as a consequence isolate, these from structures and social conditions. Other context and background information which influences personal and collective perceptions is often ignored. Further information is needed, like statements of protestors, interviews, or quantitative data sets. This would enable the acquisition of more sophisticated insight and interpretations of micro-situational dynamics and feelings.

In the Yellow Vest movement, a certain kind of tension can be seen, as an escalation of violence would be the common expectation. Consequently, the non-escalation of violence comes as a surprise, given that the scene analyzed exhibits all elements of other situations that lead to forward-panic. As the example shows, both micro and macro perspectives have to be integrated. The video footage includes exhibits the circumstances that would indicate the devolution into a needless use of force, but, contrary to expectation, this escalation of violence does not occur (Unverdorben this volume).

4 Radicalism and Protest

Several contributions analyzed the role of protest and its relation to radicalization. In this volume, the role of protest was questioned, in the mobilization on theoretical and empirical grounds" (Strunk this volume). The author argues for putting much more emphasis on opportunity structures and frames. They uncovered logical inconsistencies in existing research, where studies suggest "a positive association between protest and the mobilization of Foreign Fighters", like in Sterman and Rosenblatt (2018). The logic here is that protest and domestic terrorism are driven by discontent towards one's own government, which is different for foreign fighters as foreign fighting is most likely not a result of domestic discontent and not related to political activism. It can be said that protest events cannot predict Foreign Fighter mobilization, and that a clear conceptual distinction between domestic terrorism and foreign fighting is necessary.

More collective forms of violence can be seen in the Yellow Vest movement, which provides another prominent example of obvious connection between violence, radicalization, and protest, but where eruptions of violence are hard to predict.

Iconic visual "sequences under the Arc de Triomphe are in no way peculiar to this movement", but more to the normal level of violence at organized demonstrations. More context information would offer "possibilities to address drivers of collective violence, than interactionalist theories by themselves" (Unverdorben this volume).

5 Discursive Component

Throughout the edited volume, "extremism" and "radicalization" are taken as a communicative issue (see, e.g., Tichatschke, this volume) and measures against a radicalization of the public discourse suggested that the central question revolves around how discourses commonly legitimize violence. Discourses and the legitimization of violence received relatively little attention in the context of radicalization within Peace and Conflict Studies so far. However, the contributions in this volume enable a deeper understanding about the power of radicalizing actors. This became obvious in many contributions (for example, Clément; Tichatschke; Eftyhmiou, this volume), who all looked at radical actors and their communicative strategies, as well as reactions to it. The discursive power of actors and their strategies for communication and for the creation of narratives are crucial because limited agency can be assumed, but the communication is highly strategic.

Specifically, radicalization becomes visible in narrative emotionalization, for example, in militant Islamist actors, as "organisations mobilising for political violence draw extensively on narrative emotionalization" (Clément). These non-state organizations that operate under oppressive environments and other hierarchically structured collectives demand a high level of devotion and loyalty from their members.

Parties like ELAM [1] in Cyprus present an integral discursive mechanism of conflict's changing politics of society and state (Efthymiou, this volume). They use a specific "nationalist and militarist rhetoric" and illustrate how the "radicalization of movements during the change of conflict politics" is possible. In these situations, support for radical right politics can arise from disillusionment with the system.

Tichatschke looks more at possible receptions by the audience and what communicators can do, and how they can plan. The role of the audience where the "personality and party contexts of the people presenting the narrative and their audiences" play a role. Her analysis "points at the central dilemma and the need to balance between a clear response that fulfils the affective needs of the audience and the risks of furthering polarization and radicalization in the process." In particular, individuals targeted by recruitment efforts from extremist groups must be considered, and their possible perceptions of the narrative should be anticipated by communicators.

These considerations lead to the assumption that discursive forms of violence, like epistemic or symbolic violence, offer possibilities for prevention.

6   Prevention and Reaction to Violence/De-radicalization

The core issue regarding the relevance in society is how to deal with radicalization and enable and contribute to de-radicalization. Narratives that emphasize the tenacity of pluralist societies are more likely to link to counterterrorism and preventative strategies, which approach terrorism as a complicated political issue (Tichatschke, this volume). Several innovative approaches were introduced around the question of how to deal with violent radicalization and how to achieve resilience and decrease the normality of violence, as well as reactions to, and prognosis of, violence. Merhej and Fahed provide knowledge on how to manage the normality of violence which means, for them, a "sustainable improvement of societies resilience to political violence through addressing root causes of structural and cultural violence" (Merhej & Fahed this volume). They recommend concentrating on achieving a higher normality of violence, which entails working to further de-normalize violent behaviour and lessen its social and cultural benefits.

Concrete actions and steps could be observed in Peace Education, which can enable ways out of cycles of radicalization (Groppe) through reasonability and preventative action. The suggestion to increase "resilience within society and maintain pluralist and democratic arena of public discourse" (Tichatschke) goes in a similar direction. Peace education as a participatory approach for addressing "potentials for peace, including multiple perspectives, seems to be suitable". The starting point is to "identify entry points for, but also complicity of, peace education within conflicts over democracy" (Groppe, this volume). Peace education is not a single tool, but is meant to complement "other approaches to the prevention of radicalization" (Groppe this volume).

---

[1] Ethniko Laiko Metopo.

Reactions and connecting points as a strategy to terrorist incidents examine how they might fit into the narratives employed by extremist groups to radicalize members of their audience" (Tichatschke this volume).

The dilemmas are obvious: there is the need "to balance between a clear response that fulfils the affective needs of the audience and the risks of furthering polarization and radicalization in the process. Therefore, "the core advice would be to ask for the potential effects and risks the narratives and measures pose in relation to a radicalization of the public discourse". Awareness about public crisis communication after a terrorist attack and similar events is missing so far. This is problematic, as "it might be a lot easier to resort to clear, strong and resolute rhetoric, […] than to craft differentiated, nuanced responses that take into account their long-term effects" (Tichatschke), which is especially necessary.

The required conflict competencies are rooted in the individuals: "context specific processes can open relational spaces in order to unfold conflict competences" (Groppe this volume).

Post-Conflict settings are shown in the edited volume as unique problems with transferable lessons. Paragon scenarios, like in Cyprus, show the complexity and vulnerability for political radicalization. The "grieving of what has been lost and the hope that it can be regained can be exploited by radical organisations" (Efthymiou this volume). Efthymiou states that generally divided post-conflict societies, such as Cyprus, provide a very favourable environment for the development of radical organizations.

Positive aspects and opportunities around radicalization without violence, as mentioned in the introduction, are achievable and are possible. For example, emancipation can be a "resource that challenges the order and opens the space for political action, a fact that will give rise to possible reforms of the structures of a state" (Córdova Suxo, this volume).

7 Outlook for Studies on Radicalization

Around the globe, there are new challenges and trends which will provide interesting cases for studying radicalization and violence in the future. One primary area that will likely meet this expectation will be protests, activism and resistance in climate change discourses and political conflicts around the so-called "Climate Crisis".

While conspiracy movements might be interesting, movements which block important infrastructure as a sign of protest are of more relevance and have received less scientific attention so far. Last Generation, Extinction Rebellion, Fridays for Future and their opponents and critics are, from a German perspective, possible actors that could be studied based on an interest in radicalization. Here, once again, a prognosis about future behaviour would be interesting as well.

Scholars currently see Extinction Rebellion as "a fairly radical form of protest" (Ginanjar & Mubarrok, 2020, p. 43). So far, they use "a method of civil disobedience without violence" (Ginanjar & Mubarrok, 2020, p. 43). Their tactics include measures that "blockade and disrupt public facilities such as train stations and other public transportation" (Ginanjar & Mubarrok, 2020, p. 43). Such movements are becoming more radical due to, among other reasons, a growing time pressure due to increasingly obvious effects of climate change and a political leadership that has yet to adequately answer critical questions related to climate change.

According to the German Office for the Protection of the Constitution, these groups are not yet considered extremist (Schindler, 2022). However, experts expect fundamental changes to these organizations in the coming years (Kaluza, 2022). This again poses the question: is violence a fundamental consequence of radicalization processes? This leads back to the three different understandings of radicalization, where extremism becomes applicable as the third.

These movements, and their ramifications, embody all the issues discussed in this edited volume, such as the role of ideology, political reactions, single and group radicalization, and protest and discourses. In their current form, they can be seen as an example of radicalization without violence, and thus, they may provide a foundation upon which to build further research.

References

De la Roche, R. S. (2001). Why is collective violence collective? *Sociological Theory, 19*(2), 126–144. https://doi.org/10.1111/0735-2751.00133

Ginanjar, W. R., & Mubarrok, A. Z. (2020). Civil society and global governance: The indirect participation of extinction rebellion in global governance on climate change. *Journal of Contemporary Governance and Public Policy, 1*(1), 41–52. https://doi.org/10.46507/jcgpp.v1i1.8

Kaluza, A. (2022, November 10). Werden die Protestformen der Klimabewegung radikaler, Herr Teune? *Spiegel Wissenschaft*, Retrieved November 10, 2022, from https://www.spiegel.de/wissenschaft/radikalisierung-der-klimabewegung-die-debatte-ueber-die-letzte-generation-ist-eine-stellvertreter-diskussion-a-d3aaaaa0-81d2-4040-baf2-5a526754b6ba

McCauley, C., & Moskalenko, S. (2017). Understanding political radicalization: The two pyramids model. *American Psychologist, 72*(3), 205–216. https://psycnet.apa.org/doi/10.1037/amp0000062

Schindler, J. (2022, November 16). Verfassungsschutz: "Klimaaktivisten sind keine Extremisten", *SWR Aktuell*. Retrieved November 16, 2022, from https://www.swr.de/swraktuell/rheinland-pfalz/demokratie-forum-verfassungsschutz-letzte-generation-keine-extremisten-100.html

Sterman, D., & Rosenblatt, N. (2018). *All Jihad is Local. Volume 2: ISIS in North Africa and the Arabian Peninsula.* New America, Washington, DC.

Tilly, C. (2003). *The politics of collective violence.* Cambridge University Press.